SEEKING BALANCE

Caitlin Press Inc.
8100 Alderwood Road,
Halfmoon Bay, BC V0N 1Y1
www.caitlin-press.com

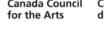

Canada Council   Conseil des Arts
for the Arts   du Canada

BRITISH COLUMBIA
ARTS COUNCIL
We acknowledge the support of the Province of British Columbia
through the British Columbia Arts Council

Edited by Susan Mayse and Betty Keller.
Front cover photograph: Inspirestock
Front cover images L-R: Jenny Kwan, courtesy Jenny Kwan; Rosemary Brown, courtesy Victoria *Times Colonist;* Hedy Fry, courtesy Patrick Tam; Tilly Rolston, courtesy Louise Rolston; Carol James, courtesy Carol James; Grace McCarthy, courtesy Grace McCarthy
Back cover images L-R: Iona Campagnola, courtesy Patrick Tam; Grace MacInnis, courtesy New Democratic Party; Dawn Black, courtesy Dawn Black; Joy MacPhail, courtesy New Democratic Party; Penny Priddy, courtesy Penny Priddy; Nina Grewal, courtesy Patrick Tam
A special thanks to Patrick Tam of FlungingPictures.com
Printed in Canada

Caitlin Press Inc. acknowledges financial support from the Government of Canada through the Book Publishing Industry Development Program and the Canada Council for the Arts, and from the Province of British Columbia through the British Columbia Arts Council and the Book Publisher's Tax Credit.

Library and Archives Canada Cataloguing in Publication
Edwards, Anne, 1935–

Seeking balance : conversations with BC women in politics / Anne Edwards.
Includes bibliographical references and index.
ISBN 978-1-894759-31-1

1. Women legislators—British Columbia—Biography. 2. Women politicians—British Columbia—Biography. 3. Women in politics—British Columbia. 4. British Columbia. Legislative Assembly—Biography. 5. Canada. Parliament—Biography. I. Title.

HQ1236.5.C2E38 2008   328.711092'2   C2008-905635-3

SEEKING BALANCE

*Conversations with BC
Women in Politics*

ANNE EDWARDS

Caitlin Press

Acknowlededgments

First, to the women members who took the time and gave their most sincere thought to our interviews.

Second, to the boosters who touted my book so many times in so many places that I couldn't, in good conscience, give up.

Third, to the generous researchers who offered their time and expertise.

Fourth, to the friends who read early drafts and offered advice and information.

Fifth, to those who put me up on my travels while interviewing.

Sixth, to the friends who supported the chores that I couldn't manage.

Seventh, to those, close and not so close, who offered leads, suggestions and experience.

And finally, to Betty Keller, the midwife of this book.

*This book is dedicated to my eleven grandchildren
and my great-granddaughter.*

Contents

PREFACE

by Darlene Marzari

A nne Edwards was elected in East Kootenay, as far east as the province extends and the epitome of rural. I was elected in Vancouver–Point Grey, as far west as the mainland of BC goes and as urban as the province gets. She protected jobs in her constituency by speaking from the backs of trucks during a mining strike and met miners at the coal face at Elkford. I worked to eradicate glass ceilings hanging over women's job opportunities and met with social activists in Kitsilano. But we bonded.

I "represented" with Anne Edwards in the BC legislative assembly from 1986 until 1996. Within hours of finding digs together in Victoria, we decided to write a book. Oh, not the one you see before you. It was to be a romance. As months progressed, and before the reality of our jobs swallowed our time, we actually created our heroine, Arbutus Pine, and set the stage for a "girl MLA meets boy MLA, girl loses boy etc," a tale of high merit indeed. Such a story it would have been!

Now Anne has written another story, and though girls do meet boys and vice versa, the outcome is not quite so formulaic. It's a deeper and richer narrative, extending over generations of women's lives, touching the foundations of how elected people make huge public decisions in very private spaces and how we deal with each other and each others' ideas in the process. Anne presents her conversations with women who have served over a span of more than fifty years in the BC legislature or the Canadian Parliament.

Arbutus Pine may have been lost in this process, and the happily-ever-after ending may have to succumb to a little reality therapy. But women who care about politics, political scientists who tabulate women's involvement in the "game," sociologists who wonder if 33 percent is really the magic number at which women start to be heard at the decision-making table, historians who chronicle the barriers to women's equality that have melted in the last ninety years and women's rights advocates who detect the underpinnings of misogyny while the melting progresses—all will win as they turn the pages here.

We all have our stories. You can't put dozens of intelligent people into old stone fortresses for five or ten years, ask them to sign elaborate codes of secrecy and give them detailed "song sheets" about what they may or may not report to the outside world and not get great stories.

Men's stories, not surprisingly, are usually about deeds and exploits. They are told in memoirs or at bars or barbecues as a veteran might recount old battles at the legion hall. The women's stories deal mainly with relationships and how we learned to live inside a military metaphor: how we struggled to reconcile problem solving with winning. Why would this be? you may ask.

After a woman has fought for a nomination in her party—often the hardest part of the access process—and she is elected, the ground tends to shift beneath her feet. This occurs despite the rules . . . well, the unwritten rule is that there are no rules. Even if she has had years of experience on a city council, a school board or professional or community organizations, she soon discovers the limits of collegiality and finds she has been seagulled, blindsided or left out of the loop. This happens to every neophyte for sure. While she is trying to level a playing field or look for fair processes (asking for an agenda at meetings, for example), her male counterparts with the advantage of long-standing mentoring routines start the game around her.

The game is a form of hockey. It matches and enhances the military metaphors of parliamentary democracy like a hand in a mitt. (My favorite story here is about a female colleague who was complemented for stickhandling an issue though a meeting. "Thanks," she said, "you're a pretty good puck yourself!") While our woman member is putting on her sweater and sharpening her skates, teams are being picked and judgments are getting made by the media and her party leader. Her male colleagues are dubbed up-and-comers, star performers or quick studies with fast learning curves, or best of all, cabinet material, while she is being asked how she manages to leave her children (ailing parents, poor husband, sick hamster) at home and where she buys her clothes (lipstick, fast food). It's a way of commodifying her before she leaves the house for the House.

Not surprising, then, that how things get done is important to her. The very business of getting to do the job, not just the doing of it, becomes her study. Also in her context are the facts that the power of the job is not necessarily an end in itself but a way of doing public service, that her experience in family and community has taught her that dialogue, discussion and fairness actually work and that the process of decision making informs the outcome. Which is not what the House is about! This book is about the distance between the paradigms of achieving or not achieving.

It's worth remembering that the Parliament itself is an eighthundred-year-old vestige of ancient power struggles between English warlords carried out in a chamber in London rather than on a battlefield. Noble venture at the time, but how little our public processes have evolved! We maintain our rules through tradition and the slow business and show business of partisan politics. Some, not all, of the "we win therefore we get the whole sandbox" mentality serves the purpose of getting on with a task at hand: delivering on an issue, keeping a promise to the electorate. But any common sense notion of creating real transparency or inclusiveness just doesn't happen. Rather like a self-licking ice cream cone, our system perpetuates itself to feed on itself. We go in with our issues, we engage in the play and we get out before we get eaten.

"But fortunately," said Charlotte Whitton about women needing to be twice as good as men in politics, "it's not that difficult."

Hockey can be learned, credit is easy to share as long as the job gets done and team play is exciting. It can even become easy to bodycheck the neophytes coming on stream after the next election and forget about mentoring, or to ally oneself with male validators to get important ideas through. Such is the business of women in politics. We may not cruise the press gallery during hockey games, as a male colleague once sincerely prescribed to "help" us get press, but women members are not shrinking violets. They dish it out with the best, stand up to be counted, stickhandle the obstacles and thump on their desks till their knuckles are white.

In the decade we were there, the women in the House or in the media or even in our party did not share the belief that an overarching patriarchy strained to perpetuate itself. Feminism to Rosemary Brown was inextricably linked to socialism. For others it did not carry a partisan label. For some it was a call to action, for others humanism with a female face. Only a handful of the women Anne interviewed would call themselves feminists. Anne rarely mentions party affiliation in her narrative. She doesn't need to. The similarities in our combined experience is remarkable. What is important here is that all of them—all of us, across the board—felt the chill as we entered the job and found we had another job to do in dealing with that fact.

What is left of the women's movement in North America can claim that women have made huge progress in achieving the right to vote, run for election, sit in the Senate or fill executive positions in upper management of business and government. All that said, the place to understand the barriers, tap into the deep resistance to women's advance or comprehend how the resistance is often inside the women themselves can partly be found in the stories of women who have achieved in the male domain. The place to find encouragement and hope—or at least a game plan—for those who wish to run for office might be in reading about those who have already been there.

This book is not a manifesto, a partisan exclamation or an exposé. Nor is it a prescription for guaranteed change towards gender fairness and equity. It contains stories formed by the winding together of answers to Anne's questions, each story or snippet or quote carrying its own validity, humor, anxiety or insight. Anne paid her dues and was tough at the table, having learned many of her skills in the process of managing gravel pits. She remains a good partisan, but she wrote as a journalist who has observed all of us and listened. Her gender lens captures the responses of some seventy women who trusted her with their stories, despite the considerable pressure women face against meeting across the floor or with female media. From a friend to all of us who have been there—men and women—and for the system we have served, it is a gift.

The task at hand begins with creating a productive space for men and women to cohabit that sits somewhere in the continuum between the secret room and the open forum. This is not the headline-grabbing issue we all crave as combatants, but a necessary one if our structures of government are to have any lasting relevance. There is more work to be done, we have said. More women are needed, we have proclaimed. On with the job!

Thank you, Anne.

Rosemary Brown, leading feminist and always a backbencher, addressing the BC Legislature. *Victoria Times Colonist.*

INTRODUCTION

Sometimes I have believed as many as six impossible things before breakfast.

—Lewis Carroll,
Through the Looking Glass

Ninety years after BC women won the vote and the right to stand for office, fewer than one hundred have ever been elected to the BC legislature or the Canadian Parliament.

The suffragettes of 1917 would be disappointed. They sought equality, but their heirs have not yet achieved even 30 percent of the seats available in either house. They have come close—29 percent once in the BC assembly—but have not reached critical mass, the point at which women's presence would lead basic change within the larger group—change which could address the flaws that citizens see in our parliamentary system.

British Columbians have elected seventy-four women to their legislature and twenty-six women to Parliament. Four women have sat in both assemblies, making the total number of women elected ninety-six. Two-thirds of the women who have represented us as MLAs or MPs did so from 1986 on. Seventeen of them have died, leaving seventy-nine participants and alumnae.

Over the course of 2002 and 2003, I interviewed sixty-six of these women about their experience and their ideas on the political system. I asked them nineteen questions that covered why they decided to run for politics, what their family had thought and done about it, the quality of congeniality in their work, what they liked best about it and what they learned. I asked their perception of the difference, if any, between women and men as they approach and execute the job—even whether men and women see the job in the same light. They told me what they thought was the essence of British Columbia's so-called zany politics. And we all considered why it is that politicians have a reputation lower than a snake's belly.

Our conversations reveal that women approach the political world much differently than men. Whereas men go boldly into the arena ready for battle, women consult and discuss, searching for a solution to problems in which everybody wins. Men established electoral assemblies and their practices hundreds of years ago, and mostly male writers have described them publicly, so it is little wonder that politicians are assessed as players in war games. The incompatibility of the system and the way women work explain much of the reason why women hold only 22 percent of the legislative seats, and 25 percent of the federal seats. Either they accept the system as laid out and work against their own grain, or they engage their own ways of achieving and work against the grain of the established system.

Nevertheless, BC has led the way across Canada by being the first to vote 10 percent of its legislative seats to women in 1941 and then 25 percent in 1991. BC made Rita Johnston the first woman premier in Canada and elected Kim Campbell, who became the first woman prime minister. Rosemary Brown was the first woman to run for leadership of a major party in North America when she stood within the New Democratic Party in 1975. In 1918 Mary Ellen Smith became the third woman elected to a provincial legislature in Canada, and in 1920 the first in the British Empire to be appointed to cabinet. Nancy Hodges, appointed speaker in 1950, was the first woman in the Empire to hold that office. Three years later, she was the first western Canadian woman named to the Senate. And in 1952, when she was named minister of education, Tilly Rolston was the first Canadian women to hold a cabinet position with a portfolio. Iona Campagnolo, who had been the first woman MP from northern BC, became the province's first woman Lieutenant-Governor. Grace MacInnis gave her life to politics and was our first woman MP. The list goes on.

Many women who held office were otherwise prominent. Before she sat three terms as a BC MP, Pauline Jewett came to the province as the first woman president of a major university when she was named by Simon Fraser University. Pat Carney was a well-known journalist and business consultant before she ran and served two terms as an MP, the first Conservative female MP from BC. After she declined to run in the 1988 election, she was named to the Senate as the fourth BC woman so appointed. Carole Taylor headed the Vancouver Port Authority and the CBC board of governors before being elected and serving as provincial minister of finance. Carole James was the longest-serving president of the BC School Trustees Association before she was named NDP party leader and became the first woman elected to the legislature as party leader. Hedy Fry headed the BC Medical Association before being elected to Parliament and is now the longest-serving woman MP.

Since electing women to assemblies is a custom that has grown slowly, it is no surprise that most of the women who have been members are alive today. Only seventeen have died. I was fortunate to have interviewed two of them before they died and to have talked to family and

In 1952, Tilly Rolston became BC's minister of education, the first woman in Canada to hold a cabinet position with a portfolio. *City of Vancouver Archives CVA 180-4323.*

friends of three others. Only one woman refused an interview, saying, "I don't see myself as a woman politician."

As I transferred my efforts from interviewing to writing, I missed eight woman MLAs and four MPs elected in the 2004 and 2006 federal elections and the 2005 provincial vote, although I did manage a phone interview with Carole James, BC's NDP leader. In all I conducted eighty-one interviews. While I am sorry to have missed the sharp observations of any of the group, I felt the women I did interview, whose service spanned more than forty years, did an excellent job of describing what a political career is like for women who, although a majority of the population, work always as a small minority when they become public policy makers.

The book is based mainly on the interviews. Although I have inserted my own "interview" from time to time, this is not my memoir. It reflects women members' views across party lines, age differences and eras from 1918 to 2008. On some things, the women agreed amazingly often; on others they expressed opinions that covered the gamut. But on the issue of seeking equality for women—equality that does not exist—they were pretty well unanimous. They believe it should be there and that time and continued effort must be made to achieve equality.

They agreed that they are glad they served, even those who left after a single term because of the difficulties they faced integrating their political work with the rest of their lives. They believe that the job is difficult, often unsung, unlike any other they have had and that it brings knowledge, wisdom and some scars. Despite the difficulties and frequent discouragement, with full and generous hearts they encourage other women to run.

They found, like Alice in *Through the Looking Glass*, that once they enter the doors of the legislature, things are not as they seem—not seen straight on. They were in a different world, where the rules of "the game" were totally different. Despite the wealth of advice offered—Alice was constantly urged to run faster, to speak only when spoken to, to learn to believe impossible things; women members are likewise urged to pick a side so they can pick a fight, belly up like a cowboy and so on—too often the only reason for what people do is that the rules of the game have somehow become engrained despite great logical gaps.

Many women remarked, "I didn't come here to defend the status quo." Woman members are eager to see new rules of the game, to base their work on the voices of their communities and to find solutions without battles or even a media performance of battles. They offer a viewpoint that has yet to penetrate practice, not just attitudes that react to the traditional system. Without destroying the benefits of a system that has served us well for centuries, they want to try fresh ideas and practise in the ways that are invading other organizations and businesses—flatter organization with more people involvement—ways that could either complement or replace the rusty parts of our assembly machines, ways that would recognize the skills that women want to exercise in politics and would balance the decisions made by our legislature and Parliament. They want balance in numbers and balance in process. They want equality.

My hope in producing this book is that more citizens will recognize the skills that women bring. I hope they will regain an optimism that has given way to a general cynicism about public life and will again join the serious activity that is public policy making through discussion, running for office and forming and following ideas that will improve our lives.

By the hundredth anniversary of BC woman's franchise, may we see a resurgence of interest in public affairs by women as well as men who regard gender equality in our assemblies—as a balance—as it should be.

Post script: News of the death of Camille Mather came as we closed the last edit of this book. She was 96, the oldest of our former woman MLAs at the time of her death in Delta, BC.

Nancy Hodges, the first woman in the British Commonwealth to hold the Speaker's chair in an assembly, was also the first Canadian woman senator from western Canada. *Image I-32485 courtesy Royal BC Museum, BC Archives.*

WOMEN TAKE THE FLOOR

BC'S POLITICAL RECIPE

"The first almighty fact about British Columbia is mountains,"[1] said writer and conservationist Roderick Haig-Brown, but the women who have joined its government found more than physical mountains. They ran head-on into its wacky, out-of-range politics.

"Provincial politics," wrote Stephen Hume in 2001, "has been considered free entertainment for the masses ever since our first premier was tossed out as incompetent after thirteen months in office in 1872—to be succeeded by a premier who was later certified as insane."[2]

At least a shadow of BC's offbeat reputation is true. The women as well as the men have been strong personalities, winning fame across the country and internationally. They have been outspoken, gritty and witty—all good qualities, according to West Coast standards. Many defend BC's reputation for rowdy behaviour inside its assembly as healthy competition, although some challenge this reputation, suggesting that a scoresheet on Alberta—or any other province—might also reveal less than exemplary conduct. But mostly we don't mind being known as bold and brawny.

Several factors have dictated the cultural differences in this province. First, BC's history began on the west coast of Canada, meaning that the colonial powers competing with Britain for what is now BC were Spain, Russia and the USA. The major competitor in eastern Canada, on the other hand, was France. Trade thrived with the Orient and Russia, which were the Pacific partners of Vancouver's Island and later the mainland trading posts in the region known as New Caledonia.

Second, when BC joined Canadian Confederation, that union was not a geographically natural progression. BC's provincial boundary was not contiguous with Canada—Alberta and Saskatchewan were still British territories—so the purpose of joining the two colonies had a focus that superseded the natural pull of neighbourhood: to build a railway and enhance the power of both Canada and BC to resist union with the US.

Third, BC not only had the most diverse aboriginal population in Canada, it had the earliest white activity that brought in immigrants from Pacific countries as soon as trading ships started visiting regularly. The flow has built until today, among all the provinces, BC has the largest percentage of citizens of Asian and South Pacific origin, making an equally diverse population of immigrants.

Fourth, great mountains rise on the Pacific coast and march range after range across the province to the Continental Divide. These constitute a physical barrier that has shaped our settlement patterns, our resource use, and most importantly, our sense of separation from each other and the rest of the country.

In 1871, BC was the sixth province to join Canadian Confederation, a hundred years after Europeans infiltrated this Pacific region and brought about trade, white settlements and white government. Still, it took twenty more years before immigrants outnumbered First Nations people. One hundred years after Confederation, historian Martin Robin described BC as "an ethnic hodgepodge with a majority of the contemporary population born outside of the province. When claims are pressed on the federal authorities, they are couched in material rather than cultural or nationalist terms."[3] BC's identity has never completely melded into other Canadians' sense of the country's origin.

The geography of BC assured the separation of regions that could be plateaus, deltas or mountain trenches. It determined aboriginal settlement, so that in the eighteenth century BC had some three hundred individual bands in ten separate linguistic and cultural groups: seven on the coast, two in the southern interior and one in the north. Complex cultures developed within these groups—many bands spoke their own dialects—but no territorial organization existed like that of the Blackfoot Confederacy across the prairies or the Iroquois Six Nations in central Canada.

Social organization in BC still hangs on this framework of aboriginal practice. In the agricultural industry of the early colony and province, for example, attempts to form an integrated farm political organization were never successful. East of the Rockies, farm parties formed governments and strong oppositions in provincial assemblies. Several women were elected with the support of these parties. Agnes Macphail, the first woman elected to the Canadian Parliament, represented the United Farmers of Ontario, and Irene Parlby of the United Farmers of Alberta held a cabinet seat in the UFA government from 1921 to 1935. In Saskatchewan the Co-operative Commonwealth Federation (CCF) became a socialist party with a farmer base; in BC it was something very different, a socialist party with a labour base.

In the interior of BC, more early communities formed around the search for minerals than around lumbering, agriculture, fishing or the search for furs. In BC men prospected alone or with other men, while on the fertile prairies whole families settled farms. The few women who came early to BC also tended to come alone or with other women, not as one of a couple. Many men who came from Asia were unable, because of laws or expense, to bring their wives. As a result, women's numbers did not match men's until the mid-twentieth century.

In these early days the resource industries—lumbering, mining, fishing and shipbuilding—brought BC its great wealth. The feast–or–famine economy it created affected both workers and companies. "The boom or bust mentality is very significant," observed Kim Campbell. "You have that powerful business concern of people who actually put a lot on the line and feel they are entitled to what they get for it. But the vulnerability of the work force is the nature of the industry." This vulnerability led to the highest rate of unionization in the country and made an impact on both provincial and federal politics. Union activists came from Britain and other European countries, and the US labour movement sent in organizers when the Canadian Pacific was building the railway through the nearly impenetrable mountains of BC.

Thus divisions between workers and owners became the class system for BC. On the prairies, a farmer usually owned his land and worked alongside his workers, often young neighbours who would later become farm owners themselves. In BC, on the other hand, resource industries were run by corporations with hired managers who were socially separated from the loggers, miners, fishers, labourers and millwrights. Early British settlers—the naval officers in Victoria, the gentlemen farmers in the Okanagan and the Chilcotin, but most particularly the Hudson's Bay Company authorities—also established class. Not only did the company hierarchy have military ranks, the officers made sure that the gentry brought from Britain, to whom they leased farms, came with their families and their employees. Because land was not given away in BC as it was on the prairies, the class patterns of the British landed gentry continued longer here.

Class division also determined political rivalries in British Columbia. Early politicians entered the provincial legislature as government or opposition members, not as Liberals or Conservatives, but the one thing they had in common was financial health, whether through inheritance or business. Labour candidates began to challenge these owners and managers of wealth in 1886, and in 1890 a Labour candidate from the coal mines in Nanaimo won election. Although Labour candidates were socialist in belief, not all socialists were members of the Labour Party. The first socialist candidate not aligned as Labour ran for office in 1900, and two were elected in 1903, the first year that candidates ran under a party label.

Labourites and Socialists rejected both old-line parties, giving rise to the right-left split that still characterizes BC politics. In response to the growing strength of the "workers' parties," Grits and Tories often chose to work together. In time the Co-operative Commonwealth Federation drew the labour and socialist threads together in one political party and began to run candidates in the 1933 election. From that time on the CCF, later to become the New Democratic Party, took enough of the vote in every provincial election to be a threat to the old-line parties. In the 1940s the CCF's electoral power forced a coalition of Liberals and Conservatives, which gave way to the Social Credit Party, a coalition of federal Grits and Tories and other nonsocialist voters. This response recurred in the 1990s with the resurgence of the provincial Liberal Party, which many people, including its own members, considered a reincarnation of the Social Credit coalition. As one editorial wag put it, "the Socreds went off into the wilderness to search for themselves and discovered they were actually Liberals."[4]

Other Canadian provinces have had strong CCF or NDP parties and governments, but in those provinces the traditional lines between Liberals and Conservatives remained stronger. Saskatchewan and Manitoba, and certainly Ontario, lack the teeter-totter that we in BC call polarization between the coalition of the left and the coalition of the right. From the time that the CCF became a force in this province, the nonsocialist right-leaning parties have formed one end of the spectrum, the CCF and left-leaning voters the other. Of course some say we are not polarized, observing that the external conflict masks a likeness we don't like to admit. Kim Campbell, for example, believed that if BC were truly politically polarized, a middle party would emerge, but "there's no room in the middle. Both parties are centrist, . . . centre left and centre right. The extremes don't really drive."

Be that as it may, BC's political climate is rough, tough and studded with large egos. It has a strong tradition of diversity in communities, personal identity and political action. Those who developed our system often had bitter struggles with the champions of old ways imported from imperial countries. All of their characteristics form the pool into which political women jump when they seek election.

SUFFRAGE:
A THIRTY-YEAR DREAM

When Susan B. Anthony, the famous US advocate for woman suffrage, spoke in Victoria in 1871, BC women were ready to begin the public campaign for their right to vote and run for office on the same basis as men. Women in Wyoming already had the vote, and a demand for suffrage was rising in England and across English-speaking North America as well as in New Zealand and Australia.

Women had no choice but to solicit male support for legislation. Some male politicians supported a franchise for women but balked at the idea of letting them run for office. Women realized they would have to win broad public support. In their public campaign, they chose to stress their gender-dictated social position as morally superior, nurturing, supportive humans: their reputation as mothers.

The difficulty of their task became clear in June of 1872, when a bill introduced in the legislature to give women the provincial franchise garnered only two pro votes on its way to defeat. In 1873 the legislature gave women property holders the municipal vote, however, and three Victoria women actually voted in January 1874, to the surprise and sometime shock of the citizenry.

The suffrage campaign started in earnest in 1883 when a Victoria minister offered his pulpit to Frances Willard, the president of the US Women's Christian Temperance Union (WCTU). Willard thought prohibition or temperance was out of reach without getting the vote for women, so she also campaigned for the female franchise. She met a warm welcome from women who soon established both a local temperance union and a provincial one.

Hope began to rise. Hon. Montague William Tyrwhitt-Drake, member for Victoria City, proposed an amendment to the Provincial Voters Act to give women the provincial franchise. Sir John A. Macdonald had introduced similar legislation in the federal Assembly. Even with the encouragement of newspapers, one of which said it would be an honour to be the first jurisdiction under British rule to grant women the franchise, the amendment failed in the BC house and in Parliament.

Hon. John Robson, provincial secretary at the time but destined to be BC premier, had signed a pledge of abstinence at the Willard meeting and was always a staunch ally of the WCTU. In 1884 he introduced a bill giving single women householders and freeholders and wives of householders and freeholders a vote for school trustees, though not the right to stand for election. His bill passed. In Victoria, where WCTU members canvassed to get out the women's vote in the next school board election, two of their preferred candidates won and a third came close. A writer of a letter to the *Daily Colonist*, probably a member of the WCTU, wrote that "there had not been any loss of dignity or 'womanliness' in the election process."[5]

By 1889 legislators allowed women to stand for school board—very likely the legislating men could see that education was within a mother's ambit—but in 1891 the members of the legislature decided to appoint school trustees in the cities, although elections continued in the rural municipalities. Governments spent two more years changing the rules and the possibilities for women before Maria Grant of Victoria became the first woman elected to a school board in the province.

Women met a similar see-saw response from government over the municipal council vote, which had been granted in 1873. After a lobby against woman suffrage by the Victoria Property Owners' Association, which included saloon keepers, the right of women property owners to vote was repealed in 1908. The excuse was that it would allow women who ran houses of prostitution to vote. The WCTU, concerned that saloon keepers would now gain ascendancy, overcame any scruples they may have had about supporting madams and mounted a spirited defence of their rights. The WCTU and the Local Council of Women (LCW), which the former had engendered, raised a thousand-name petition in three days opposing the move, but their efforts did not prevent the amendment.

For the provincial franchise, the women of the Victoria WCTU—

who by 1885 had encouraged the formation of unions in other places such as Nanaimo and New Westminster—led the gathering of names on a petition to the provincial government asking for the vote. The petition carried fifteen hundred names, but by a margin of five, provincial legislators still refused to accept it. From 1885 forward, women petitioned the legislature annually until they got the vote.

In 1891 the WCTU was instrumental in establishing the National Council of Women, with Lady Ishbel Aberdeen, the wife of the Governor General, as its first president. Three years later, when she visited the West Coast, she encouraged women to found local councils (LCWs) in Victoria and Vancouver. By 1909 Victoria had the largest LCW in Canada, with an average 150 women coming regularly to meetings. Soon the council—nationally, provincially and locally—had become the most influential Canadian women's organization to support the franchise for women. The Victoria LCW led the way when it became the first branch in Canada to come out publicly in support of full woman suffrage.

In the 1890s, members of the BC legislature voted five times—in 1891, 1893, 1897, 1898 and 1899—on giving women the franchise. The 1898 women's petition for the franchise had twenty-five hundred signatures, twelve hundred of them men voters. The member who introduced a woman suffrage bill in 1899 was Hon. Ralph Smith, whose wife, Mary Ellen Smith, was later to become the first woman MLA in BC. The *Daily Colonist* ran a headline before the vote saying, "Woman Franchise Close to Success." And indeed it was close, with fifteen for and seventeen against. Member Richard Hall confessed later to a reporter that he had been confused about the vote; he had intended to vote for the bill but voted against it because he thought they were voting on a different question. Had he voted as he intended and tied the vote, the speaker—following general practice for speakers in the parliamentary system—would have cast his vote on the side of the government, giving the bill approval.

That close call aroused both those in favour of woman suffrage and those opposed. In the first decade of the twentieth century, women were organizing within the BC Trades and Labour Council, where members encouraged them to political action. Other women organized the University Women's Club of Vancouver, which lobbied for a university but also became the leader of the suffrage campaign in Vancouver. Suffragettes were spurred on by the fact that women were winning the franchise in other places—in New Zealand in 1903 and very soon after in the US states of Utah, Colorado and Idaho. In 1908 the WCTU conducted a membership campaign and over the year more than doubled its provincial membership to 1,107. An executive member said at the annual convention, "We intend to get the franchise and there is no power in British Columbia that can prevent our getting it."[6]

In 1909 Hon. J. H. Hawthornthwaite, who three years earlier had introduced an Act to Extend the Franchise to Women, reintroduced it, but was again unsuccessful. The campaign for woman suffrage was now at a peak, however, with "public and parlour meetings, essay and speech contests, letters to clergymen, articles for newspapers."[7] A women's parliament, staged by the Victoria LCW, had various activists taking the parts of parliamentarians in the Land of the Happy Parallel, debating a bill to grant the franchise to men on the same basis as women. One of the honoured guests was a visitor from Mars, where a successful campaign had just been carried out.

At the first woman suffrage conference held in BC in 1911, a Washington state senator told about women's successful battle for the vote in his state. By the following year, both the Political Equality League (PEL) and the Voters' League (VL) had been formed in time to welcome Emmeline Pankhurst, a leading suffragist from Britain. One in eight women in Canada belonged to a women's group by this time, and most of those groups would have favoured woman's franchise. The Women's Institute, which had taken root in BC's rural areas, was a public exception; the government superintendent for the WI declared suffrage off-limits because government funding precluded any "political" slant. The most active women's organization, the provincial WCTU, had sixteen hundred members in 1912, only one hundred short of its all-time high in 1914.

The annual petition of 1913 gathered ten thousand signatures, but the government rejected it, suggesting a private member's bill instead. When the Hon. John Place responded by proposing such a bill, however, it failed twenty-four to nine. That same year the BC Federation of Labour officially endorsed woman suffrage, while in the wider world Emmeline Pankhurst was incarcerated in Holloway Prison just before bombs exploded in London in support of the suffragettes, and thirty-five thousand women marched down Fifth Avenue in New York to demand the franchise.

In 1914, Place, this time supported by an Alberni member whose local PEL had gathered seven thousand names on a petition, once again introduced a woman suffrage bill. LCWs across the province wrote letters and approached their members to support it. But when it came up in the house, according to local newspapers, debate took only minutes before it was defeated. The *Champion,* organ (newsletter) of the PEL, timed the debate at twelve minutes and observed, "The suffrage bill was a source of merriment in the house, which of itself shows the lack of respect these men have for the women of the Province."[8] The Conservative premier and the Attorney General were among the twenty-three who opposed the ten supporters. Mary Ellen Smith, who was president of the PEL and a member of the WCTU, spoke to the annual WCTU provincial convention to raise the morale of the women, echoing the prediction of the *Champion* that "this present sitting of the Legislature may try to stop women approaching the Government by a referendum, but in less than eight years the women of this Province will be voting for the representatives in Parliament."[9]

The Conservative government, preparing to announce an election, said it would not support woman suffrage, but the Liberals adopted suffrage in 1915 as an election plank and formed a Liberal women's organization in Vancouver. It drew women of all backgrounds and beliefs who supported woman suffrage, including Smith who belonged to the party and Laura Jamieson who did not and later ran successfully for the CCF. The following January, women in Manitoba won the vote. By April, Saskatchewan and then Alberta women were also enfranchised. BC women campaigned to pass a referendum that Conservative Premier John Bowser had promised on women's suffrage. Election day was September 14, 1916. The referendum passed with a polling day majority of twenty-one thousand to ten thousand, and although the soldier vote that was counted later came out opposed, the numbers were not enough to change the outcome.

The Conservative government was thrown out in the election, and the Liberals, led by Premier Harlan Brewster, took over the administration. Even in defeat at least one Conservative member made no apologies for opposing woman suffrage. The Vancouver *Province* quoted him as saying, "I can tell Mr. Brewster . . . that if he is called upon to form a government he is going to have an awful time deciding which ladies' husbands get portfolios. When the Liberal members took their seats here I half expected them to appear in kimonos."[10]

Although wrangling continued over the count of the soldier vote, Premier Brewster introduced the long-sought suffrage bill on March 27, 1917, and announced that royal assent on April 5 would involve a special legislative ceremony. The galleries were full, and invited women—most of them members of the Victoria and Vancouver Liberal clubs—were seated on the floor of the house. Cecilia Spofford of Victoria, one of the most active women in the suffrage campaign, spoke at an evening reception.

Delighted with the result, she was also pleased to remember the campaign's beginnings in Victoria with women she knew, women active since the start of the WCTU in 1883 and the LCW in 1894. She reminded those who attended that she had been "on the job before Vancouver was on the map."[11]

Maria Grant, our first woman school trustee, also held a pivotal place in the decades-long campaign, and was honoured at a recognition night about a week later. The Victoria *Daily Times* quoted her as saying, "I felt like St. John when he said: 'Whether in the body or out of the body I cannot tell.' It took three days to come back to mother earth. A dream of thirty years had come true. When the full returns were in showing a majority of 21,000 in favour of woman suffrage, I said: 'God bless the men of British Columbia'"[12]

Cecilia Spofford of Victoria was active in the woman's suffrage movement "before Vancouver was on the map." *Image I-51701 courtesy of Royal BC Museum, BC Archives.*

That same month, Louise McKinney, president of the Alberta WCTU, was elected in a general election to the Alberta legislature along with Roberta McAdams, who was in the Armed Forces. McKinney took her seat as the first woman in a Canadian assembly, preceding by ten months BC's Smith, who was elected in a January 1918 by-election and took her seat February 11.

Just as the campaign to get the municipal vote folded into the work for the provincial franchise, provincial campaigns folded into the federal effort. Bills were introduced several times in Parliament, beginning in 1883 and continuing until the vote was finally granted to women at the end of World War I.

Typical of these bills was the one introduced to the House in 1895 by Nicholas Flood Davin of Regina. Davin's friend and "companion," Kate Simpson Hayes, was a strong feminist and some MPs would have denied any support for the bill because of the couple's unsanctioned relationship. "That the motion would not be popular was quickly apparent and those who opposed it argued that voting women would magnify political differences and disrupt homes. Arguing righteously against the motion, most honorable members were sure that equal voting rights would have a degrading effect upon women."[13] The surprise was not that the bill was defeated, but that it garnered forty-seven votes, nearly half the total of 105 opposed, after a long and flowery debate in which most of Canada's governing men explained that they must preserve the "moral purity and sweetness" of the fairer sex by saving her from exercising a franchise.

When women finally did get the federal franchise, they had reason to tout their moral superiority, at least over Prime Minister Robert Borden and Secretary of State Arthur Meighen. The latter had framed both the conscription legislation and amendments to the War Time Elections Act that won the December 1917 federal election for the Conservatives. In the previous September, to assure approval of conscription, they had legislated the vote away from recent immigrants who had come from countries at war with Canada's allies, at the same time enfranchising female service members and mothers, wives, widows, sisters and daughters of servicemen. The manipulation was successful, and the Tories had stayed in office. The following year they extended the franchise to Canadian women on the same basis as men, almost simultaneously with Great Britain and the US. In 1920 they passed legislation to let women stand for election. The moral and spiritual sweetness of Canadian women was no longer to be preserved by the best efforts of their male governors.

In fact, the women were intent on improving the moral and spiritual environment in our Houses of Parliament by their votes, if not their presence. One of the principles of the WCTU, for example, was that "as woman is the natural conservator of home, she should be endowed with the use of the ballot as a means of protection for her home."[14] For many BC suffragists their Christianity was the motive and the moral anchor for their activism. Maria Grant was such a Christian. "She believed that women, in their natural role as mothers, ruled the world through the cradles they rocked. Enfranchised women would rock these cradles with an enlightenment which would benefit everyone."[15]

The activists' alliance with their churches was often strained, however, as not all clergymen advocated temperance when it appeared as prohibition. Many clergy invoked Queen Victoria's views opposing any move by women away from the accepted behaviour of loving, subordinate wives. The Queen had said publicly that she was "most anxious to enlist everyone who can speak or write to join in checking this mad wicked folly of Women's Rights, with all its attendant horrors, on which her poor, feeble sex is bent, forgetting every sense of womanly feeling and propriety." Suffragists responded defensively. Cecilia Spofford, for example, told a WCTU convention in 1885 that women had been called by their Redeemer to temperance as a cause and explained that "by taking a forward stand in the ranks of temperance workers, we are not stepping beyond our sphere as women but are only using such ways and means as will accomplish the work which God has assigned us."[16]

But at times these maternal feminists resorted to equal rights arguments to make their point. At a citizens' meeting in 1907, called to resist a move to take the municipal vote away from women, Spofford said, "If women are to be debarred on the ground that they are not intelligent enough to vote . . . then let us demand that only intelligent men be allowed to vote. If we are to take the standard of morality—and there seems to have been some fear that the extension of the franchise in this city would have put undue power in the hands of immoral women—then we have the right to demand that only moral men vote. If the Property Owners' Association who are so careful of the morals of the city will undertake to look after the morals of the men of the city, the ladies will undertake to look after those of the women." She couldn't help adding that she thought "of the two the ladies will have the easier task."[17]

THE PARTIES' PART

The attitudes of political parties have a robust impact on women's success at the polls, observed Linda Trimble and Jane Arscott, who have written and critiqued the history of Canadian political women. "Where parties of the left that champion equality have assumed a dominant position electorally, other parties in the system feel competitive pressure to provide opportunities for women in their parties as well. Conversely, in systems where parties of the right and center right have dominated politics, few women have gained access to legislatures, even as representatives of the left."[18] Despite the fact that until 1972 the CCF and NDP never attained government in BC, they "assumed a dominant position electorally" from the founding of the CCF in 1933 and have strongly championed the election of women.

Studies in Canada have revealed that it is far harder for women to win party nominations than to win elections once they're nominated; they win elections about as often as men do. Since party members make the policies on gender equity and choose party candidates, they create the most difficult barriers to gender equity in government representation. No party has yet offered the voters a gender-equal slate. The best any has achieved in BC is the 42 percent of its nominees that the New Democrats put up for election in the 2006 federal election. With that in mind, it is interesting to look at the political parties' roles in winning the franchise for women.

The Tories under Sir John A. Macdonald proposed several bills to allow universal—or at least two-gendered-for-most-whites—suffrage. Finally Tory Prime Minister Robert Borden's government passed the legislation that gave most Canadian women the vote in 1918 and in 1920 the right to stand for election.

In British Columbia, party politics was not introduced into government until 1903. From that time, it was Conservative Premier Richard McBride who repeatedly rebuffed the annual petitions of women suffragists until his resignation in 1915. His successor as Tory leader, Premier William Bowser, put the issue to a referendum in 1916 but was not called upon to legislate the women's franchise because he lost the election.

BC Conservative Party women have reflected their party's reluctance to accept woman suffrage by being slow to take up the opportunities offered by suffrage legislation. Provincially a Tory woman ran in the 1920 general election and in the next two elections, but efforts after that were sporadic until 1986. Since then no woman provincial candidate has labelled herself Conservative. As the Social Credit Party emerged in BC under the leadership of a former Tory, two Tory women switched allegiance and sat as Socred MLAs. A few Tory women ran even when Social Credit was in its heyday as the provincial party for right-leaning voters, and Tory women have run and been elected to Parliament. Federally the first BC Tory woman ran in 1953, and four more ran in elections over the next twenty years. BC voters returned three Tory women to Parliament in the years between 1980 and 1993.

Preston Manning established the Reform Party for disgruntled Tories and other right-wing voters in 1987. A number of women were among candidates—and MPs—for that party and its successor, the Alliance Party, between the 1988 election and 2004 when the Conservative rift healed. The Reform-Alliance Party had no official policy encouraging women to run. Stephanie L. Montgomery cited this fact in her 1997 master's thesis for the University of Western Ontario, confirming what she called "the male-centredness of the Reform Party in its ideology, policies, organization and electoral base."[19] Sydney Sharpe, in her critique *The Gilded Ghetto*, wrote that "The Reform Party has a large quota of sexist men, but its women can be surprisingly strong (maybe because they have to put up with the men)."[20] Many women helped form the party, and several were asked to run when its organization was new in 1988 and 1993. In BC two who were central to their local organizations agreed to run and went to Parliament in 1993, and one was re-elected in 2000 after Reform became the Alliance Party. Under both banners the party ran a total of twenty-eight BC women in four federal elections, three provincial elections and one provincial by-election. In 2004, when

Alliance members united with the Progressive Conservatives and ran as the Conservatives, an Alliance member was re-elected as a Conservative and one woman was newly elected. In the 2006 federal election, four BC women were candidates—11 percent of the total—and the two incumbents won.

BC WOMEN PARTICIPANTS

BC Women's Participation in Federal and Provincial Politics, by Party Membership				
Party	Candidates	Elected	MLAs	MPs
CCF-NDP	176	48	37	11
Liberal	157	33	27	6
Conservative-PC	76	6	1	5
Social Credit	60	10	10	0
Reform-Alliance	27	5	0	5
Other	341	1	1	0
Total	837	103	76	27

Note: Although British Columbians elected seventy-six women MLAs and twenty-seven women MPs, four of those women sat in both houses, and three sat in an assembly for two parties, so the actual number of women is ninety-six. Subtract one for each of K. Campbell, G. MacInnis, P. Priddy, J. Murray, B. Hinton, T. Rolston and M. E. Smith.

The other old-line party, the Liberal Party, followed a more activist path. After the 1916 BC referendum succeeded, Liberal Premier Harlan Brewster passed legislation in 1917 allowing women to vote and to stand for office. He even recognized women's interests in setting the next election date in 1920, if we suppose he paid attention to a letter from his Speaker, John Keen, member for Kaslo. Keen recognized that a date earlier than December 1 would be inconvenient for the women, who would be voting for the first time, because in the autumn they were "all so busy with fruits, and preserves, pink teas, outings etc etc."[21]

The Liberal Party of Canada, in response to activism among women in the party—much of it led by Mary Ellen Smith—agreed in 1923 to set up a national federation of women's clubs. In 1928 it held a founding convention in Ottawa, which elected Smith as president. The goal of the federation was to "give persons an opportunity to become imbued with Liberal principles and to learn how to conduct a political club and eventually be able to join with other Liberal organizations, either as a club or as individuals, in the support of a candidate during election contests."[22] Notably, electing women—or even getting them to run in elections—was not an explicit objective.

Grace MacInnis (centre) and Dorothy Steeves (right) with Harold Winch, CCF party leader when both women were MLAs. One writer called Steeves a peacock and MacInnis a guinea hen to describe how they worked. *City of Vancouver Archives, Major Mathews Collection Port P809.*

The delegates spent most of their three days at convention fawning over and memorializing male Liberal leaders, living and dead: they ceremonially placed three wreaths for Sir Wilfrid Laurier, and every speaker lauded the broad-minded, enthusiastic support of William Lyon Mackenzie King, the current prime minister. Their organization, under Smith's leadership, nevertheless set up action committees and put members in touch with each other.

From the 1920 provincial election, when Smith ran provincially as a Liberal rather than an Independent with Liberal support, Liberal women have missed running in only one BC general election. Their absence in the legislature occurred only during Socred governments. Federally, women's participation was sporadic until the mid-1970s. Since then six candidates have become MPs.

Liberal Prime Minister Jean Chrétien tried to address the gender imbalance. In 1993 and 1997, on party convention resolutions, he appointed candidates to increase the number of women and of visible minority candidates. He had set up a leader's task force on women in politics which decided, as MP and committee member Hedy Fry noted, that "if you were going to really support women in politics you had to support them at a nomination level and you had to support them to run in winnable ridings." Chrétien named thirteen Canadian women candidates in 1993 to winnable ridings. Twelve won. In 1997 he named Sophia Leung in a new riding, Vancouver–Kingsway. She won and held the seat for one more election.

Prime Minister Paul Martin nullified the success of that affirmative action in 2004 when he arranged for five uncontested nominations of candidates for what critics called his

Dream Team. Although Leung had told me she planned to run again, she stepped aside for BC business heavyweight David Emerson, who won in her solid Liberal riding. Five other women were organized out of nominations to make way for Dream Team members, and the only nominated woman in the group lost in the election. In the 2006 election, seven women ran for the Liberal Party, or 19 percent—6 percent short of the federal party's general goal but close to the national average. Veteran Fry was the only woman to win election. Within weeks, Emerson left the Liberals to become a Tory minister.

The provincial Liberal Party disappeared from the legislature in 1975 when Liberal MLAs joined the governing Socreds. As the Socreds faltered before the 1991 election, the BC Liberal Party formed a separate provincial party, and since then has used a Women's Liberal Commission to assist and promote the role of women in the political process. The party made a serious effort to encourage women to run in elections in the 1990s and the first half-decade of the twenty-first century. It has been the second most successful party in BC at electing women to assemblies.

Socialist parties have always advocated equality for women. The founder of the CCF, James Woodsworth, regularly invited speakers on women's equality to the discussion groups he led in the early years of the twentieth century as a political organizer and leader. When the party was founded in 1933, strong women leaders were among the active BC members. One ran and won in 1933, and women have run for the party in every general election since then, running for the NDP after 1972, when the party changed its name and enhanced its ties to labour. Federally, CCF women started running in 1940 and have missed only three federal elections since. In 1965, Grace MacInnis became BC's first woman MP. The party has put forward more candidates and elected more women provincially and federally than any other BC party.

The New Democrats have an active Women's Rights Committee, established in the 1970s with the second flowering of the women's movement. In 1975 it backed the candidacy of Rosemary Brown as the first woman to contest a major federal party leadership and took a large part in running the campaign. It has successfully supported gender parity in executive positions both provincially and federally. Although it has also set its sights on gender parity in candidate selection, it has never achieved higher than 42 percent. Still, that is the highest percentage of women candidates yet recorded in a Canadian election, and the BC women did well, six going to Ottawa with four men in their caucus. At its 2007 convention the provincial party adopted an affirmative action policy to achieve at least 30 percent women candidates in the next election. For one thing, each constituency in which an incumbent retires must nominate a woman candidate. The balance will come from volunteer or assigned constituencies that do not have an incumbent running.

While the Socreds didn't necessarily encourage women to seek nominations, they were generous in giving cabinet appointments—albeit without portfolios—to women who had been elected. In 1952, the first year of the Social Credit government, Tilly Rolston was appointed minister of education, and from 1953 until 1972, Premier W.A.C. Bennett appointed the five women elected by his party as cabinet ministers without portfolio. In Socred administrations from 1975 to 1991, four of the five women MLAs held cabinet portfolios. The fifth was Kim Campbell, who resigned her seat for more interesting work in Parliament with the Progressive Conservative Party.

Although BC women candidates have contested 1,250 federal and provincial seats, many women ran for more than one party and appear on more than one party list. In fact only 837 BC women have run for election provincially or federally. Just more than 40 percent of them ran either independently or for fringe parties—which have never elected a member. That includes the Green Party, which has run 108 women since it began to put candidates forward in 1983, and the Progressive Democratic Alliance, which ran twenty-two women in the single provincial election it contested in 1996. Many of the candidates in smaller groups have belonged to strong labour or communist parties, although women also ran for the Rhinoceros Party, the BC Marijuana Party, the Family Coalition, the Natural Law Party, the Sex Party, the Work Less Party and others. It may well be easier to get a nomination in a fringe party, but women's willingness to run, sometimes more than once, for parties that have never elected a member also clearly shows grit and commitment to principle.

"You bring skills that your male colleagues don't bring," said Penny Priddy. "Our kids will be worse off if those skills don't get to the table." *Courtesy Penny Priddy office.*

ALL IS FAIR...

THIS IS THE ARMY,
MS. JONES

When Johnny comes running because big brother Bob has locked him in the closet for an hour, a mother doesn't say, "Well, Bob is bigger and smarter than you. Don't whine to me. You'll just have to do what he wants until you're bigger and smarter and the tables are turned. Get your licks in when you can. You might be able to whack him on the shins with a lacrosse stick now and then because you can run pretty fast."

Men don't do that in their families either, but they do it in the wider world. They do it in the assemblies of the nation.

Male politicians, the media and the public who feel uneasy with women politicians lament that they don't fit the mould of traditionally successful politicians. They might also notice that women don't organize their lives or their families on the military model.

"The arrogance of male dominance is to be found, naked and un-ashamed, at the heart of our democratic system," the *Globe and Mail* said editorially in 1997.[23] Many male members are somewhat surprised to experience the raw force of power as it is exercised in our assemblies. But women in the BC legislature and the Canadian House of Commons express shock.

April Sanders thought being in the BC legislature was like "being in a foreign country, feeling completely from another planet with respect to how things were run: the rules, the way decisions were made," and her sense that the debaters showed "no real commitment" on either side of the house. And Evelyn Gillespie said, "We were under attack from the time of the election. It was war mode. You didn't let your guard down for a second." Agnes Kripps remembered somebody saying, "You don't wound a tiger; you kill him," but that was not her "political instinct."

Government and our democratic system evolved from ancient models created by the men who governed nations and conducted wars. Our houses of assembly work on a military model, which rewards winners and consigns losers to the margins of the world.

Politics is a war game, like hockey or football or polo, and the only object is to win: winning warriors command the hill. To political parties and the scribes who monitor and report the battles, a victory that is compromised by some other value is just unfinished business. In war and in politics, you are a sissy unless you find something to fight about every day.

The armies are political parties, which any citizen can join. They do the difficult work of gathering societal interests into platforms of beliefs and values. Different as the parties are, each one brings some kind of order to what would otherwise be chaotic. As critic Thomas E. Patterson put it, the great virtue of effective party competition is "not that it always produces the best leadership and provides a full discussion of the issues, for it does not, but that it offers a steady and relatively coherent set of ideas and traditions for the voters to choose from."[24] To win office and put into effect their platforms—or at least to articulate them publicly—parties gather candidates and campaign teams and raise money for campaigns. And in elections where voters do not know the candidates personally, they can count on the candidates' party affiliations to guide them in their choices. Thus, the parties fall into place as do the competing armies in a war, and when members take their seats in the chamber, they line up across the floor from each other in battle formation—two sword-lengths apart.

This characterization of politics was evident at the 1928 organizational conference for the National Federation of the Liberal Women of Canada. Mrs. Peter Heenan, wife of the Minister of Labour, told the new members, "Local organizations are indispensable to a party. They are as necessary to it as regimental organizations to an army. Whoever desires to see Liberal doctrines prevail in the Government of the country will find the weapon nearest at hand is membership in the Liberal organization of her district.... After all, it is not enough for us to be Liberals because we were born that way."[25]

From nomination as a candidate to service in an assembly, fighting is the pattern of behaviour that has worked before, is approved by the media and is expected of members. Elections, public statements, caucus organization and chamber business are all adversarial. Barb Copping made this blunt observation: "The current system, the adversarial system, is testicle-driven. Women would be more consensual, and the parliamentary party system would not exist, if only females were members." When she entered the legislature, Copping thought that members might work together for solutions to problems, but found "you weren't to agree with any of the opposition. In some cases I did, but I quickly had my knuckles rapped." Copping thought that in this polarized environment, too much of the talk was just filling time by repeating party positions, and she wanted to see instead "the bringing together of the best of both sides."

Linda Reid tried to set an example in the BC house when she was critic for women's equality and Penny Priddy was the minister. "I stood up in the house and shocked people when I said, 'Nothing would be worse in the house than two women squabbling about women's equality. There's a ton of issues we agree on; let's get it done. There are issues that are just good public policy that should be common to every walking, breathing person in this province.'" Reid thought the women in that assembly did some good work across party lines; unfortunately she lost her women's critic role only a short time later.

The highlight of the assembly every day is question period, when the champions of the teams are sent out, like Agamemnon and Paris under the walls of Troy, to carry the important battle of the day. The action is raucous, loud, overly aggressive and boastful. Heckling, desk-pounding and pointed interjections tax the authority of the speaker to maintain what all members say they support in the chamber—dignity and decorum. Before Joy MacPhail retired from a legislature in which she and Jenny Kwan had been for more than three years the only NDP members in a House with more than seventy-five Liberals, she told an interviewer, "We would do everything we could to support each other, including, in the early days, holding each other's hand under the desk. Any time either of us showed weakness, they would increase their attacks on us."[26] Neither MacPhail nor Kwan were rookies, and no one would ever accuse MacPhail of being a shrinking violet.

Mary Collins said, "I hated question period. I felt it was just to make everybody else look stupid. . . not to elicit any interesting information. Your own colleagues never applauded [unless you acted aggressively]." If she said, "That's a really interesting issue; I'd be glad to . . ." she was reproached. "They liked it when you stood up there and gave 'em hell!" Collins didn't like being bombastic but often played the role.

"You're not supposed to answer the question," said Cathy Mc-Gregor. "Get into your message, go after the other guys and score. It's about scoring, animosity, conflict, confrontation and being able to get in a good shot." It's a culture, she said, which values beating up the other guy. And it reaches beyond question period. "When you introduce a bill, you're never supposed to amend it. It doesn't matter what they say on the other side—it doesn't matter, it doesn't matter—just ignore them. Make up reasons why changes shouldn't be allowed. Stand up and speak against [any opposition suggestion] and tell your colleagues to vote against it. Because making change is a total sign of weakness." You are never to agree with the other side.

Jan Pullinger felt it was indicative of her success in the house that "in all my years in cabinet, I think I had one question from the opposition. . . . And my estimates were the shortest of anybody's. My absolutely hard-nosed, in-your-face attitude in the legislature worked."

In contrast, Joan Sawicki said she was often confounded "because

Joy MacPhail was interim leader of a two-woman opposition in the BC legislature with seventy-seven government members. "We would do everything to support each other" against tangible aggression. *Courtesy New Democratic Party.*

I don't deal well with conflict." Faced with any aggressiveness at all, she would back off but be angry with herself "because there would be no reason why I had backed off." She didn't back off as often at the end of her ministerial career, "but I'm not sure that the other tool I used, which was just to forge ahead, was any more successful. [I never] figured out how to achieve what I so passionately believed we should achieve."

An assembly and its armies do not have perfect military discipline. Occasionally some soldier brings in a consensus decision, for example, which creates an organizational problem because it is inconsistent with military structure. It has to be accepted by the hierarchy in order to have force, but even if the hierarchical leader withholds his veto, it is clear that a community decision is not final. This is so even though the whole tenor of good community action and good management in the wider world is moving toward flatter organizational structures and more consensual decisions.

"All our institutions, church or state, are military," said Iona Campagnolo, "all hierarchical, a military construct." Campagnolo does not like that construct, but it's the legacy of an all-male institution that is "hierarchical, military, command and control, not inclusive. [With it comes] a built-in power mechanism where you don't just attempt to overcome your opponent, you attempt to annihilate him—I've had people threaten to annihilate me—to make him economically unable to survive, so that he can't rise again. The whole pattern of rewards, checks and balances is to moderate who can stay afloat and who can't."

Darlene Marzari, remarking on our British beginnings, said, "The systems that were invented in 1265 no longer suit the day. A bunch of guys riding down to London after the crops were in and the women were locked up, to make the decisions about who got what share of the pie, doesn't work anymore. They built the structure around the lowest common denominator of male teenager, which was war, fighting for land and turf. It was a system built for tribal chieftains, and it still operates, though now they're economic tribal chieftains."

Canadians try to operate in our electronic age within the parameters of a system built for feudal lords, she said. As a result "we have a system that is completely corrupt. I don't mean individually corrupt, but it encourages individual corruption. It's redundant and archaic and anarchistic, and you have to lie to make it meet your needs. You have to distort the truth because the system was built on a military model. And you know there's the right way, the wrong way, and the army way.

Parliament is structured on the army way with all the components. You have a general, and whatever happens, you are loyal and you don't mutiny. And your so-called freedom of voice becomes subsumed under loyalty to a master and the master's gatekeepers. To make the structure operate, a chieftain puts in a series of hierarchies, all reporting to him. And any notion of consensus building, any notion of working inside a community so that the decision makers reflect what the community needs and wants and asks for is virtually impossible. If a consensus process works, it works despite the system."

Gretchen Mann Brewin agrees. "Consensus bumps up against the traditions of the parliamentary system with its hierarchies and adversarial ways of doing things."

Marzari found a phrase to describe it all. "John le Carré remarked that the British secret service operated during the Second World War in 'the windless heat of a secret room.' That extrapolates into the larger system. A secret room is dominated by bullies. No matter who the tribal chief is, he has to rely on his bullies to keep him safe from those who would take his position. Lear, Macbeth—they're all based on that. And you want to know why women have difficulty in that system?"

"It's not a rational process," says Darlene Marzari of the way we use our parliamentary system. *Courtesy New Democratic Party.*

The answer, said the pragmatic Marzari, is that "you've got to learn to play hockey sometimes. It's a skill and you can do it. Some women hear that message and understand it. Others are hockey players to start with." Knowing how to play hockey means knowing "how to get things on the agenda, pushing them through, linking yourself with the right person at the right time. It's not a rational process; it's an army process.

So you drape yourself in the flag of what's going on at the moment, and you get your initiatives through. And that is timing. Never accept the position of loser. Maintain equilibrium and get in there for the next fight. Constant positioning."

Pullinger called it constant competition. Like Campagnolo and Marzari, she considered the military shape and practice of parliaments one of the major difficulties for women and the way women prefer to work. Pullinger, who was elected in a by-election and came into the legislature alone, described her first day at "the testosterone tabernacle" as getting hit in the face with a bucket of ice cubes. "I didn't comprehend any of it. It probably would have been easier to walk into Tenerife in terms of cultural difference."

Old wives believe the first rule of war is that there are no rules. Pullinger came to the same conclusion. Wherever she'd worked or studied, there'd been written rules and a language. Pullinger thought there must be a handbook titled *The Art of War: Women's and Men's War Games* or at least a book covering those subjects, but she couldn't find any such thing. She had just been immersed in women's studies and had read the available literature on women and power and women in politics. Our legislature wasn't there.

"I went to see [the house leader] and found there was nothing to help anybody, which is part of the war game, right? I was completely overwhelmed by the fact that I was so far aside from what was going on. Ultimately I had two choices. I could continue to behave in the way that I prefer to behave—which is to negotiate with people, to do things collectively, to set up the goal and do my bit to reach the goal—and be ignored, or I could play the boys' game and be labelled a bitch or some version thereof and have some influence. So I chose the latter. I didn't come here to be liked. I came here to make things happen."

Pullinger concluded—with caveats about not all women or men being the same—that "men (a) understand the rules of the game and (b) are way more comfortable with the fact that it's competitive at every level. The objective is to catch the general's attention . . . by being better than your colleagues, and the way you get to be better than your colleagues is to frequently pull the rug out from under them, ignore them, whatever."

Bonnie McKinnon suggested, "Go and learn to play chess really well and then look at politics the same way, because whether people like it or not, politics is a game to see who's going to back down first." Chess may be the most appropriate comparison. World champion chess master Bobby Fischer has been quoted as saying, "I like the moment when I break a man's ego."[27]

Neither Marzari nor Campagnolo can see this war structure surviving through the globalization that is upon us. As Campagnolo put it, "We live in an adversarial society. Partisan politics, competing ideologies and various belief systems generally oppose co-operation" and negotiation. The media "pits opinions against each other to stimulate debate and elicit maximum disagreement. It is a pattern designed for entertainment, not results. Our past tradition of elite decision making—the men-in-suits syndrome—is characterized by winners and losers, and we all know winner takes all! But in an anxious age of change, losers will prolong any process until their views are incorporated into outcomes that affect them."

Such processes take time, but people will not accept noninclusive decisions anymore and will use protests and other means to see that their input is recognized. "In my experience the time taken is generally the same in the long run." Campagnolo concluded, "In the old world, conflict was a way of life, but today conflict is tolerated at great risk."

Marzari noted that our governmental systems "do not have public policy infrastructures to match the globalization of capital, so they have to be fabricated. But they won't be created by the existing decision making structures because they just survive to save themselves. Armies do that."

On this issue and in many of their other comments, women politicians strongly suggested that communities—communities of interest and of common concern—must become the basis for decisions, particularly as the world's business continues to become more and more global, and the impacts become more and more local.

The Media—It's Not All Romance

Members and the press gallery have a symbiotic relationship: the media and politicians need each other for healthy survival. Judi Tyabji Wilson pointed out the danger for politicians: "You do your work as a politician, but nobody knows about it unless they write about it. But if they tell the world that you're an incompetent dork, that's all the public hears."

The relationship started once "scribblers" began using the printing press to circulate their political ideas. Originally as a jest, the press was called the fourth estate in Britain. The lords spiritual (the church) were the first estate; the lords temporal (the nobility), headed by the king, were the second estate and the commons had recently won the right to be the third estate. The name "fourth estate" refers to the press's role as a watchdog to keep the others honest. The press took the name seriously enough to try to do that job, and the label stuck, leaving it the only part of the modern public world calling itself an estate.

Today's citizens expect the media to keep a public eye on the people elected to run the state; such scrutiny is one of the important checks in a democratic system. The public wants the media to ascertain facts and opinions, provide a balanced view of our public business and so shape a perception as close as possible to reality. Reciprocally, politicians depend on the media to recognize their part in the process and carry to the public their message as representatives of citizens.

We are not dealing with the print-media press of old, however. Posters and billboards, radio, television, email and satellite transmission make news reporting faster and faster and now nearly instantaneous. Local ownership of newspapers and broadcast outlets has virtually disappeared. Consolidation of news outlets and the expense of technology have led to a degree of corporate control that has never before existed. Now too often corporations value the slowly accumulated wisdom of an editor less than the marketing know-how of businessmen as they vie for the most dramatic—read "conflictual"—presentation of news to hold the greatest market share. The media needs what a critic recently called "adversarial narrative." Conflict is seldom positive, and Patty Sahota noted that the media's practice of "selling the negative before they sell the positive has a huge effect on the psyche." Politics is "a blood sport and it's entertainment," Joy MacPhail said, "and therefore it's in the interest of the media to make us larger than life and give us personalities that are larger than life. People react to that."

Complexity has become a victim as the requirements of speed, breadth and conflict have inevitably led to increasing distrust among the media, governments, political activists and the public. Even experienced editors, reporters and columnists with integrity cannot escape the demands of a public expecting instant reports. They often succeed in offering only information that resembles reflections in funhouse mirrors, emphasizing, distorting and hiding various parts. "When there's a scandal," Sharon Hayes said, "[the media exploit it] to sell copy." Often a politician has overstated something and appears to be scheming, so "people don't believe either side but think they're all trying to connive to their own end." The public response is often to stop participating in political action.

The media's appetite for conflict fits neatly into our adversarial system of government. "It's the whole system" that contributes to the sensationalism, said Sue Hammell. Politicians, cast into conflict with members of other parties, must win their battles publicly, preferably in front of media who will spread the word. For politicians the easiest way to get the attention of the media is to look like the winner in a conflict.

No praise comes to those who avoid battles for the sake of a cause, or even more essentially, to those who extend a civil word to a colleague. This isn't physical war—politicians don't usually fight with fists—but it is verbal war, savoured by the media and many members of the public, who like it to be as close as possible to the drama of blows. As a result, when one politician calls another an idiot or a shyster, the public doesn't blink but says, "Oh, just another politician; they're all idiots, they're all shysters," and awaits a more telling blow from one of the combatants.

Joan Smallwood said, "You don't defeat a government or an individual because you disagree with their values or their ideology. You defeat them by smear campaigns."

As well, the media has a strong habit of reporting politics as they would a horse race, focussing more on the technical success of the players than on the policy dialogue. When Stephen Harper made no media appearances for three days in February 2006 after he was sworn in as prime minister, the subject of the day for reporters and columnists was his failure to cement a good first impression with them: what he should have done, what he didn't do and where that all might lead. World and national events, as well as Conservative Party policy, took second place.

When Rosemary Brown conducted a personal five-day filibuster of human resources minister Bill Vander Zalm's legislation to end the Vancouver Resource Board in 1977, the media reported on her achievement by congratulating her for having broken the standing record for length of filibusters. The *Vancouver Sun* opened a story headlined "Weeping Brown Ends Her Record Filibuster,"[28] with the time of her quitting and a description of her tears, and then reported, "Brown had spoken for about 13 hours and 45 minutes, a modern-day record, surpassing current economic development minister Don Phillips, who talked for 12½ hours in 1973 against the NDP's Land Commission Act. Including time taken up by points of order raised by fellow NDP MLAs so she could sit for a few minutes and rest, Brown held the floor for almost 16 hours." The Victoria *Daily Colonist* of the same date, in a story headlined "Sobbing Rosemary Surrenders to Exhaustion,"[29] added more statistics. "The spirit had carried her past the modern-day BC Legislature debate record . . . set by . . . Phillips. But, if old reports are correct, she was a little short of the 16 hours recorded by Leonard McLure in 1866."

No wonder Brown wept—after such a campaign to be remembered only as the one MLA more windy than Don Phillips, a notoriously loud and blustering member, but still not as successful as some heroic filibusterer of more than a hundred years ago! Her objections to government action were significantly overshadowed by media reports of the competition to get media attention, including Vander Zalm's response: "I didn't notice any [tears]."

The media's drive for immediacy encourages the human tendency to stereotype. Too often they base their reports on expectations that (a) politicians never speak the truth, (b) they don't deliver on their promises,

(c) politicians will do anything to hog the spotlight, (d) they waste the time of the legislature at great expense by probing points—with no relevance or importance—only for "the politics," (e) they went into politics for their own financial benefit and are now reaping huge rewards, (f) they take every opportunity to sponge off the public.

The media many times pointed their finger at Glen Clark as one of our youngest MLAs, for example, and added up the total amount that he could receive as a pension from the Crown after serving two terms—which would have made him eligible for a pension—or after serving three terms, which he did, some of that time as premier. It always added up to more than a million dollars. The same is true, however, of pensions for many workers with good pension plans who begin to collect as soon as they are eligible and live to an average life expectancy. The rewards of anyone doing private-sector work with similar responsibility to Clark's would be much higher.

Then there are prejudices about married couples. The media are still delighted to bring up the old-fashioned idea that married couples, when working for government, should not have their pay and pensions considered separately. When Nina Grewal was elected MP in the same election as her husband Gurmant was re-elected, the media made a great fuss about whether each should have a capital living allowance, despite the number of MPs who over the years had bunked together for convenience and economy. Jan Pullinger and husband Dale Lovick, both MLAs, could count on seeing speculations and tut-tuttings whenever they were the subject of media reports on pay and allowances.

"The media loves to portray politicians as corrupt. They love to talk about our pension plans and perks and free trips," said Margaret Lord, who saw no special benefits when she was an MLA. Before she went into politics, she left a good job and severed her pension plan. "Just as I got [into the legislature], our pension plan was cancelled by our own government, and nothing was put in its place. So here I am at age fifty-three with no pension of any sort." Lord resented the media's "unfair" approach. "The media know how hard members work. They know what our life is like." Characterizing members as bad guys sells papers, she said, but it's a real disservice to democracy. "I guess the other side of the coin is that the public has a responsibility to do some critical thinking of their own." On this point Brenda Locke agreed. "The public doesn't take the time to understand politics."

Lynn Hunter remembered press gallery members asking politicians why they act so belligerently in the Commons, especially why they make such an event of question period. One of them said, "'You're just a bunch of babies down there, yelling at one another.' And Jim Fulton asked them, 'Do you ever report on anything substantive happening in the House? What we're trying to do is get the profile of our party elevated. We can't do it by asking substantive questions because you never report it.' So round and round and round it goes. It's more than just the politicians to be blamed." Hunter nevertheless recognizes some of the constraints endured by the media. "They have a job to do and a deadline to make, and if you want your story out there, you've got to work within their rules. There's a lot of misinformation—a lot about politicians—but there's a lot of misinformation out there about media too. They don't necessarily have an agenda. They're trying to get a job done."

Privacy for elected people has shrunk to a tiny island in their lives. "At one time, we didn't talk about anybody's private affairs," said Grace McCarthy. "Whatever they did was their business. That was an unwritten rule and better, because we don't know what goes on in people's minds and hearts and bedrooms and living rooms, and honestly I don't want to know." Now the media reports very personal things, which destroys families, marriages and lives without adding a thing to the political process. Such reporting adds a terrible, undeserved aura to politicians. McCarthy said coverage of "the whole Wilson thing"—the affair and subsequent marriage of Gordon Wilson and Judi Tyabji—"was just an abomination. It didn't need to be on the front page every day for weeks and weeks and weeks."

Coverage by some of the most influential members of the press gallery often happens without benefit of personal contact. The journalists are confident they have gleaned enough—from party publicists and others who cultivate the acquaintance of press gallery members and have no qualms about sharing their gossip—that they can get it right in a hurry. Experienced male members and party functionaries often encourage rookies, especially female ones, to get friendly with gallery members, to go for a beer with them after work. "That's part of the culture, too, if you want to be a 'successful' politician," noted Cathy McGregor. "have little secret meetings and give little bits of information." It was a game she was unwilling to play. In fact the high proportion of males in the gallery who see politics primarily as conflict—in the face of which some women collapse—makes it difficult for women to contemplate such cultivation. A chummy beer after work does not beckon with the same force as a phone call home to the kids, even for those women who enjoy chatting in a bar with co-workers. On the whole, women politicians do not closely cultivate members of the gallery even if they have a hard time getting media attention. "The media tend not to come to women for questions. They go to the male members," said Margaret Mitchell. "Except for the odd woman reporter, they very rarely give you interviews," although such coverage is important to MPs from BC.

The media misses the point with its emphasis on conflict and its encouragement for politicians to be aggressive and to simplify their positions, said Jan Pullinger. "People who understand politics understand it's about compromise." When Pullinger told a talk show host at a private gathering that she personally would prefer the province be free of gaming, the host said she was dishonest by not stating that position publicly. She told him that this was a narrow view. "I have another personal opinion—that we should alleviate poverty. And we have something like seven hundred million dollars of British Columbia money going north, east, and south of us to

Grace McCarthy, who served six terms over 20 years: "At one time we didn't talk about anybody's private affairs. That was an unwritten rule." *Photo courtesy Grace McCarthy.*

jurisdictions where people can gamble. My personal opinion is also that this money should stay here to help us deal with poverty. How could I express this complex issue to the public through the media? I couldn't." The view that compromise and trade-offs are sellouts is reinforced and exploited by government critics. Pullinger added, "The condemnation of politicians who don't take simplistic stands on complex issues has been exacerbated by the global concentration of media and other corporate interests who share the same ideology."

When the media gets a story wrong, redress is far from easy. Grace McCarthy contemplated suing for what she claimed was a libellous story about her. When she led the Social Credit Party from 1993 to 1994, "I never took any money for being leader of the party—didn't take a salary, didn't take expenses. Except once. I think it was seventy dollars or seventy-five dollars."

Brenda Locke answers questions with visiting Liberal leader Stéphane Dion. Locke ran twice federally after her legislative career. *Photo courtesy Patrick Tam/FlungingPictures.com*

A member of the party's board of directors, however, "gave a story to the *Vancouver Sun* about how much money it was costing them to have me as leader. He quoted figures that were absolutely phenomenal. Well, can you imagine waking up to that in the morning after my husband had written cheques and I had written cheques for every single thing I did? If I took people to lunch, if I took them to dinner, I wouldn't think of putting in a bill. If I travelled to Vernon or if I travelled to Prince George, I never put in a bill. I didn't put in for gas, and gas was a big thing. I was all over the place. And he accused me of costing the party money!

"Well, if the accusation is there in black and white, it exhausts you to disabuse people of that idea." Many haven't even read it themselves. McCarthy went to a lawyer who said, "Everybody knows you. . . . This is something that is going to pass in a day or two. Do you want it all brought up again in a trial, in a court case?" Her first reaction was to clear her name publicly, but after talking it over with her husband, she concluded that she didn't want to give anyone the satisfaction of having the whole thing regurgitated. "We didn't do it because I was tired of the whole thing, because the party executive weren't co-operating, and because of all the other things." And then McCarthy quoted an old nostrum: "That newspaper would be wrapping fish by tomorrow."

WHO'S PLAYING THE GAME

"There was a time when women politicians didn't feel all that much collegiality with other women because there was a peril to it," Kim Campbell observed. "An example: if a few men stand in the corridor talking, nobody thinks anything of it. If a few women stand in the corridor talking, men will ask 'What are you girls talking about?'" Campbell saw how a group of people who differ from the norm seem to provide a threat if they gather to talk among themselves. The predominant group has no way of knowing what the odd ones out might do or say, and their control might be threatened.

The prancing penis affair drew interest when a gathering of women engaged in what is usually men's recreation. The media response it drew was instructive both for what the media said of MLAs in general and for its coverage of the women involved.

It all started after the May 1996 election, when the legislature sat through July. Estimates debates continued in night sittings, but most of the members had finished their major work in the house. Penny Priddy had just finished a series of treatments for breast cancer, so the NDP women who were gathering to celebrate with her decided to invite the Liberal women too. Joy MacPhail was the instigator. With a sense that the women in the NDP caucus were "very close amongst ourselves," she wanted to bring that group of eleven and the eight Liberal women together, as well as some female staff and media. "It made for a good party." They had refreshments in the legislature buildings in case a vote was called during the forestry estimates debate. In that term the legislative numbers were very close, so attendance at the session was closely monitored. The

MLAs were tired, but if one critic wanted to grill one minister whose estimates were not completed, all members had to be present.

Among the gifts Priddy received was a windup toy shaped like a penis that danced on two feet. It was a stupid, cheeky little item that got most of the women laughing. "We decided we'd go down and put it on the desk of whoever was talking," said MacPhail. "Everybody could watch on the remote TV."

Forests minister David Zirnhelt was up. MacPhail went down to put the toy on his desk while most of the women stayed in Priddy's office and watched a television monitor. Zirnhelt was not rattled, and nobody except the women and some in the chamber knew what had happened. "It was a great laugh internally," MacPhail concluded.

A year later, in 1997, so many women planned to attend the second women's gathering that it was held in the Ned de Beck Lounge, a room reserved for members' social events. The gathering of the women was, to Evelyn Gillespie, "rare, a kind of a trust" that developed because all members of the house "become like a family" after being in the chamber for months at a time; they eat together, celebrate new babies and mourn deaths and illnesses. "Party didn't matter with those kinds of things. People announced grandchildren in the legislature. And that gave us a sense of humanity—that we weren't enemies all the time."

Priddy came to the Ned de Beck Lounge that night carrying the toy as an icon, draped with a cloth and flanked by candles on a tray. Historic echoes of phallic symbols in early civilizations contributed to the humour. Two Liberal MLAs said it was their turn to put the item on the desk of one of the Liberal men. The TV monitor showed that the Speaker was Ted Nebbeling, so Bonnie McKinnon and Linda Reid took the toy into the chamber. As they opened the door to execute their mission, the laughter from the lounge could be heard invading the solemn space of the chamber.

The object of the prank could have been any male in the Liberal caucus, although it was agreed that Nebbeling was a lucky choice because he could take a joke well. As they took seats beside him, he paused in his speech and commented on their arrival. Reid curtsied. The toy was set to dance on his desk. According to several of the women, Nebbeling kept the dancing penis after the prank. "He had it displayed in his office."

The story got out because one of the women MLAs who did not attend the soiree was offended and went to Michael Smyth of the

Province and to her leader, Gordon Campbell. Smyth reacted like a coiled spring. "Just an innocent prank in the house? This week some of our women legislators got up to something that sets a curious example," said the *Province*'s front page. Pictures of MacPhail, Priddy, McKinnon and Reid loomed from newsstands. In his column, after warning those "easily shocked and offended [to] stop reading now," Smyth went on with his "weird story about what is and isn't acceptable behavior by our politicians" based on reports from "more than a few of the women who were there" who had given him "a detailed morning-after description of the raunchy proceedings." Smyth claimed he would have ignored the prank "until a couple of MLAs quietly started complaining to me that the prank was inappropriate and in poor taste." They pointed out that a similar prank, pulled on a woman by men, would have created "an uproar."[30]

Having finally got the point, Smyth initiated an uproar himself with a broadside attack, speculating that the women had chosen Nebbeling because he is openly gay. Also noting that the MLAs' capital city allowance had just increased from a hundred dollars a day to $150 a day—they had been sitting for sixty days, and it was the tourist season—he suggested that MLAs were trying for financial reasons to extend the session. And he pointed out that the event happened as proceedings were being televised at a thousand-dollar-an-hour production costs. The next day, under a story reporting that Nebbeling had accepted McKinnon and Reid's apology,[31] Smyth kept the pot boiling. He framed the prank as "politicians who treat your parliament like it's their own private playpen."[32] Premier Glen Clark may have inadvertently bolstered Smyth's reader response and given his words momentum by saying "Look, it's July and people are working hard and working late nights, and if MLAs got together and if there were a few jokes pulled, it doesn't bother me at all." Smyth then called Clark and Campbell as well as Speaker Dale Lovick to task for not disciplining the women. He also related that "some of my reporter colleagues actually criticized me for writing Friday's column. That disappointed me."

Smyth quoted from the 365 phone calls and emails he had received, 341 of them condemning the women's prank. "You ask if there's a double standard? I say there's no standard. This incident is disgusting and has sunk our legislature to a new low," said one. Another said, "If Gordon Campbell had any moral courage, he'd suspend McKinnon and

Reid and call for the resignations of MacPhail and Priddy, but I won't hold my breath." And another said, "As a feminist, I'm heartbroken. This only hurts our cause and is an insult to the legacy of women like Rosemary Brown who brought such dignity and passion to the women's movement. I'm ashamed for them."[33]

Smyth's *Province* colleague, Susan Martinuk, chimed in on Sunday under the heading, "Double Standard of Legislative 'Sisterhood,'" saying "the women's shenanigans were an embarrassment to women and gave justified support to the argument that women are promoters of a double standard when it comes to sexual harassment." She added, "The pitiful performance of these women has virtually ensured that BC's legislators will continue to be treated with the contempt and disrespect that is increasingly evident among British Columbians. The girls have given us just one more public demonstration of the self-serving nature of the ethical standards that BC's politicians live by."[34]

Martinuk also condemned the foolishness more severely for having been executed on an openly gay man, and for coming at a time when the media was running stories criticizing MLAs for "meaningless debate" that extended the session in order to profit from an extra fifty dollars a day in capital living allowance. She was careful not to say they were generating meaningless debate, only that some unidentified media sources were accusing them of it.

The following Monday, the third day of Smyth's coverage, he quoted Rosemary Brown, calling her "a near-saintly figure in the NDP and among BC's social activists." He quoted her as saying in a "soft, trembling" voice, "I didn't dedicate my life to electing women to Parliament to see them act like men when they got there. I am so disappointed in them. . . . It had all the earmarks of sexism and I was appalled by it." Brown refused to "separate anyone out" for particular blame. "They were all involved. It really hurts. It really sets us back." Three days later, Smyth corrected his quotation from Brown. "After reviewing my notes, I found I had made a very unfortunate omission in transcribing her remarks. The accurate quote, with my emphasis added, should read: 'I didn't dedicate my life to electing women to Parliament to see them act like men who have no respect for women.'"[35]

Writers to the *Province's* editor also gave the women MLAs a drubbing, one of them going so far as to label the prank a "debauched exhibit of hedonism."[36] The *Vancouver Sun*[37] and Victoria's *Times Colonist* chimed in the day after Smyth made the incident public, but with a lighter touch. Sun reporter Jim Beatty lumped the prank in with one that Liberal Mike de Jong had pulled the next night. De Jong had presented MacPhail, as NDP house leader, with a box wrapped in plain brown paper, implying without saying so directly that the box contained a bomb. De Jong suggested that MacPhail take the box and open it later that evening at an event where most of the NDP caucus and their families were attending a fundraiser. MacPhail accepted the box, suggesting that she would go to the Liberal caucus room to open it. The box did not contain a bomb, of course, and whether or not they laughed, everybody let the prank go. Beatty attributed the two events to stress "brought on by late-night sittings of the three and one-half month legislative session."[38] Two days later, after Beatty had spoken to a union official who handles sexual harassment charges and a professor of business at Simon Fraser University, he reported that both had said the situation was handled typically. "Men would be embarrassed by it and would accept an apology," said professor Steve McShane, adding that women might demand more than an apology, given that they suffer about 95 percent of sexual harassment cases.[39]

The *Times Colonist* sent Susan Chung out to do street interviews about the prank on the Friday after the party. People called it "ridiculous," "in bad taste," "immature," and "a waste of taxpayers' money" though they did not identify how any money was spent or wasted.[40]

On the same day a *Times Colonist* editorial deflected blame directed at the women for wasting legislative time, noting that Nebbeling was at the time "continuing his filibuster against forestry spending, while on parliamentary television." The editorial admitted that the prank was in poor taste but added that "most really good pranks are." It pointed out that Nebbeling himself had offended the house earlier in the session by saying, *"Gong dye wah,"* Cantonese for "tell a big lie," when Jenny Kwan was making a speech. It concluded, "Maybe it's time we all lightened up . . . let's stop being so darned sensitive and recognize that sometimes human beings, male and female, will do stupid or tasteless things in a spirit of fun. That's part of life and not worth getting into an uproar about every time it happens."[41]

Further into the *Times Colonist*, senior press gallery reporter Les Leyne commented on the de Jong prank. "The bouncing windup plastic penis that was a highlight earlier in the week was funny. Bombs are not.

De Jong should take his toy to the next Air India memorial service and see how funny it is."[42]

By the time the *Times Colonist*'s Jim Gibson wrote his weekly column eight days after the prancing penis prank, he had checked out local joke stores to find that there had been a run on toys like the prancing penis, but no run on "the prank's female counterpart." Redirecting the discussion, he said, "The female MLAs should start stockpiling more politically correct windups for next year's presentation," such as a racing car for Moe Sihota, an avid collector of speeding tickets, and a pugnacious kangaroo for Gary Farrell-Collins, known for his combative ways.[43]

The next day, another weekly columnist, Jody Paterson, took a hunk out of the women because "I don't want my MLA to be the type who presents somebody with a dancing penis in the legislature ... I want MLAs who not only show me their decent side but in fact are pretty decent all the time, even when they've had too much to drink."[44]

Letters to the editor continued for nearly two weeks. Most of them disapproved of the prank because it was in bad taste or because the women were drinking. Few identified the point that sexual harassment of males was inappropriate for a group highly vocal in opposing sexual harassment of females. By the time I talked to the women MLAs about the incident, half a decade had passed. McKinnon's only regret was that her picture was on the front page of the *Province* on Friday morning, the day her son was to graduate from a course. But other than the timing, McKinnon still felt that it was all just a funny prank. "You know, so many politicians are forced to sit in this little box. Everybody's sense of humour is gone. Everybody has to find something wrong with what you said or what you did. It's just getting too ridiculous for words, and I'm not one to be fit into anybody's box."

MacPhail, who took most of the criticism, said, "You know, we had a ball that evening. It was very collegial; it was completely nonpartisan. If we were taking the mickey out of anyone, it was our male colleagues on both sides of the house."

The gathering had created a different dynamic among the women members. Women of both parties denounced the tattling as a "betrayal" by "one of us." One accurately reflected the mood of many of the women by saying, "We felt betrayed by one of our own who chose not to come to the event." Probably for the first time that session, the "us" was a group that crossed party lines. Gillespie said, "With that sense of betrayal, we never met again. I really regret that."

Lynn Stephens said, "It had been women supporting other women; one woman made a fuss about it. The rest of us thought it was funny, all in fun. As did most of our guys. I thought, 'What's the big deal here?'" The morning Smyth's outburst appeared on the front page of the *Province*, Stephens dug around so she could answer questions about how the report got past the party. Some indignant men in her caucus asked accusingly, "Well, what were you doing?" To the answer that the women were having a drink and a bite together, came a stern reprimand: "Well, you shouldn't be fraternizing." Stephens was riled. "What do you mean, we shouldn't be fraternizing? How many times do you go out and have a drink? Does that mean we can't?" She found some of the men "really embarrassed to have their women, of all people, on the front page of the *Province*—with a dancing penis. Like the world had come to an end. I thought, 'Grow up!'" In sum she had appreciated the opportunity to talk with the other women and regretted that "it was spoiled by one individual."

Rosemary Brown was right, I believe, when she expressed her regret that a group of women leaders in the province had slipped into the trap that led to belittling men as sex objects—the same trap that men fall into and women label a misdemeanour. Besides defending the decades of work put into resisting sexism, Brown said, "When I was elected an MLA, we went there to change the world, not to play games. We went there to change the balance of power among men and women, not set it back." Brown's arrows were on point, if ungenerous in the circumstances. Equally ungenerous were the many charges made by the media scribes, and many of them went far beyond the issue of "bad taste" the *Times Colonist* identified. Smyth himself didn't even recognize what the women did until it was pointed out to him, but once he recognized that he had found a conflict, he used every weapon he thought would hurt. Martinuk and Paterson joined him with a series of clichés about politicians. The women members were costing the taxpayers money, they said, ignoring the rules of the house, neglecting their duty by escaping to a gathering during debate, unfairly groping for media attention, harassing a gay man, embarrassing a near-saint and so juvenile in their behaviour that they should not be allowed to manage public money. The columnists got encouragement from writers of letters to the editor who criticized the women for every peeve they harboured. And most letters to the editor were about MLAs in general—lazy layabouts and extravagant spenders—not about the issue of one sex objectifying the other.

I wasn't at either of the parties that launched the rude toy, but I have abundant and considered sympathy for the women involved. There is a cost to the stress of a legislative session when members average ten-hour days and seven-day weeks for months on end. When the women relaxed, they didn't use the judgment they would have brought to their usual routine.

The reactions of the party leaders, the speaker and most of the media constituted a measured response. Premier Glen Clark accepted the misdemeanour with equanimity, as did Liberal leader Gordon Campbell and Speaker Dale Lovick. Perhaps if the forest estimates debate hadn't gone on so long without a news hook, the penis prank would have garnered less ink. To be fair, feminists decry such activity, and women who want freedom from sexual harassment shouldn't publicly make fun with a model of a male sex organ. On the other hand, it hardly called for discipline by the senior male members of the house as some critics reflexively demanded.

Another remedy championed by Paterson was a requirement that every action by members be on the record. "MLAs wouldn't do things that would leave them ashamed if the public knew. And media would be watchdogs, not censors who hide their charges' offensive behavior from public scrutiny." It is hard to detect how this differs from current practice, even harder to imagine how Paterson would have it enforced. Since the prancing penis was so enthusiastically on the record, it is also difficult to see how her suggestion fit the case.

In general, members do not drink alcohol while on duty in the house, though these women were arguably neither the first nor the worst offenders, and those immediately involved wouldn't call the party a "debauched exhibit of hedonism." Smyth's assumption that "the gossip and drinks were flying thick and furious" fit his prose better than his knowledge.

Obviously the prank upset Brown, but those of us who knew her wondered where her sense of humour was that day. Smyth's characterization of Brown as "a near-saintly figure" and his description of her phone voice as "soft, trembling" seem manipulative. Brown spent fourteen years in the legislature as a feminist, and she didn't win any ground by being faint or trembly. Nor did she do it without gaining enemies and collecting baggage. Brown would surely have been offended to be characterized as a sorry victim of someone else's sin.

Many writers objected to the prank because the penis was "an icon," and that objection bears a particular twist. When Priddy carried the toy into the party on a tray, flanked by candles and swathed in a cloth that she ceremoniously removed, she was mocking no present-day religion. The phallus in ancient mythology was a symbol of male power. These women of the late twentieth century could, with true irony, dress the icon up to make the point that they do not worship it and thus establish a clear identity for themselves as women. The phallus, now called by more common words, is seen in locker-room jokes as an icon that males still worship beyond all sense. The expression "Does size matter?" clearly has rude implications and an assumed positive answer.

The premier saw that aspect of the story and said with consummate irony, "If men had done it, it would have been a bigger penis."[45]

Not a Gentleman's Sport

"I cannot image a woman coming out of an assembly unscathed," said Sue Hammell. "Now I have to say that's true of men, too, but they come out with different scars."

Women go away scarred because their carefully honed skills are not the ones that bring recognition in the provincial and federal assemblies. What has brought them considerable success in municipal or regional politics and community organizations—being able to make an idea work, bringing people together to achieve a goal and sow co-operation in the soil of community diversity—takes second place to winning battles.

Betty Hinton, who started her political career in municipal politics eighteen years before she went to the House of Commons as an MP, said, "I naively went there believing we were all there for the same purpose. It was a big surprise to me to find out that's not what this is about." She couldn't even trust her fellow members; she told me that she watched a women on the other side of the House vote pointedly contrary to what she had said privately.

Women members observed that gender differences nearly always involved male aggression and the structure of politics that reflects aggression: competition, hierarchies and dominance. Psychologists have said that "the greater aggressiveness of the male is one of the best established, and most pervasive, of all psychological sex differences."[46] Male aggression is more frequent, more violent, flashier and riskier than the limited aggression that females practise, and it nearly always occurs in front of an audience in order to establish dominance. While women may call each other names or start rumours, men grasp their weapons and wield them with as much strength and damaging effect as possible.

Because of our evolution, says psychologist David M. Buss, "Women tend to be more egalitarian, men more hierarchical. Men and women also differ in the actions through which they express dominance. Whereas women tend to express dominance through prosocial actions (e.g., settling disputes among others in the group), more often men tend to express dominance for personal gain and ascension (e.g., getting others to do menial tasks rather than doing them themselves). As well, when given a choice of roles to take, dominant women tend to appoint men as leaders, whereas dominant men take the leadership role for themselves."[47] Women are satisfied to have chosen the best leader, but men want the status of leadership.

My own recognition of the male ambience of government began early. We went into the chamber where the mace, a lethal cudgel from medieval times, was carried in as the sign of power in this talking place. The seats were set two sword-lengths apart to assure that, should sword-play threaten, it could not occur in the chamber. Settled into my chair, I looked up at the ornate, recessed ceiling. Light shone in through eighteen round windows arrayed above the wood panelling, each with its own plaster embellishment: two bare-breasted maidens supported each of these windows, one dainty arm under the curve, the other reaching over her head to the top of the window, giving a graceful tilt to the breasts. One washroom for members, converted for the use of women, still had open urinals. In another, urinals were boxed but not removed. The one with boxes still has them, though the open urinals were finally removed.

In the worldwide scheme of things, no single one of these things matters—the urinals, the bare-breasted ornaments, the ominous mace to protect governors from the governed or the threat of sword fighting—but together they demonstrate that the legislature was built for men, made safe against their tendencies and decorated for their enjoyment. This physical fact reflects the social fact, and few changes have been made since women began to frequent the premises, supposedly as equals.

The political system emphasizes gender differences. Women entered electoral politics in BC ninety years ago but still lack strong enough numbers in our assemblies to change the pattern of men's governing habits. They haven't achieved critical mass. They have had limited success in their attempts to join the decision making processes with behaviours that succeeded in their previous lives, and whenever they have tried to join as full members with behaviours that work for men, they have also met with qualified success. The political system that men built for men has proven to be stubbornly stable, and it limits and qualifies women out of their equality.

Iona Campagnolo saw a benefit in the gender difference. "My thesis is that men and women are two halves of human consciousness. When we put ourselves together, the decision-making process is better." Rosemary Brown saw a more specific divide. "I've always looked at how feminists do politics and how other people do politics. Non-feminist women do politics exactly the way that men do, and some feminist men do politics the way women do. So I think it's the ideology that makes the distinction." However, she added, "on so many issues, the women speak from experience,

Rita Johnston at her first cabinet meeting as Premier of BC, April 1991. Carol Gran is on her right. *Photo courtesy Rita Johnston.*

while the men have to speak from learning and observing."

Division of labour through a hundred thousand years of evolution has wired women to be more collaborative and nurturing, and more prone to seek support networks, Joyce Murray said. "Some wiring leads men to seek to fight wild animals, protect the family and go out on adventures to find new territories. Our society gives more status and recognition to the behaviours that men are more comfortable with: overt competition and accomplishment."

Carol Gran also noted men's desire to fight for fun. "Men like the game. It's made for men by men—a big game, high stakes—a war game for sure, just like Nintendo. They love it. It makes me sick."

Blood sport is a common description of politics, but women see little fun in the conflict. Joan Smallwood said, "When women go to war, it's not a sport." Daphne Jennings agreed. "Women don't do politics as a game. It's pretty serious."

Having braved conflict or even initiated it, men garner the rewards—dominance, status and power in their hierarchy—but women, said Lynn Stephens, "generally want to get things done and will just do it. Men are more ego-involved, more embracing of power." "Building an image," Jackie Pement called it, noting that men choose issues to build that image, whereas women politicians enter politics to assist and help. "Men do good work, lots of them, but I don't see that they need that image and that ego."

"Seagulling" is Joy Langan's word for something she's often seen as a member, the political male's tendency to appropriate women's ideas to build his own image. Anyone who has been a member of a caucus—political or otherwise—has seen it happen. Linda Reid said, "I'm sure you've been in a meeting where you say something and there's no reaction. They're doing what they're doing—reading, chattering, whatever. Five minutes later a male counterpart says exactly the same thing, and they go, 'Hah! Great idea!' I always say, 'Is there an echo in here?'"

The difference may depend partly on men's motivation; they often see a personal future in politics. Agnes Kripps and Gillian Trumper agreed that men went into politics as a career, or at least for advancement in their occupation, whereas women used it as a vehicle of community service.

If in that sense politics for men is often personal, said Reid, "politics for women is often process." Seeing women's life role as "crafting a sense

of belonging," wanting people to fit in and have opportunities and choices, women are interested in "how people were rolled into the decision making." Another difference she saw was that men had confidence. "Asked to run for election, women want to learn about the job and be sure they have the skills, but "men don't worry about that." They just say yes.

Confidence creates distinctive political behaviour. "Men might often be wrong in what they say, and they'll often say things just for the sake of saying them," Wendy McMahon observed, "but women are pretty sure before they have their say." Elizabeth Cull remembered that "the men stars were brash and individu-

Elizabeth Cull, here with leader Mike Harcourt, found the male stars were "brash and individualistic...incredibly strategic and very sure of themselves." *Courtesy New Democratic Party.*

alistic, incredibly strategic and very sure of themselves. I don't ever remember sitting down with a Glen Clark, a Dan Miller, or a Moe Sihota and having them express any doubts to me about what they were doing, where they were going, how they were doing. They just didn't do that."

And men fake confidence really well, Sue Hammell reckoned. "In a culture that allows them to present confidence as part of their *raison d'être*, and where women do not have that built into their training and therefore have to fight to get it, it is the central issue around politics." People will not vote for a candidate who lacks confidence, so it is a core political issue. "I think it is the defining issue between the two genders."

Many women blame the party system for heightening the conflict in assemblies. Some accept that the party comes first, Carol Gran said, but that is a huge mistake. The concept "can take away your individuality and compromise your values." April Sanders agreed. As long as members must toe the party line under a party whip, with a caucus system which forces voting strictly on party lines, "you may as well go home—we won't have better government."

Using an assembly as a battlefield does nothing to improve political decision making. "Politics is not a gentleman's sport," said Sharon Hayes after listing all the same problems as Sanders, "although it may be a man's sport." When everything is confrontational "it's not constructive; it's the opposite."

Polarization is another method that male politicians naturally deploy.

"How did Glen Clark win the 1996 election?" asked Elizabeth Cull. "He polarized."

Polarization forces people to choose one side or another on an important question. The subtleties of policy statements disappear when voters are persuaded that one team or the other is not to be trusted, so polarizers use wedge issues to split voters into us and them. The object is to get the opposition to say it doesn't agree with what the government proposes, even if it shares the goal; each side then argues that the other is perfectly unreasonable and wildly ungenerous.

When the Liberal government in October 2004 brought forward legislation opposing aggressive panhandling on the streets of Vancouver, for example, it declared that closer management of panhandlers would bring a measure of comfort to shopping pedestrians in downtown Vancouver and protection to retailers. The New Democrats opposed the law as an unwarranted attack on poor people—panhandlers—and they wanted measures to address poverty. In fact both parties wanted the aggressive panhandling to stop, but their solutions were kilometres apart.

Women will naturally move away from polarization, said Cull, because they are uncomfortable with it. "It is a macho style of politics, which unfortunately serves political parties very well."

Katherine Whittred noted that, when women deal with issues, they "tend to work more towards consensus than towards an adversarial position where one side wins and the other side loses." But pressure follows any attempt to flout the adversarial tradition. "We tried to network differently," Cull said of the women during her legislative time. "In some things we tried to do, particularly across the floor, we got shot down by the men on both sides who didn't like us collaborating." In fact a lot more work than usual was done among the women, who were not afraid to say, "I'm bringing this forward, what do you think? Will you support me? Can we work on this together?" It wasn't what men tended to do.

Politics and government are competitive at every level, Jan Pullinger said, and although "the New Age guys" function differently than those steeped in older traditions, they "still grew up in a male culture and they understand the rules of the game." She felt competitiveness is easier for men. Women tend to focus on the outcome: getting the ball through the goalposts. "So there's a lot more willingness by women to negotiate." Men have a lot more drive to stand out. "Certainly, after twelve years' reflection, that's the piece I'm most uncomfortable with."

"For the most part," Jenny Kwan said, "Women don't go about intimidating you into a decision and manipulating you so that you support it. Male politicians value aggression as a characteristic in their day-to-day work." And their aggression is appreciated, according to Libby Davies, who has noted that successful male politicians, "who can be ruthless and authoritarian, rigid and non-inclusive, are often described as 'strong,' 'decisive,' and 'visionary.'" Betty Hinton observed that many male politicians "take a stand at the beginning and don't back off, no matter what they hear." She hasn't found that in women politicians, who are "born problem solvers."

Gillian Trumper perceived that most women in politics do a much better job of stopping fights based on party differences. "They are able to make the difficult decisions but at the same time get people to work together. I'm not sure men are able to do that in the political world."

Dawn Black told of a cross-party relationship that in some ways puzzled her but showed women's distinctive approach to political differences. Alberta MP Edna Anderson used to knit in the House and was a down-to-earth person with whom Black felt comfortable. Anderson was

"Women don't go about intimidating you into a decision and manipulating you so that you support it," said Jenny Kwan. "Male politicians value aggression." *Courtesy Jenny Kwan's office.*

Tory and Black was NDP. Black's father-in-law had been arrested as a member of the On-to-Ottawa Trek in 1935 and charged under Section 98 of the Criminal Code for unlawful organization, which was considered treasonous. The penalty was death, and in what historians perceive as an attempt to intimidate the protestors, the charges were not withdrawn until a year after the event. The experience was central to the Black family's sense of politics.

One day Anderson got up in the House and talked about her family and its Tory roots. She was proud of the fact that a relative had been a member of the R.B. Bennett government—which had ordered the arrest of the Trekkers in 1935 in Regina—and she was obviously proud of her family's long association with the Conservatives. "And there was I, another woman MP who saw the Conservative Party and the Depression years in a diametrically different light. My family members had certainly experienced those years very differently. Yet we both served on the status of women committee of the House, and there were some ways in which we could co-operate to advance women's equality."

Historian Jean Scott chats with Carole James in Victoria. Gender imbalance has shone through the history of women writers, too. *Courtesy Carol James' office.*

JUST THE WAY IT IS

You Ain't as Good as a Man

A coalitionist MLA once demanded hotly of Tilly Rolston,
"Do you think you're as good as a man?" She said firmly,
"Yes." He blustered, "Well, that's too damn bad. You ain't."

The sixth woman in BC to hold an assembly seat, Rolston was elected in 1941 as a Conservative MLA—the first woman of her party elected in Canada—and sat continuously until 1953. In 1952 she left the Conservatives to be elected a Social Credit member along with W.A.C. Bennett and became the first woman in Canada to hold a cabinet seat with a portfolio. As minister of education, she brought in what became known as the Rolston formula for funding of public schools in BC, reducing some of the cost differences between rural and urban school districts. When she ran with Bennett in 1952 some media commentators dared to suggest that she, not he, should have been the leader. She died in 1953, and her funeral cortege in Vancouver was the largest the city had ever seen. She had reasons to think herself "as good as a man."

Rolston's story shows only one of the putdowns thrust at women politicians, from before they gained the vote until today. An up-to-date version of that attitude would be, "Girlie tough ain't tough enough."[48] It reflects the long-held belief that public life, where people are recognized by others for their skills, was made by and for men. Private life—home life—is the venue for women, whose value will be judged in a kindly way by family, neighbours and friends. This ongoing prejudice means political life gives women more problems than it gives men with similar goals, because too many people still assume that politicians will be men and—with astounding irrelevancy—should be men.

When Dawn Black was elected MP and went to Ottawa, she needed a car to get around, so she bought Pauline Jewett's "little old Toyota" in Burnaby and shipped it to Ottawa. "When it arrived in Ottawa, an assistant took the call that my car was available and asked me to call them. My assistant said, 'Well, I'm sorry she can't call you right now; she's in the House, but she'll call you when she's free.' This person said to her, 'Well, if she's in the house, give me her home phone number; I'll call her there.'"

Black also remembered going to one of her first committee meetings, filling in for Svend Robinson. "They're all so polite in Ottawa, you know; it's different than Victoria. Everybody has a veneer. The Tory chairperson welcomed me very graciously, saying how wonderful it was to have me there because I was much better to look at than Svend."

Political men who assume women are out of their element in politics frequently offer paternal flattery and protective attitudes. In public they will jump to the defence of a woman politician who

Dawn Black asking a question in the House of Commons. Her leader, Jack Layton, right front, and House leader Libby Davies just visible left front. *Courtesy Dawn Black's office.*

has been asked a question, making her own statement inoperative. Defence is a frequent posture in warlike politics. Some voters tell women outright that they have no place in public life; their place is at home tending to the children. This is why Nellie McClung, one of Canada's earliest and most-loved women politicians, always told her audience before she started to speak at an evening meeting that her children were all safely home in bed.

Matters of appearance and manner are kept strictly to females. As Sydney Sharpe wrote in *The Gilded Ghetto*, "The urge to justify physical appearance simply never occurs to male politicians because their sexuality is not an issue."[49] Ida Chong observed that the media, when writing about a male, describes "his actions, even about a decision that he made." But when journalists write about women, "they usually write about how old they're looking now, how much weight they've gained since they got into politics, or something that has nothing to do with their abilities or their minds."

Pre-election workshops offered for women candidates differ from those for general attendance because they are larded with advice about how not to offend the men that women are likely to work with or the broad range of voters to whom they want to appeal. What would offend them? Earrings that dangle in any way, of course. Open-toed shoes. Dresses with a line that is much softer than a tailored suit. Giggles. A thin or high-pitched voice. Sharon Carstairs is always the negative example of this, though I don't recall anyone mentioning that she is an intelligent, skilled politician who led her provincial party for years in Manitoba before she was named to the Senate, where she served as Liberal house leader. Libby Davies told of a colleague who went to one of the workshops for women newly in politics and came away feeling "her shoes were all wrong and her hair was too big." Without ever having to make a specific reference throughout our ten years in politics, Darlene Marzari marked our response to the workshops by suggesting acidly that something I had on was not "tastefully feminine or discreet," a line from a workshop we attended before we were even elected.

Women have been elected despite dangling earrings, open-toed shoes and big hairstyles, but they haven't yet convinced the public that women belong in politics. Besides avoiding the most flagrant characteristics of their gender, they must also avoid being manlike. Joy MacPhail, an aggressive fighter, is aware that her manner brings disapproval. "The Liberals try to undermine me by talking about my loud voice. They say it's grating and I'm strident." Their criticism didn't prevent MacPhail's success, but it illustrates that too few people have digested the difference that women are making in public life. Walter Cobb, MLA for Cariboo South, ignored the sincere recognition MacPhail compelled in the legislature when he said with innuendo that he pitied her fiancé because "it would appear she can never be satisfied."[50] He did later apologize.

Crying, which is allowed women in private life, cannot be countenanced in public life. In 1959 Camille Mather, a nurse with graduate work in psychiatry, was a leader of the Burnaby Women's Committee on Radiation Hazards and actively campaigned against nuclear weapons even before her term as an MLA. She was best known for an incident in Burnaby when she was a city councillor. An Air Vice-Marshal's civil defence report to council, which said the residents could not count on any warning of an intercontinental ballistics missile attack, brought her to tears. The report recommended preparation of an evacuation plan, but Mather warned that "evacuation is not the answer" and pleaded for the city to take a more powerful stance.[51]

Three years later, as an NDP MLA, she prodded the education minister about the state of Jericho Hill School for the Deaf, saying the students deserved better. When she refused to accept the minister's response that Eton and Harrow, renowned British schools, also operated in old buildings, another Socred minister shouted that she was "playing politics with human misery." He refused her request to withdraw his statement until the speaker forced him to, and the house broke into a "midnight mulligan"[52] involving all the heavyweights. Premier W. A. C. Bennett, his ministers, opposition leader Bob Strachan and his veterans and the leader of the Liberal Party all erupted during a late-night sitting of the legislature. The speaker was reported to be "himself close to tears" as he appealed, "Please . . . please . . . let's have some order."[53] During the fracas, Mather "quietly wept in her seat,"[54] although she continued to press her point when she found room on the battlefield.

The outcome, according to Ed Cosgrove in Victoria's *Daily Colonist*, was that "gentle-voiced Camille Mather found herself on the front page of every prominent newspaper in the province."[55] Expanding on that point, he went on, "It was a return engagement for her. Several years ago, while a member of Burnaby council, her tears brought her the same prominence." The impression was so ingrained that in 2002, when I asked an NDP staffer of the 1960s—a feminist—about Mather, she went back into her memory and said, "Oh, yes. The woman who cried."

In the late 1950s, a local editor recruited Grace McCarthy to run for parks board. "The first time I ran, I had somebody come into my shop and say, 'I see by the paper you're running for the parks board.' I said, 'Yes, I am. First time.' 'Well, that's great, Grace, and I'd vote for you if you weren't a woman.' Just as blatant as that."

A decade later, Karen Sanford put up her name to be a candidate for a provincial election. "There was a big controversy in the papers. It started with a letter to the editor saying I should not be elected because there were several days every month when I could not be counted upon to make a sane decision. [The papers] published it! It became quite an issue. That was 1971, don't forget." Sanford thought the incident helped her get elected because "a whole lot of women were so infuriated by this." When she won the nomination, a local headline read, "Mother of Three Wins Nomination." "Mother of three," Sanford spat out. "Had one of the men won, would they have said 'Father of Four Wins?' No." The editor of that paper always referred to Sanford as Karen Baby.

"The first thing that happened when I got elected [in 1969]," said Agnes Kripps, "a mother phoned me saying that her daughter had given birth. She was from the high school in the constituency and the girl wanted the grandmother to adopt it." It was a big issue involving social services, adoption agencies and others, and "the girl didn't know what caused her pregnancy." Kripps believed such girls needed "something" in the schools to help them, so she proposed a course in biology.

In the legislature, she realized, "the men's mentality was different than mine," and she wanted to avoid the "stigma attached to the word 'sex.'" To address the men's probable response, Kripps did not use the term "sex education." She proposed "a course on Biology on Life Today." The acronym BOLT took on a life of its own, of course, and the male members hooted and punned, after which the media reported it all and embroidered its own version. According to a male witness some thirty-six years later, one MLA said, "I sat bolt upright, and then some." Said another, "If you've got the bolt, I've got the nuts."[56] When I asked Kripps about it, she said, "I survived it, and we got sex education in the schools."

A decade later Joan Smallwood was active in lobbying the local council on land use issues. One evening the husband of one of the women Smallwood worked with on civic issues visited her and her husband Larry. He thought the group should run a municipal slate and asked Larry if he would run. "Larry was never involved with municipal issues, was never part of a delegation to council or petitioning or anything like that. I said, 'Pardon me? What's that about?'" After that demonstration of ingrained political preference for males, "we women set up the campaigns ourselves, but we continued to run into that kind of gender bias."

About the same time Gillian Trumper—former school trustee and board chair, former city councillor and current mayor, former college board member and current chair—was vice-president of the BC Association of Colleges. "I was to step up to be president. But the senior management and some of the college board representatives were not going to have a woman, and I wasn't elected."

During the 1989 federal campaign, Dawn Black's husband went canvassing door-to-door, where a constituent confronted him and said, "What kind of man are you that would allow his wife to run for politics?" Black said, "He was shocked."

In the provincial election of 1991, Jackie Pement encountered "guys that wouldn't talk to me because they weren't going to vote for a woman. It was very clear: 'You cook, you sew and you clean, but you don't do this stuff,' and it wasn't just men. It was women too."

In 1996 April Sanders found "people saying to me, 'You should be at home. What do you think you're doing leaving small kids and going to Victoria?' They said it to me openly. One of the groups that said it was a women-in-business group that I used to support—my own group, which was the least supportive of all I visited." Sanders called it "my first shock about the gender issue," and she traced it back to the roots of liberal democracy. "Even in ancient Athens, women slaved and men owned, and here we are, . . . still in a liberal democracy where men are allowed to be in the public realm, and women are supposed to stay in the private realm." Even though women have moved into the public realm, they're still judged by the standards of the private realm. Sanders was "amazed to recognize how often not just myself but other women were judged on how they looked, what their hairstyle was, what they wore, whereas for men that isn't an issue at all." She'd never experienced that before.

April Sanders saw the gender defining line was the same as it was in the Greek city states. Men were in the public domain; women stayed in the private domain. *Photo courtesy April Sanders.*

Given that married women with children have these problems, you might think that single women would find politics easier. Not so. In the mid-1960s, when Pauline Jewett first ran in Northumberland riding in Ontario, her single status was brought up at the nomination meeting. As

Dawn Black told the story, "The fact that she wasn't married had become a huge issue. People said, 'It's one thing to vote for a woman, but to vote for a woman who's never been married, that's different.' Suddenly a farmer got up from the back row and in a no-nonsense manner said, 'Oh, for God's sake, if that's such an issue, *I'll* marry Pauline!'"

Jewett used to tell another story about a party meeting where she was being considered as the candidate. Somebody mentioned that she was single, as though that were a slight case of acne, unfortunate and ugly but not catching. A man in the audience wanted clarification.

"You're not married?" he asked her.

"No."

"You've never been married?"

"No."

"Are you sure?" was his last question. Jewett didn't need to answer.

Gender language is still a controversial issue, although not with Pat Carney who was named Oil Man of the Year in 1985 by *Oilweek,* a respected industry publication. She said she felt honoured. After all, no other woman had been Oil Man of the Year, so the naming was done in her honour. She said she felt every word that ends in 'man' need not be changed just because women are now taking some of the positions that were habitually filled by men.

Others were not as comfortable about being called names designed for men. Joan Sawicki was elected to city council when all the councillors were called aldermen. Resenting that sexual assumption, Sawicki drafted a motion for council, to go forward to UBCM, to change the title to "councillor." But her own caucus stalled. "They were furious with me because—so they said—I had done this without their approval, without their permission." As well, they had all sorts of reasons not to change. "I

Pauline Jewett's single status was a big issue for some. At one meeting, a man volunteered to marry her if it made that much difference. *Courtesy New Democratic Party.*

was shocked. I had never really run into that gender bias in my life." But Sawicki's initiative eventually led to the change she wanted.

She didn't have such longstanding success when in 1992 she be-came the second woman speaker in the BC legislature. "There was the debate about how I would be addressed. I was adamant that we use the gender-free term, Honourable Speaker. The system did not agree." While the clerks had no problem with Sawicki packing away the dishes which bore the words "Mr. Speaker," she said, "It seemed I was striking a mortal blow to the very foundation of the British parliamentary system in throwing off not only 'Mr. Speaker' but their preference for 'Madame Speaker' as well." Sawicki persevered, "believing strongly that as long as the salutation reflected gender in any way, then gender, not the office, would be the focus." This was shortly after her successful campaign to have municipal representatives called councillors, "so both my arguments and my resolve were strong. 'Honourable Speaker' it became—though regrettably not for long." With encouragement, most members adopted this gender-free term, more women members than men. "My sense of achievement at this small victory was short-lived," because when Emery Barnes, Deputy Speaker, assumed the chair, "as if on cue, most of the house quickly reverted to 'Mr. Speaker.'" When Gretchen Mann Brewin assumed the chair four years after Sawicki's term ended, the house adopted "Madame Speaker."

In the House of Commons, Margaret Mitchell reported, "I was on the members' committee at one point, and they always referred to the members as 'gentlemen,' and all the wording in the documents was masculine. I used to raise the issue, and the clerks got me off that com-mittee pretty soon; they weren't going to have any such impudence." Mitchell challenged members in the House, particularly Prime Minister Pierre Elliott Trudeau, "who had a very patronizing way of saying, 'The Honourable Lady such and such.'" Fruitlessly, as it turned out, she would say, "I would appreciate it if the Prime Minister would address me as Hon-ourable Member, as the male members of the House are called." Trudeau's practice showed no respect. "It was putting me down as a little girl."

Women also resent being called by their first names when the caller means to indicate lesser status, not warm affection. MLA Jan Pullinger always bristled at the greetings when she walked down the legislative corridor with her husband, MLA Dale Lovick. "Hello, Mr. Lovick. Hi, Jan." When the party leaders debated on television during the 1993 federal election, Preston Manning called both Kim Campbell and Audrey McLaughlin by their first names. He did not extend the same discourtesy to Jean Chrétien. McLaughlin said, "I've never felt so patronized by anybody or so put down as I was by Preston Manning during the debate. He was lecturing me!"[57] We must remember Camille Mather too; after the debate about Jericho Hill School for the Deaf, the government two weeks later committed a million dollars to the school for building improvements, and the province's dailies found it adequate identification to use only "Camille" with the word "tears" in their headlines.

Just after I had been appointed minister of energy, mines and petroleum resources, I had an interesting experience with Mayor Charlie Lasser of Chetwynd, who presided when I visited the town. In the basement area where we met, a dais had been placed in a large open space so that he could sit on it in a large chair. Once enthroned, he turned to me, seated with everyone else in a line of folding metal chairs below, and said, "Welcome to Chetwynd, Mr. Minister!" He then proceeded to lay out what he wanted, despite the fact that I was so surprised that I had not responded to his greeting in the moment he left open. He didn't correct himself, and I've never really figured out what the incident said about what he thought of me, the political system or the constraints of grammar.

Six Hours of Sleep —or Less

The work of representing voters in a house of assembly has never been an easy job, although sometimes it has been seen as a prestigious one. In early times only those who were independently wealthy enough to spend part of their year as members sought election to Parliament. As years went on, practice dictated a modest stipend. Although more citizens have a realistic opportunity to offer themselves as representatives if the job pays a reasonable salary, MPs received no salary until the twentieth century, and BC MLAs have been paid for a full-time job only since the early 1970s. That has allowed elected members to immediately disengage from their former employment, professional practice or business ventures to avoid the possibility of conflict of interest and the appearance of conflict. Neither is ethically acceptable, and most members disengage.

But neutrality can be compromised by family as well. A caucus member whose spouse is a doctor, for example, may find it difficult to comment when doctors take job action. In fact, in today's public climate, a doctor may find it easier than the spouse of a doctor to participate in politics. In my time in cabinet, when the government was passing legislation that affected teachers, cabinet asked the Conflict of Interest Commissioner for advice for those members whose spouses were teachers. He okayed involvement with issues that affected all teachers as a group, but the conflict line is not always so easy to define. As for issues related to acquaintances, members needn't renounce their friends but must look at their involvements in a different way. A member who writes a letter of reference for the troubled child of family friends, for example, may find herself accused of trying to influence a judge or another powerful civil servant.

Only after election does a member see that campaigning wasn't the most consuming activity she ever experienced. Sometimes even before the last gathering of campaign workers, the leader calls members to caucus to begin planning the work for annual budgets and legislation and to work toward being an effective machine. Once her specific duties are assigned, the member begins meeting with stakeholders in her area of interest, with other members on common issues, with civil servants who have knowledge and influence, with councils, boards and commissions in the riding and with chosen advisors. To make these meetings effective, members have to be alert, informed, ready to listen and prepared to make decisions about what they will take back to caucus and to the legislature.

Carole Taylor, April 2007, at the ground-breaking ceremony for the new Ecole Secondaire Francophone de Vancouver, which opened September, 2008. *Courtesy of Carol Taylor's office.*

In the capital, assembly and committee work consumes a member. At home she accepts invitations to ride in parades, to attend citizenship courts as encouragement to new Canadians and to drop in on picnics, 4-H Club beef auctions, high school graduations, women's celebrations, Rotary meetings and any number of other events that help her stay in touch with constituents. She advocates to government for individuals, trying to solve the problems that flood in at her office doors. She may even occasionally make a speech, but usually she simply carries greetings or congratulations. Most of her time is spent on the phone or in endless hours of meetings. Time, stress and pressure from being in the public eye—where no one likes to make a mistake—keep a member at a high pitch of urgency.

No handbooks exist as a guideline for the job itself. A member's personality and experience determine her approach, and her constituents' characteristics determine her success. What works in Peace River North or Columbia River–Revelstoke may not work at all in Vancouver–Kingsway or Okanagan East. To represent her constituents in the assembly, however, she must say what most of her constituents want to be said about gun control or closing schools or gay marriage. All the nuances of such issues have also to be balanced with party policy and personal beliefs. Even when a member has been totally open about her position in an election campaign, the complexities of issues may make her stance hard to articulate and sometimes harder to square with the ideas of the majority of those who voted her in, with her caucus and party, and with influential interest groups.

When Cathy McGregor supported the 6-Mile Ranch resort proposal near Kamloops, she was dancing with an octopus. Before her term, property bought by offshore developers had been taken out of the Agricultural Land Reserve and an agreement approved for resort development. That agreement had expired, but a new owner bought the property and reapplied just as McGregor was elected. Many of her constituents saw the development as a benefit, since it would bring jobs and boost the economy. Besides, much of the property was "steep slope and rock, and you couldn't put cattle on much of it," she told caucus. Then, too, some of the parcel remained in the land reserve. She opted to support the agreement with the new owner but said, "I know the [provincial] environmental community was very unhappy. It was highly symbolic for them." She also had to face fierce resistance from inside caucus. Still, McGregor made major environmental gains, because the outcome was recovery of water rights from the surrounding ranches, including 6-Mile. "Fisheries experts in the ministry of environment were ecstatic," she reported, at the significantly reduced threats to that fishery. Nevertheless, McGregor paid the price politically with the environmentalists, within her community and her party. Every MLA finds at least one such controversy.

When members take the opportunity—and accept the obligation—to speak out on controversial government issues, they must also ensure that their comments circulate widely through media coverage, member reporting in newspapers, radio and TV, or via news releases, newsletters or other general mailouts. As well, the decisions of the party's and member's must be put to the constituency regularly; in either government or opposition, the member wants her constituents to be aware of what is going on in the capital. Many members see advocacy and public education as their main role. Overall, members try to reach solutions to public situations, improve the job that government does and help constituents who ask for assistance.

People respond well to requests from MLAs and MPs for information and for meetings. A member is soon launched into a round of information gathering and sharing to facilitate community solutions and party policy. A caucus research department helps every MLA, and parliamentary or legislative libraries cater particularly to current members. Eileen Dailly told me, "I believe that you get things done better if you take your time than if you try to ram something down somebody's throat. Do some base work first—your research—then build a consensus." One of Margaret Bridgman's greatest enjoyments as a member of Parliament was "picking up the phone and just saying, 'I need information on this, that or the next thing' to the parliamentary library. Oh, that was phenomenal!" Bridgman recognized the power inherent in being an MP. "You could walk over to Carleton University and just say, 'I'm Margaret Bridgman, MP, and I'd like to speak with So-and-So,' and my god they'd come running—or within ten minutes, you know. But you had to be able to say MP."

Daphne Jennings, who had been a high school teacher, tried to be a model in handling her paperwork, but it wasn't easy. "Even with staff helping you, there's just not enough time. It was important that you knew these bills, that you knew them well, and that you had your own opinions." Something had to give, namely the French lessons she took for her first six months, even though cancelling those lessons bothered her so much that she still plans to attend night school courses in conversational French.

"The reading is an amazing challenge," said Brenda Locke, "and trying to keep up with all the meetings, all the technical stuff." She wanted to have the confidence of "knowing every single thing, because I believe the devil is in the details." She wanted to be confident that when an agreement went for framing, what came back was what was intended. "I don't think I'm a control freak, but I truly want to know where it's going to end up." The biggest barrier for Wendy McMahon was finding information. McMahon, a first-term MLA, wanted "to figure out how things worked before I asked the questions," but was sometimes stymied because government services—and the people who could provide her answers—were sparse in her huge rural constituency.

Within their constituencies, members hire at least one assistant who will keep in touch with public issues and private problems that need the member's help, keeping lines of communication open with the public. And while it sometimes feels as if they create more work than relief for the member, assistants provide extra pairs of ears. Hedy Fry described herself as a professional listener. "I don't know if it's because I'm a woman or because I was a family physician for twenty-three years, but I believe that one must listen to communities, to people, to groups because if you're going to make meaningful change that will affect their lives it can not be 'one size fits all.'" Listening to individuals teaches more than any book, and nobody knows it all before they listen. "My patients

Author Anne Edwards, MLA for Kootenay from 1986 to 1996, took former Premier Dave Barrett (left) to see a new addition to Fort Steele's purebred Clydesdales. *Photo courtesy Anne Edwards.*

taught me not to judge, that people live the most absolutely different lives, and that you can't solve a problem because the book says so." People will be debating the same things in thirty years, she said, if members use the House of Commons as an ivory tower where they just write gorgeous bills.

Some meetings that a member must attend will be neither at home nor in the capital, and she must drive or fly to meet organization or industry representatives across the province or country. Almost every party meeting—local, provincial or federal—will take place on a weekend. Hotel rooms of every description and quality all fade into stereotypes: hair conditioner, soaps and lotions; getting a hair dryer, iron and ironing board; trying to get the dripping tap or constantly running toilet fixed; the view of the parking lot that inspires even less than the music of the guest next door or the bar downstairs.

A member is often up at 5:00 a.m., nearly always by 6:00 a.m., and her workday may go on formally until 10:00 p.m. or later. In a single day a member could attend a breakfast meeting with or as the minister, participate in a motorcycle toy ride in the morning, lunch with a corporate executive, tour a gravel pit in the afternoon, and dine at the Lieutenant-Governor's residence to honour long-serving civil servants in the evening. Such a day would be unusual, but not unheard of. The challenge of fitting everything in—while maintaining the polish on her shoes, the smile on her face and an informed mind—excites a new member but exacts a toll as it repeats day after day. Six hours of sleep is as good as it gets.

Briefing books must be read, people phoned and another versatile wardrobe assembled before each day. More and more as the years in office proceed, buying clothes for work happens in a spare hour between meetings. That means it happens whether a member is in Prince George or Ottawa, Winnipeg or Penticton. Keeping a hair appointment is fraught with uncertainty. Sewing on a missing button is a small task that may take weeks to happen, given a need to assemble the garment, button, needle, thread and scissors at the same place during a free moment. Cleaning out a drawer or closet may have to wait for retirement. Provisioning two residences, one at home and one in the capital, taxes the ingenuity, as does spelling off the few clothes in the capital or the few clothes in a suitcase every week and keeping a few at a friendly house in Vancouver for overnight stays. The member's assistant or family is likely to have to organize servicing her car.

Some caucuses want to be sure women are represented on most, if not all, committees and platforms and at meetings, which creates a particularly heavy demand on women members' time. "There were five women in our caucus," Lynn Hunter reported. "I offered at one point to provide [Dave] Barrett with a sex change operation if he volunteered one more woman for one more task, because the work load is just incredible."

New members need to learn by being there how the legislative chamber works: what brings approval, and what leaves one leaning on a wall of indifference. When the house is sitting, members must attend in the buildings unless they have approval of their party whip, although they usually sit in their seats regularly only for morning prayers and afternoon question period. They lead estimates debate on their assigned ministry, ask appropriate questions or make

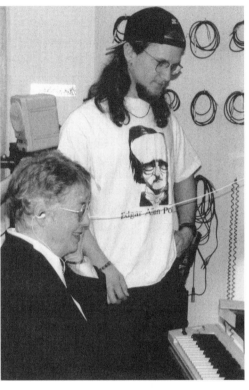

Anita Hagen listening to Phil Thomson's computer composition at Port Moody Senior Secondary school. She felt she was the first MLA to specifically promote issues for seniors. *Photo courtesy Anita Hagen.*

statements on their portfolios or on interests from their constituencies, and respond to the throne speech, the annual budget address or any special issue of broad interest. The whip assigns duty time so that her party has a minimum number of members present in the chamber to call for votes; otherwise members work in their offices, monitoring the house debate by radio or television, or attend meetings within the buildings. Committee work must be done outside of house sitting hours, so committees—which frequently travel—meet in the evenings, after the session is finished or on weekends.

Advocacy for constituents, which includes meetings with other members, ministers, and civil servants, has to be done around sitting duties. When the house bells ring, meetings are interrupted until the vote is over; then a member may return to her office. Lois Haggen, who sat in the 1950s, used to regale her friends with a story of hosting a group in her office when she was chair of the BC Historical Federation. Appropriately for those days, she wore a hat for the meeting, but when the bells rang, she had to take off the hat somewhere out of sight of her visitors and get to the chamber uncovered for the vote, return to reclaim the hat and put it on before rejoining her meeting. This happened three times during an hour-long meeting.

Although Canadian assemblies, federal and provincial, adjourn for Christmas and for more than a month in the summer, members cannot just go home and relax because—understandably—the public's demands on a member continue every day, month after month. The only respite comes when the member goes away on vacation. The public may think members are an extravagant lot, often vacationing far from home, but the real attraction of faraway places is that extreme distance manages to lessen—occasionally stop—the flow of communication into the consciousness of the member. But taking a vacation out of the country is possible only if the member can find a block of free time. The word "annual" doesn't usually apply to members' vacations, but that does help to make out-of-country vacations affordable.

In 2001 the BC legislature adopted sitting rules that relaxed demands on MLAs to a level closer to that of MPs, who regularly sit Monday to Thursday, with one week of every month free of parliamentary business. Although MLAs can expect to sit spring and fall—something the BC legislature has not always done—they can usually count on having July and August free for other activities. These new BC rules also freed members from Friday sittings and set a timetable of about one week off after three weeks of sittings. The government has also set a timetable to mark in advance the date of the Throne Speech, the Budget Speech and adjournment day. This change has moved some attention from the assembly to constituency business.

Far from being a sinecure for charming but shiftless people, political office demands hard work. Said Margaret Lord, "I worked really hard to be out there, to keep dialogue going, meeting with groups, bringing people into the office on any particular issue. Figuring out where people stood on issues by being totally open to them. So even when I see the media trashing the Liberals, whom I love to hate, I have a certain amount of sympathy because I know they've left their families behind in their community, and they're working twenty-four hours a day, and they're stressed out. They're exhausted. I don't think the general public knows that." After three terms in the legislature Rita Johnston remarked, "I hear people complaining, 'Politicians are going to have to work harder.' I don't think most people know the hours that politicians put in. It was not unusual for me to get my first phone call in the morning before I was out of bed, at 6:00 or 6:30." Like farmers and parents, politicians can only dream of having "working hours," observing weekends or booking time ahead for a task or break and knowing the booking will stand. You have to be able to dedicate your life basically to your responsibilities as a member, said Mary Collins. "It's not an appropriate lifestyle for a lot of people. Nor is it necessarily a good life, but it's what you need to do to do the job." Simma Holt was most succinct. "I worked like hell."

Being on alert is a state that persists throughout a member's career, and it demands huge attention and concentration. In an interview a year after she lost the 2001 election, Joan Smallwood—having put in fifteen years as an MLA—said she was still recovering from burnout. "It's taken a full year just to focus on regaining my own health. For a woman it's a tremendous sacrifice personally—and for her family."

And it can be lonely. "I've always felt very isolated," said Jan Pullinger. "Part of it is geographic. The people that I like very much and who were on the same wavelength would go home to other corners of the province. You don't get to know each other in meetings. It's a bizarre workplace; I've never before worked with people for twelve years and never known any of them really well. It was incredibly uncomfortable and stressful."

When Joy MacPhail left office in 2004, Jeff Lee interviewed her and wrote, "Politics itself can be a nasty, brutish affair that will break all but the strongest."[58]

ON THE ROAD

Distance is a weekly obstacle for BC members of Parliament, with four thousand kilometres between British Columbia and Ottawa. In the fall of 1988, Joy Langan remembered, "We were elected in November, we were recalled to debate the Free Trade deal, and we got out on the twenty-third of December. I flew home on the twenty-fourth and did my Christmas shopping in an hour and a half on the way home from the airport."

"When you consider it takes me eight hours door to door to get one way, that's a lot of travel," said Val Meredith. "And with delays and limited flights and all the rest of it, it becomes a real chore. Certainly distance is a barrier." Pat Carney reported, "A trip to Ottawa can take nine hours, what with security and waits at the airport," and she still had to ferry to and from the Gulf Islands. Iona Campagnolo, who represented Prince Rupert, took nearly as long to get home from Vancouver as she did to get there from Ottawa. Still, she deliberately refrained from complaint. "Yes, it was horrible travel, and yes, we're tired all the time, fatigued, but being an MP can be great fun if you don't whine about it as you do it." Margaret Mitchell called it "recycling your jet lag." She was blessed because, until he became too ill to do so, her husband met her at the airport every Friday night when she arrived home from Ottawa.

Because of the time difference, members could leave Ottawa on Friday around noon and still arrive home before bedtime. But getting back to Ottawa was a different story. Hedy Fry missed Sunday dinner with her family every week. "If you leave at eight o'clock on a Monday morning you don't get into Ottawa until five o'clock and miss Monday's votes."

Even getting to Victoria for legislative sessions takes a lot of time.

Interior MLAs or those from northern Vancouver Island must fly to Vancouver and take another flight to the capital. Karen Sanford of Comox always drove. "I spent a tremendous amount of time on the road. It took just over three and a half hours, and in those days we sat Fridays until six." A member from Golden would have a three-hour commute to Cranbrook or Calgary, but although Calgary offers more selection—even nonstop flights to Victoria—the legislative comptroller frowned on approving expenses for trips originating in Alberta. It took Jackie Pement two and a half hours in good weather to get from her home in Burns Lake to the Prince George airport. "You know how hard you worked?" she said. "And you had to work hard just to get there." Just to show up and be seen in her Skeena riding Pement often had to fly charter, and she told of pilots swooping down to read road signs to orient themselves during flights.

Sanford's riding included all the north end of Vancouver Island. A hundred miles of gravel logging roads stretched between Gold River and Port McNeill. Sometimes her meeting at a community such as Woss Lake would last until 10:30 p.m. "It would be pouring rain, and it was so dark, and the roads are not very well marked. I had visions for years afterwards of driving those logging roads. What would I do if I got a flat tire? I was on my own. I don't know that I would want to do that again."

Some Lower Mainland members take the ferry to the capital. The ferry terminal is closer than the airport, and they have a better stretch of time to do their briefcase work. When the BC government owned a fleet of planes used for ambulance work and cabinet member travel, public resentment was always easy to raise against cabinet members flying to Langley or Abbotsford rather than taking regular airline flights to Vancouver International, despite the overall efficiency in time and money to fly Lower Mainland members closer to their homes.

Fog plagues the airports on BC's coast. In the fall and winter, MPs travelling from Victoria are wise to overnight in Vancouver rather than risk being caught in morning fog in Victoria and missing their connecting flight out of Vancouver. The north coast is more hazardous. I remember trying to fly to Terrace with a committee for a meeting in Kitimat. The fog didn't stop us entirely, but we were rerouted to Prince Rupert airport, which is on an island. The ferry to the mainland had closed for the night, but workers were brought in on overtime to operate it. We then found cars to drive to Terrace, about 150 kilometres away, where we held the meeting late in the evening after those we were to meet in Kitimat also drove to Terrace.

Another problem is that there are so few MPs—BC's per capita representation has consistently lagged behind that of eastern provinces—which creates problems in articulating BC's distinct viewpoint. Pauline Jewett, her former assistant said, felt frustrated sometimes about the way British Columbians and westerners were treated in the political system. And Pat Carney for years was the only British Columbian in the inner cabinet. "There was no echo effect. If you make a point to say 'British Columbians don't like nuclear-powered submarines,' there's no one to say, 'Yes, she's right,' or 'I hear that, too.' When you're the only, you're always the oddball."

Carney remembered the coast-to-coast attention she got on a marijuana story. "I was saying if the government of Canada has a health policy—I wasn't endorsing it, just saying that if we have a health policy that says we provide marijuana for medical purposes—why don't we provide the best BC bud instead of trying to grow it at the bottom of a mine shaft in Flin Flon? When the crop fails, it costs a million dollars. We have a government policy that doesn't work, why not make it work? Of course, I was treated like a kook. I got coverage in Halifax. But here in BC—at least in the Gulf Islands—it was considered quite a reasonable thing to say. In Ottawa, it was 'There's that kook Carney again, bouncing off the wall.'" Carney refused to live in Ottawa. In BC she could spend "six days out of eight going to things—like the premier's congress this week. People come up and tell me things." That happened only if she'd recently been in Nelson and Gold River and other BC towns and cities.

Geography was the first thought that came to mind when I asked two MLAs from Prince George about barriers. Lois Boone represented the area for fourteen years as a New Democrat, and Shirley Bond succeeded her as a Liberal. Both referred not only to the physical distance but also to the different perception that residents of the southwest corner of the province have of the reality of the North. Bond said, "The challenge is for those who live beyond Hope to get issues to the centre." She meant the metaphorical centre, because Prince George is the geographic centre of BC. "Decisions and policy are generated by the Lower Mainland," said Boone. Those decision makers in the Lower Mainland or southern Vancouver Island could be either "politicians or bureaucrats, their point of view was the same. To me that was a constant barrier—in the political realm, within your own party, and within the bureaucracy."

Once when I was travelling north from my own riding in the extreme southeast corner of the province to officiate at a mine opening, I stopped for the weekend to visit Boone. By that time we had both had about eight years of travel back and forth to the V-cities, with not enough time at home. I accompanied her to the Prince George Exhibition, where one of the hawkers was particularly eager to stop us on our perambulations. When he finally did, he said with bright enthusiasm, "You look like winners! How would you like to win an all-expenses-paid trip to Vancouver for a weekend?" The poor young man hadn't expected us to simultaneously break into gales of laughter in a clear rejection of his prize.

Time limitations plague members. "Provincial things always happened in Vancouver," said Grace McCarthy. "I always felt the party should be represented, so if I was asked to do it, I would." Then, thinking about the members from outside of Vancouver, she added, "But in a smaller community, you can't miss anything, can you?"

Wendy McMahon, who represented Columbia River–Revelstoke, one of BC's largest constituencies, felt rural members are squeezed for time because constituents go to the MLA's office for answers they would get at government offices in large cities. She had thought about the problem before she was elected but concluded, "'Oh, this won't be too bad.' But it's bad. It's a struggle."

"As politicians, we do a lousy job of taking care of our families and friends," observed Sindi Hawkins. "Time is a huge barrier. Once I wasn't home for a month, so I changed my habits. At the end of this, I want to know I have some people who care for me." And Christy Clark said, "Time is the number-one barrier for me at the moment. You need to network to be successful. You need to meet informally, to bring people along to a policy before decision time, but my evenings belong to my son and my husband."

COOKING WITH PRESSURE

Margaret Bridgman accurately described the stress of holding office when she remarked that one of her greatest achievements was surviving.

"When you're new at it, it's a whole new world and you go in feeling this tremendous sense of responsibility and you think, 'My god I don't know anything about this!' So you make all sorts of adjustments, and then you start to see the power struggles within groups, within politics, and you listen to your colleagues. And then the little power struggles and the backstabbing occur in your constituency because 'you didn't hire me as manager of your office' or whatever. And here you are being pulled all these different ways, and you know somebody somewhere is just waiting for you to say the wrong thing or upset somebody so that they can run to the press or the other party. You're walking on eggshells, and it's a wonder you don't become extremely paranoid and just regress into a room somewhere and lock the door. People that you met thirty years ago suddenly arrive as your long-lost buddies. . . . Other people, they're shaking they're so excited. And you haven't changed; you're the same. I used to joke that three months ago I'd walk into a room full of people and I'd have to stamp my feet or yell to get their attention; now all I have to do is open the door, everybody looks at me, and they expect me to say something brilliant.

"So when you suddenly go into that and you manage to come through it unscathed to a certain degree and still not cynical or it hasn't taken away that love of life you had before you went, you're a little wiser and you're a little more oriented as to what's going on. You can read between the lines in the paper, and you can see the spin doctors coming, which you may have never seen before."

Stress was immediate for Evelyn Gillespie, and she learned what a panic attack feels like. Gillespie had three children at home, the youngest three years old, when she was elected in 1996. She found the work in Victoria heavy, the gender bias disorienting and the parenting from afar difficult. "I was taking chances with my kids, in terms of being there when they got home on the bus. My brother was coming to stay. Everything was mounting up. I couldn't talk to my nominating committee because I didn't want to appear weak, and I certainly couldn't talk to the executive. Everyone I knew was a member of the party, and they were expecting me to perform. I'd gone all-over numb, tingly. I called up this counsellor and asked if she would see me." Sitting in the counsellor's office with her three-year-old sleeping in her arms, Gillespie realized she just needed somebody she could talk to. "That's all it was."

Sometimes she didn't feel strong, Gillespie admitted. She worried about whether she could do the job, caring for her children and taking chances. One day she lost her car keys. "It was six o'clock, and I'd been looking for my keys for an hour." She phoned the daycare and said she'd be there, but not until she found her keys. "I had to just stop and think about things for a while, and then I found my keys and I went and got my daughter. At that point the counsellor really helped me through. But the next thing was—oh god, the recall campaign here!"

Gillespie holds the questionable title of being the first woman MLA to be subject to a recall campaign. She was not the first MLA targeted, but she was one of two MLAs threatened with a second recall after the first one failed. Her recalls were launched by "an individual who didn't like it that I would not advocate for him in a child custody situation—something that any half-intelligent MLA would never do. But he could go and launch a recall campaign against me! Against any MLA! I mean, anybody can."

While Gillespie was going through this, MLA Paul Reitsma from Parksville–Qualicum was found guilty of sending phony letters to the editor but denied doing it. He too was challenged under recall legislation. At that point, said Gillespie, "Gerard [Janssen, NDP house leader] was saying to us, 'If any of you have anything touching you, let me know.'"

Gillespie returned home for the Easter weekend while the recall campaign was in progress. "Oh god, what a weekend! . . . My constituency assistant met with me and told me he'd written a letter to the editor with a phony name and handed me his letter of resignation. And I found out that our nanny was not taking care of our children. We had to fire her that weekend too. And I had to go back to Victoria, and we didn't have a nanny. Well, gee, you wonder why someone would have a panic attack?"

Her constituency assistant's letter-writing venture was intended as a spoof—he used a phony name but his own telephone number and address—but had extended repercussions. Because of the Reitsma incident, she called her party whip and talked to the premier's principal secretary. When all of that was done, she still didn't want to accept the assistant's resignation "because he was such a good CA and it was such a stupid thing," so she decided to pursue the union process, which eventually failed.

A month or so later a newspaper reporter noticed Gillespie's ad for a new CA and asked what happened. She said he went back to teaching, "which is just exactly what he did do." Another couple of months after that Vaughn Palmer got hold of the story and accused Gillespie of lying because the assistant was fired over the phony letter. "That's when I had another panic attack. I could hear music in my ears, I went all tingly, and I couldn't eat for a week. All I could take was little sips of warm water."

Gillespie didn't ask for any counselling help at that point. She had to deal with it. "Do my interview with Vaughn Palmer, and then do big media and all that stuff." When the same fellow launched another recall campaign, ads ran in the newspaper saying Gillespie lied. "Oh God, that was awful. It was a horror show from beginning to end. I believe in my heart of hearts that I didn't lie, but I wasn't going to say I accepted his resignation because he had written a phony letter to the editor. It was so obviously a phony name—Charlie Redneck or something like that."

I asked Gillespie what the letter said. "It was just a joke. It was about two people sitting on the front porch chawin' tobacco and talking about the recall campaign. 'What's it all about anyway? What's the matter with that guy anyway—somethin' about a child custody thing, isn't it?' 'Yeah.' 'Well, what's that got to do with an MLA?' It was just that."

Gillespie was deeply hurt by the accusation that she lied, which assumed she should have told the reporter that her CA had written a letter under a joke name and that he retired over that issue. Her opponents claimed that she evaded the truth, and "That's something I'll carry with me forever. But you know what?" she added. "I survived. And our children survived, and our marriage survived."

The event clearly demonstrated to Gillespie the hardening effect of having been an MLA. "I used to be nicer than I am now. I'm a little less polite and a little less sensitive." You can't turn it off and on, she said. "You can't expect me to be thick-skinned to the kind of abuse you're going to throw at me and then expect me to be sensitive to your personal needs." The effect on her personal life was her greatest regret. A year after she lost the next election she still considered herself "in recovery when it comes to having an emotional relationship with my children and my partner. It takes a long time." What she would never do again is "be too nice." She would "just stand up and say, 'No, it's not appropriate to talk to me this way or write about me this way, and I won't take it.' Because I have enough respect for myself that I know I'm not what they're saying." Summing up, she said she found her term in office "a profoundly isolating experience."

Sheila Orr had her own methods of resisting gratuitous criticism but was surprised at her husband's reaction when he was subjected to the same treatment. "Three weeks ago my husband phoned me to say he'd had a letter of criticism from someone. My husband never gets criticism. He is an Irish lawyer that people love. He was horrified. He fussed over it for three days. Finally I said, 'Get over it. It's not a big thing. Take that letter and multiply it by twenty times a day every day seven days a week,' which is what most politicians get. He said, 'I couldn't handle it. I couldn't take it.' So I think what happens is that you grow a shell over yourself."

Personal integrity is "constantly at issue—and it's a public issue," said Sue Hammell. "People think they own a piece of politicians," Shirley Bond explained. "By casting a ballot they own part of you." Elizabeth Cull believed the blaming worsened since she entered politics. "Right now, politics in BC has got very nasty, very personal. You really run the risk of being dragged through the mud and your family too, no matter how hard you try to be honourable." And Gillian Trumper reported, "You get threatening phone calls. It certainly happened to my family. It happened when my husband was ill, and it terrified him. He came home a couple of times beside himself."

Women in politics, no matter what their rank, are considered the intruders. When Joan Sawicki became Speaker, she found it very uncomfortable sitting in the speaker's chair as her feet did not touch the floor. "If they lowered the chair, Deputy Speaker Emery Barnes's knees would be up near his chin. BC Building Corporation carpenters very creatively invented a button-operated retractable step, although the clerks and carpenters saw this as 'accommodating' the Speaker rather than the Deputy Speaker."

The speaker's robes were also an issue. "The tailor who traditionally made the robes didn't have any patterns for women, so I designed my own and hired someone else to make them." These inconveniences were minor compared to "more subtle barriers and challenges" facing her as a woman speaker, but she found them the most difficult to articulate. Sawicki found the good old boy network was more prominently entrenched in the legislative precinct than in government as a whole. Tradition was a common excuse. Two practices revered for their longevity were an open bar in the speaker's office—called vespers, like an evening prayer service, by regular invitees who dropped in following the afternoon chamber session—and frequent invitations to the speaker's dining room for lunch or dinner. Sawicki called the expenditures from previous speakers' regimes "absolutely outrageous and indefensible," and made it clear that "the speaker's bar was not a twenty-four-hour free liquor store, and decisions on having members join the speaker for lunch or dinner would be on a more fair and reasonable basis."

She was "perhaps naïve," she admitted, and in honourably intending to do things differently as a woman speaker, "I probably cut off my nose to spite my face. My isolation increased because few members came to visit, and I felt so awkward and uncomfortable walking into the speaker's dining room alone, I grew to dread it and seldom used it." Her isolation came partly from the fact that speakers do not attend caucus meetings and so they seldom meet even their own party colleagues.

Cathy McGregor responded to public exposure by devoting herself to detail. Having been "burned a couple of times" early in her career, she said, "I was always worried about what questions might get asked, what answers were the appropriate ones to give, how to make sure I didn't make a major *faux pas*. I was always on edge, trying to think through possible consequences to decisions that had been taken and possible angles that the news media might take in exploring those issues, and being able to respond effectively." To avoid ridicule for "being stupid or not getting it," she was meticulous about going over questions and answers, even outside the context of the particular event she was going to. The task took huge amounts of time and was "highly stressful." McGregor also found at home that getting buttonholed by constituents meant "even just going through a grocery store took me two hours, so I started going at 9:30 at night."

And there's the issue of weight gain from the eating habits de-manded by the job. "It certainly happened to me," said Mary Collins, "and to a lot of women I know, because your eating habits are very bad. . . . You eat out so much." April Sanders looked at it profession-ally. "In my experience as a physician, women are much more health-conscious than men, but the system completely destroys the ability to maintain a healthy diet, get your exercise or be in a balanced environ-ment where you are mentally healthy—all of those things are completely unavailable when the house is sitting." She cited an example. "Poor Judy LaMarsh was a slim woman in the first part of her career and a large woman at the end. The abuse, the scorn she took for that, despite the fact she did many, many wonderful things! If people are fat, they're not noticed for who they are. It makes them invisible, nullifies them."

Susan Brice said one of her barriers was exposing her private self. "Not my private life—I've found that by and large people aren't that interested in your private life." But, said Brice, "You wear your heart on your sleeve. Elections put you up for disappointment and rejection." It's

Joan Sawicki as the second woman Speaker in BC found it nearly impossible to break habits based on gender differences. *Courtesy New Democratic Party.*

not like that in private enterprise. "Most people who are making decisions in their careers make lots of mistakes. No one knows about it because you can rework a piece. In politics, everything is so open."

You can't keep your personal life out of it, said Sophia Leung. "It's no life. You eat junk food. I used to have a lot of interest in music, opera. Now, nope. Nothing. Soon I won't even have friends—I don't have time for them."

Collins agreed that a member really doesn't have a personal life. "Brian Peckford had been my mentor and we'd been friends for forty years. One day he said, 'What you have to be really careful about is your reputation, and you only get that once.' I said, 'Absolutely.' So I took my vows, which I kept. I decided that at least they couldn't tell stories about me as a single woman with kids."

A similar message came from Margaret Mitchell. "Women MPs found they were so far from home and didn't have time to have any social life. The men would go out to the press club or just hang out somewhere, but you couldn't go and hang out in the press club as a woman, or they'd be saying you were having affairs or doing this or that."

Women members sometimes found themselves trying to be polite without getting patronized as members unable to defend themselves in the arena. "I'm not a very aggressive person or assertive," said Shannon O'Neill, "and I think you need to use your elbows a little bit when you're in politics." And Mitchell explained, "There was an element of patronizing if you weren't a woman who, like Pauline Jewett, was independent and successful in her own career and well known." Jewett didn't take any nonsense about anything, but Mitchell thought sometimes she herself was "kind of patted on the head and given the so-called soft issues to deal with inside our caucus by our leader, a man at that time." She learned "to be more assertive and more confident."

"I get so emotional about stuff," said Carol Gran, "and I think that was a barrier for me because people could read me so well. Everything that was going on in here," she said, pointing to her heart, "was there on my face. You have to be able to control your face. I could never do that."

Penny Priddy reckoned she was not good at saying no. "Women keep giving away pieces of themselves until suddenly there's nothing left, and they've got to find a way to fill that bucket up again. The harder it is to say no, the faster that bucket is going to drain. So that was a personal challenge for me."

Advisors have told Jenny Kwan time and again that she's too idealistic, a dreamer, utopian, suggesting that she is a bad politician and what she really needs to do is focus on the world here and now. "But I'm not prepared to be fake to do my job—even to the degree of being the macho person I guess I could be—and from time to time I have lapsed into those moments of weakness. But if I became that and that's how I portrayed myself, then I would think I had betrayed myself. . . . I've decided every time that I don't want validation if that's what it means. But it's a barrier as a politician. I don't fault others who do it. Good on them."

Kwan seems to be a magnet for trouble. When she was a city councillor, she drew strong criticism and a caution for wearing blue jeans with her blazer in the council chambers when it was not in session, since a photographer wanted a picture. But another councillor, Kwan observed, drew no comment when he wore his cycling shorts to council meetings. When Kwan spoke Cantonese in a speech in the legislature, MLA Ted Nebbeling called out in Cantonese, *"Gong dye wah,"* (tell a big lie). Nebbeling had previously spoken Dutch in the chamber, yet he saw no problem in demanding that Kwan use a language all could understand.

She was loudly accused and nearly prosecuted for drawing a daisy in water-soluble paint on the boarding of the Woodward's building in Vancouver's East Side at a time when homeless people were tenting beside the building to request low-cost housing space in the redeveloped building.

As one of two opposition NDP members in the house, Kwan sat on a lot of legislative committees. At the time I interviewed her, Liberal members were threatening to boot her out because she leaked a document from one of the committees to the BC Teachers' Federation. She had already apologized to the house. No other MLA or official who was questioned about the issue could remember such severe threats being made—ever—over that level of misdemeanour. Kwan thought she was subject to such attacks frequently because of her youth—she was born in 1966—her ethnic status and her gender. "If they can't silence me, who can they silence?"

THE HOME FRONT

Finding the middle ground can be difficult for women MLAs and MPs with families.

"When my family was happy and had enough time with me," April Sanders said, "I would suffer at work. And when I was doing the job so that all my caucus was thrilled with me, my family was totally alienated. It didn't seem that there was any in-between. No matter where you turned, you were punished, and not even on a conscious level. You were punished by role strain. There's no way to service those two completely divergent and important issues—trying to walk the line and trying to absolve the guilt that I would feel, regardless of which area it was."

For Margaret Lord the hardest part about the job was leaving her family behind. "I carried that with me all the time." Lord's kids were little, and she had no idea what she was getting into that way. "I know it's hard for men to be away from their kids, too, but I don't think it's that same soul-wrenching thing." The government would insist the legislature sit over spring break and in the summer. "It was like the military, you know? It didn't matter that you hadn't seen your kids since mid-March. Your kids are out of school, so what?" Government wants to get its work done. "So your husband gets a week off work and brings the kids down to Victoria so you can see them. Too damn bad. 'We're going to sit till midnight every night. You'd better not leave.'" Lord found that such constraints made holding office "impossible for a parent of young children." Like Sanders, she did not run for a second term.

Rita Johnston said, "I watched Darlene Marzari, now I watch Christy Clark—I don't know how they do it." Marzari had two very young children, and Clark delivered a child while in office.

But being a parent, despite the difficulties, generally expanded what women members thought about their political work. Judi Tyabji Wilson ran partly because of her opposition to the Free Trade Agreement. "When you have a baby, you start to think, 'Okay, everything has to be at least as good for my kids as it is now.' And I didn't think it would be with that agreement." Joy MacPhail had grown up in a community-minded family and worked as an economist for the BC Federation of Labour. She had been a political activist for years before her son was born. "Prior to his birth, policy initiatives were theoretical, esoteric exercises," recalled MacPhail. "All of a sudden, with Jack there, health, education, environment, the quality of air in the community all became extremely important."

About one-third of women MLAs and MPs have had children at home while they were members. Susan Brice's children were small when she began in Saanich municipal politics. Her husband, who was raised in the 1950s, was supportive "as long as the family never looked as though it was being neglected," she said. "We had a lot of babysitters, but I made sure the kids were ready for bed, and sometimes they didn't even really know I was gone." But sometimes she knew she'd really pushed her limit. "So I'd do a high-profile weekend—with housekeeper, family dinner—just to make sure everybody was happy."

Karen Sanford's family of three was young when she was first elected as MLA for Comox. "Kids are far more capable of taking on things than I would have given them credit for. Before I got involved I was up first, I made the lunches, I made them breakfast, and I kept saying, 'Where is your homework? Why aren't your shoes polished?' It wasn't necessary. It all got done. So I was very lucky." Her husband was supportive, and her son's comment about trips to Victoria and touring the legislative buildings was "What a gas!" Her daughter, who was younger, "probably felt my absence more, although I don't imagine that there were any long-term effects."

Brenda Locke tried to keep her routine. "When I'm sitting, the first thing I do in the morning for my kids is get them out of bed and ready for school, even though their father is there to do that. I used to be a cookie-bakin', apron-wearin' mom, so despite the support, it's pretty traditional." On the day of her election, Locke reported, her husband was scrutineering somewhere and she was locked up in a hotel phoning when her youngest daughter, aged ten, phoned to say her hamster had died. "She was just devastated and she phoned me to come. I didn't know how to get out of the hotel room because all these people were there visiting me, but my kid's hamster was dead and that wasn't good. I mean, I'd had enough of the hamster anyway, but that's not the point. How could I let her down when she was pretty upset?" All she could do was ask her older daughter, aged eighteen, to "Give your little sister a hug."

Lois Boone, who has two daughters, said they accepted her political activity, partly because she tried to keep them out of the whole situation as much as possible. Boone noted of rural members, "When we're away, we're away." Everything has to be done by phone, and members—male or female—really depend on their spouse. Boone often arranged special events. "On Sonia's sixteenth birthday, I brought her to Victoria and we went to dinner. And then the family travelled with me sometimes, for example, to New Brunswick for a parliamentary conference."

Grace McCarthy had three school-aged children when she started on parks board. "My husband said, if that's what you want to do, we'll support you all the way, and he did." It made a big difference that he was his own boss. The children grew up thinking, "Doesn't everybody take an interest in politics?" But McCarthy said, "With maturity I think I wouldn't have gone in it so early, and I wouldn't have stayed there so long. Every day I was there, I accomplished something—I didn't waste my time—but still it was a huge effort to keep everything running. Huge." Through history and convention, she observed, it's still the female who "must look after those little babies in the crib."

Agnes Kripps, who grew up in a Ukrainian-Canadian home in Manitoba, had four children, two of them at university when she was elected in 1963. "On the home front," she said, "I had no nannies, no maids, and I expected my husband and my university-aged son and daughter to absorb many of the homemaking and childcare responsibilities. Such an arrangement was very radical, considering the traditional patriarchal culture my husband and I came from."

In the 1990s when Evelyn Gillespie agreed to run for the nomination, her family living arrangements were difficult for her. "We run a resort and were living in a six-hundred-square-foot cottage with three children and Bruce working away five days a week." In this small house, the kitchen table had to accommodate homework, artwork, meals—and election planning. "We had to move to a space where I could actually work and make telephone calls and have the children in another place while election planning went on." After her election, Gillespie's husband reduced his working activity, although his employer accommodated only some of that reduction, and they hired in-home child care.

It took April Sanders's family a year to make the decision for her to run. "I had their full support," she recalled, but the reality of politics was a very different story. "Your family definitely becomes an also-ran. There was a lot of unhappiness about me being away Monday to Friday, abrogating responsibility for everything, being the centre of attention within the family regardless of the fact I put no energy into it." Those things wore so heavily that the family was "very relieved" when she decided not to run again. A year after she was back to her medical practice in Vernon, her little girl saw the legislature on TV at about nine o'clock on a Sunday. "She turned to me and said, 'I'm really glad you're home and not there.' That meant a lot to me because I still had rebound anger and grumpiness over the fact that I had made my decision for the benefit of other people."

Cathy McGregor had a sixteen-year-old daughter who thought her mother's election would "inhibit her capacity to be anonymous and not draw attention to herself." Although she was annoyed, she eventually came around. McGregor was elected in May, and her daughter started high school in the fall. "She didn't want anyone to know I was her mother. She was living with her dad for the first time since we split because she didn't like being alone so much and she could be anonymous, but in November she wanted me to come to parent-teacher interviews, so then everybody knew."

When Jan Pullinger decided to run, her fourteen-year-old son wasn't happy. After she talked with him and told him what it would mean in terms of time, he more or less agreed—at first. Pullinger recognized that "it had been just him and me for all his life, and all of a sudden I was gone, canvassing for the nomination and so on. He was very angry." As a single mother she needed someone to look after him "for the first year, particularly during the session, or I couldn't have done it," and her stepmother was "wonderfully supportive." Although her son was always "kind of close to the chest," Pullinger said once he got through the first anger, "I think he thought it was kind of neat. He was proud."

Jackie Pement's husband Al was supportive in many ways but felt some ambivalence, and the rest of their family were not comfortable with her being an MLA. "When I asked Al how he viewed my term, he said, 'Absent. You were just absent.' That's all he said." Their twelve-year-old daughter was "getting into that wonderful teenage stage." Pement had been home when the other kids were raised and knew her husband wasn't used to dealing with the vagaries of such young teenagers.

"I do have to worry about the orthodontics for my son," said Elayne Brenzinger. "I do have to worry about graduation day." While she described her husband as "fantastic," she also felt he "wouldn't quite catch the subtleties" that told her when her thirteen-year-old wasn't telling them everything. She and her husband talked every night about their son taking showers and having clean clothes every day, and "you have to have the relationship to be able to do that. Three kids—two of them teenagers—need guidance." Brenzinger's mom lives with them. "She's a great help, but I also have to concern myself with her."

Carol Gran had two teenagers, and "the beautiful part of it" was that her husband and the two kids worked right with her during her term. In hindsight, however, "I can't count the holidays, the special occasions that just went by the boards because politics had to come first." Gran remembered her first day in caucus, when her leader said, "If you have to make a sacrifice, the party comes first." It took her a while to decide she didn't agree. "I began to see how you could get caught up in this party stuff. And for what? It isn't a religion. It's a band of people coming together for a common cause, and it doesn't even mean the cause is right." But she worked to that concept. "Maybe not everybody made the sacrifices that I did, although I suspect a lot of women do."

BC's women MPs had an even harder slog than the MLAs. Pat Carney's solution was one of her proudest achievements. "As an MP, I made a significant breach of the male culture by forcing Parliament to change its rules on who could travel to Ottawa with an MP." When Carney was elected, only spouses could travel to Ottawa at the expense of the government. Even though she had no spouse, she couldn't take her fifteen-year-old son to Ottawa unless she paid his way or put him on a military aircraft milk run which gave priority to military families. Carney was the only mother in the whole Parliament west of the Lakehead, "so no one thought that was important except me." She announced she would not sit in her seat in the House until the rule was changed because it was grossly unfair to families and women. "When I was starting to worry that I would never take my seat," Speaker Jeanne Sauvé phoned, asked her to tea, and then changed the rules to say "designated next-of-kin" rather than "spouse."

"All sorts of other MPs, everybody, said, 'Thank you. This means so much to me.' Ian Waddell could bring his widowed mother." Others could send the oldest daughter or son back or forth. "It made a great, great difference to members of Parliament—particularly from the West." About 25 percent of the families in Carney's riding of Vancouver Centre had a single parent. "To every one of them it was a symbolic move. For years after, they'd stop me in the street, and they wouldn't talk about free trade—they would talk about having the rules changed for children's travel to Ottawa."

Carney's son "loathed and despised Ottawa." When she was first elected a friend lived with him at their home in Vancouver during the week. "But when we lived in Ottawa, he said I was away half the time, so he'd be alone in a strange place with limited support systems— other MPs—and they all had the same problems." In one year he went to four schools.

Iona Campagnolo's sister gave her a great gift. An accountant for BC Packers, she gave up her job and went to Ottawa with Campagnolo. "I still owe her. She took a job in a dress shop and cared for Jennifer (fourteen) while she

Pat Carney, a single parent, fought to have her son travel to Ottawa just as spouses of others could. Speaker Jeanne Sauve answered her concern and allowed funding for "designated next of kin." *Michael Bedford Photography*.

went to high school and did all those things I didn't have time to do."

Mary Collins had three daughters still in school when she was elected in 1984. They were fourteen, twelve and eleven. A national caucus meeting in Ottawa was called for September 4, and her three children, travelling with her, had to get enrolled in school. "My kids tell this story more often than I do, about sleeping on the floor in a hotel because the plane was delayed and living in Ottawa in this little Hill apartment hotel with one bedroom for a while." Collins was a single parent; she thought she would be in Ottawa during the weeks and would return to Vancouver on the weekends. It was not a perfect solution, but, she observed, there is no such thing. When one daughter was in grade nine she moved back to Vancouver and went to private school for a year, then boarded with a family for a year. "By then, she was, well, supposedly old enough—hm, hm—to find a place here on her own." Collins thought the situation was "very hard" for her daughters because "they didn't have the kind of traditional family life that I think would have been nicer for them." On the other hand, "they certainly are more aware of politics and what life is about than their friends or colleagues."

Even when a woman is sure her care arrangements are okay, there are what Lynn Hunter called "constant considerations." She told about being on a mission-for-peace trip to El Salvador with a Tory and a Liberal at the time of the presidential elections. "I had been in other war zones when I was working with Oxfam, but this was really something. There was gunfire every night and every day. From our hotel room we watched a helicopter gunship in a civilian neighbourhood. We didn't know it was going to be that bad. I was very glad I had those MP letters after my name because it would have been an international incident if we'd been killed." A BCTV reporter was to interview Hunter, and her husband had told their kids she would be on the evening news. They went into the television room to watch. "You could hear machine-gun fire outside and predictably BCTV made it more dramatic than it was." Hunter's daughter turned on her heel and said, "I didn't know that was what Mom was going to do when she became an MP.""It was hard on them," Hunter said. "They were worried about me all the time. Hunter was also stalked, which happens to women in the public eye. "I guess that's a barrier that men don't have to deal with. Not as frequently anyway."

Joy Langan's daughter was twenty-two, but she was affected by her mother's move to Ottawa in 1988. "She hated me being an MP. You know—small town, everybody knows you're the MP's kid, and you do something at the pub and the whole town knows about it. She always felt she was being watched, and probably she was, because I was certainly always watched." Her daughter had encouraged Langan to run, but living in her mother's house, she received awful phone calls. Langan ended up getting a second line "because there were really some ugly things said. She had to live there alone in a big house that was broken into the first week we lived in it."

Elizabeth Cull's son was four when she was elected. She recognized the benefits that women in her caucus enjoyed thanks to the young fathers in it, who made decisions based on family responsibilities that men of a different age would have dismissed. "When we went into government in 1991, we had more women than ever, lots of young people with young children, school-aged and younger. At a Treasury Board meeting early in 1992, Glen [Clark, minister of finance] said, 'We're not meeting Tuesday nights because my son has swimming lessons, and I'm going to be home for that.'" As well, Moe Sihota often left meetings to pick up his daughter. "If we as women had suggested we had to leave because of child care arrangements—well, we would have never dared because we thought if we made an excuse for that reason, we would have been looked down on because we weren't able to be full participants in government. But because the men in our party forged the way for us, we were all able to do it." She felt their actions gave her and other young mothers "some breathing room."

Judi Tyabji Wilson was the first of four women who upset hallowed parliamentary ways by having babies while they were members. She was carrying her third child during the 1991 election campaign, and baby Tanita was born three days before the spring session in 1992. Tyabji Wilson took the baby to the opening. "I was twenty-seven,[59] and this was exciting for me." She called a friend, who agreed to be nanny for the day, so they flew to Victoria from Penticton. "Who ever gets a rest when you have kids, anyway?"

Tanita "slept all the time," so she was an ideal baby to spend time in a crib in her mother's office, unless she was taken for walks or to Tyabji Wilson's nearby rooms by a caregiver. Tyabji Wilson found she could schedule breaks for nursing and otherwise arrange for the care of her daughter when she was in the chamber. But the media were not generous. "In the *Vancouver Sun* following the opening of the legislature, I was portrayed as a mother taken up with the fashionable trend of toting a nanny into the workplace to whisk the baby off while I leisurely went about my MLA duties. The columns . . . recommended that I resign my seat before my child was neglected in favour of my career. In fact I remained her primary caregiver throughout the four-month session of the legislature. I did all the planning and all the scheduling,"[60] as well as the laundry.

An article by Carolee Chute, headlined "You Made Your Bed,

Judi," gave a negative critique. "Your claim to fame, other than being a rising political star, seems to be bringing your newborn baby to work—showing us that women can do it all. You'll never know how other working mothers resented your action—they must find child care outside the workplace—and there stands a political representative flaunting political privilege by bringing baby and nanny. . . . Special rules for special people."[61]

BC MLA Linda Reid delivered a little girl in Victoria on February 3, 2000, and was back on the job when she was four days old. She cared for Olivia in much the same way Tyabji Wilson had done: with one caregiver in Victoria and one at home and a pram in her office. Under the Legislative Assembly Allowances and Pension Act members accumulating more than ten days of absence when the legislature was in session were subject to fines of three hundred dollars a day. Not surprisingly, there was no clause making allowances for members having babies. Government reacted after the fact by amending the act so that MLAs may without penalty miss sitting days for pregnancy, illness or another reason approved by the speaker, such as a death in the family.

On August 25, 2001, Christy Clark delivered her baby boy Hamish. Clark was the first cabinet minister to deliver a baby. She had just been appointed minister of education and deputy premier, and the media gave

Linda Reid was the second BC woman MLA to give birth—to both her children—while in office. In 2007, from left: Olivia, Reid, Will, and Reid's husband, Sheldon Friesen. *Courtesy Linda Reid's office.*

her lots of attention leading up to the birth. "Everybody says, if I had any experience with children I probably wouldn't be doing all this stuff now. But ignorance is bliss,"[62] she told an interviewer in June. Clark was able to have a small room across from her office for Hamish, but otherwise she used the same set-up as the other two new mothers. "It's expensive," she told me, reporting that she used a caregiver in Victoria every Monday to Thursday and in her riding every Thursday and Friday to assure no gap in care.

Like Tyabji Wilson, Clark was criticized for keeping her baby at the legislature, using supposed privilege. Anna Elphinstone of Halfmoon Bay wrote in a letter to the editor of the *Vancouver Sun*, "How nice that the deputy premier has been able to balance motherhood with her political career. She might try grabbing a bus at 6 a.m. to take her son to child care, then get back on the bus to go to work for minimal wages, then repeat the process eight hours later. This is the reality of single-parent employment. It's unfortunate that she's made it so difficult for other working mothers by supporting cuts to child-care subsidies and by supporting changes to labour laws governing hours of work that separate mothers from their children."[63]

Clark felt the labour movement in particular opposed her child care arrangements. "I got a lot of criticism from opponents, surprisingly on the left, about my decision to take my child to work." She said union protesters outside her office were not there to protest her activities as a mother, but part of their message track was that she was getting a free ride on child care. "They said, 'Why was I taking my baby to the legislature?' and 'Not everybody can do that,' and all that, and I'm just trying to have a baby and go to work at the same time, and trying to figure it out like anybody else is."

Jenny Kwan's daughter, Cee-Yan, was born March 11, 2003, and Kwan took eight weeks off before returning to the legislature. In a house that had seventy-six Liberals, one Independent, and only herself and Joy MacPhail representing the NDP, her maternity leave took away half the caucus, but she had strong support from MacPhail as leader. Kwan's mother usually travelled to Victoria to care for the baby when the legislature was sitting, and the rest of the family pitched in at home.

With little fanfare Reid had her second baby, Will Nicholas, on March 3, 2004. This time she took a month before she went back to work.

In September 2004, Christy Clark announced that she had

resigned from cabinet and would not run in the next election because "my family needs more of me than I have been able to give them."[64] Jim Beatty, *Vancouver Sun* reporter, noted that Clark had been the first politician in Canada to have a baby "while maintaining her formidable cabinet responsibilities as both deputy premier and education minister. For three years, Clark successfully juggled the heavy demands of motherhood and cabinet but finally decided to quit politics following a summer of internal struggle." Clark said the decision was personal, not political. "I decided I needed to find a different balance in my life."

Clark strongly rejected being "a symbol of whether women can be mothers in politics. That's the last thing I'd want to be," she told me. She still recruits women to run for politics, noting that "everybody's family is so individual." She admitted that she might go back into politics some day and characterized her action as "quitting while her blades were sharp." In fact she made an attempt to get the Vancouver Non-Partisan Association nomination for mayor of Vancouver in 2005 before she took up a new job as a radio talk-show host.

Sanders, who did give up politics for her children, rejected missing a big chunk of their lives. They were in grades one and three when she was elected in 1996, and when she contemplated running again in 2001 they were in grades six and eight. After ten years she'd have been away for the entire schooling and maturation of her children. "I think the hardest decision I've ever made was to look at the big picture—what was not necessarily best for me but was best for other people—and to say in ten or fifteen years from now, I cannot look back and say what the price of my career would be for two terms. My decision not to run again ... was very, very difficult."

Several men politicians remarked fatalistically on Clark's resignation, accepting women's biology and regretting such difficulty. Tyabji Wilson and MacPhail, whose son was five when she took on the social services portfolio, instead claim the problem lies with the failure to accommodate women, something that could be done for the good of the province. Still, Sue Hammell said, "I don't think women will have equality until men and women accept the responsibility of raising their children as an equal partnership."

KNAVES AND SCOUNDRELS

"You and I know that politics is not a corrupt business," said Pat Carney when we talked about the poor reputation that politicians endure. Nevertheless, when St. Peter asks BC women politicians, "What was your occupation?" few will own up to their choice of electoral politics.

In polls to see which occupations employ people most trusted by the public, politicians usually end up with car salespeople at the bottom of the list. About 10 percent of respondents are willing to trust them. Corporate chief executive officers and trade unionists score about twice as high. The "press" along with lawyers is some 10 percentage points up again. Professionals such as pharmacists, doctors and teachers rate in the top 20 percent with airline pilots.

So why do voters still elect car salespeople and trade unionists, lawyers and CEOs to public office? And when they elect pharmacists, airline pilots, teachers and doctors, why does election plummet these people to the bottom of trustworthiness polls? After all, according to the pollsters, voters chose to elect them because above all else they want honesty, integrity and reliability in their elected representatives.

Christy Clark has experienced a whole gamut of responses when she tells people she's a politician. "I wait for the look on their faces. Sometimes they look excited; sometimes they look disgusted; sometimes they look like they want to confront me." A negative public view of elected representatives has consequences. "Young people are raised to believe there's something dishonourable about politics. People can imagine themselves becoming a politician as much as they can see themselves becoming an astronaut." She thought such an attitude about politicians "fundamentally undermines democracy," which depends on the idea that anyone can see herself equally worthy among citizens, and if she chooses, running for public office.

Ida Chong helps start a seismic upgrade project at École Margaret Jenkins School in Victoria. Chong who felt she got more respect as an accountant than as a politician, wanted people "to know me before they know my status." *Courtesy Ida Chong's office.*

If we want people to believe what we do is "important and meaningful and responsible," she said, we have to take the time to actually talk to them about it. When Clark co-chaired the Liberal election campaign in 2001, she found it's getting harder to recruit female candidates. "I think that's partly because women are less likely to get into a profession that's held in such low regard."

Few women look at politics as a career, that's why I mentioned St. Peter in my questions—to offer a wide perspective. For some women, being a politician constituted a very short period in a life of doing many other things, and when I asked, they named another job. Some felt one aspect of one of their jobs was the role that fit them best. But their answers were larded with confessions that being labelled a politician was not a socially pleasant fate. Even if a member believed that the overwhelming majority of MPs and MLAs are hard-working, good people who ran for election so that they could serve a community, she knew the public's stereotype of a politician.

Crooked, amoral if not immoral, lazy, skiving, conniving, manipulating, sleazy, rotten, opportunistic, blowing with the wind, arrogant, unwilling to listen, self-important, a scumbag, a low-life, a liar, a corrupt bastard and a self-serving scoundrel: every one of these words came from women members describing the public's attitude toward them. No wonder they avoided being labelled "politician." In the right circumstances, however, most would confront the inappropriate stereotype which harms the system and interferes with the work of those sincerely committed to our democracy. Margaret Lord said with regret, "Such an important position, but held in such low regard—it's so ironic." But to St. Peter or any other gatekeeper, she would still say no, she was not a politician.

"I don't see myself as a politician now," said Elizabeth Cull, "even though I am political. I sometimes say I'm a recovering politician, which is good for a laugh." Cull gave two descriptions of how she sees the job of an elected member. "A person of ideas," was her first answer. "We don't hand out money or write laws very often. What we do is come up with ideas. We get them from our community, and we make them happen by selling them to other people. We convince civil servants, communities and colleagues this is the right thing to do. We're salespeople." Cull comes from a long line of salespeople, and when she went into politics, she found herself using all the sales techniques she ever saw her parents use. "A change agent" was her second definition. "I have never been involved in a political action to preserve the status quo." In her political roles as government minister, MLA, school trustee and union rep, she said, "I was always working for change. Still am."

Sharon Hayes, who retired as a member in 2000, doesn't volunteer that she was a politician because from the time you enter politics, "whether you go to a meeting or whether you send a birthday card, you are maybe a conniver." Five years after she resigned in good faith and "didn't swindle anybody for a hundred million dollars," in some people's minds, she is still a politician, and "they are always thinking 'What is she trying to get?'"

Ida Chong got more respect as an accountant than she does as a politician, and she wants people "to know me before they know my status." She's a servant of the public, she would tell St. Peter. When people ask what she does, she says she "works for government," which is the same phrase Sheila Orr uses if she's out of the province. Jenny Kwan admitted, "When I was working as a city councillor, if they thought I did therapy counselling, I didn't tell them any different." But Anna Terrana reacted vigorously. "I would never say politician! A politician is more sophisticated than I am. I am a volunteer. I think I would tell St. Peter I was a mother."

Other women like the label "mother." Grace McCarthy said, "I've been a mother and a grandmother; I think that has to be the highest calling. I've had a number of lives. I was very good at business; would I say I was a businessman? I spent a long time in the political game; would I say I was a politician?" She concluded, "If I'm to be judged, I'll be judged on that. The other things are fleeting." Camille Mather decided she would say housewife. "I have been a nest-builder all my life. I enjoy making a home. Even my daughters feel that." Karen Sanford would make all roles in her life equally important. "I would proudly say teacher, homemaker, politician. It would be hard to choose one because I think the others are important too."

"It seems to me I'm always in the teacher role," said Jackie Pement. "When I picked up a skill, I seemed to be in a place of passing that on, so I feel more like a teacher than a politician." Katherine Whittred would also probably say a teacher, "simply because that was my profession for most of my life. Politician is sort of an avocation."

Hedy Fry deals with politics as a physician, making things better, "and if not having the power to fix things and heal the condition of people's lives, at least being able to mitigate whatever else is going on so that it is more bearable." People have come to tell her, for example, "My only sister is disabled and living in the Ukraine. All of my family is here and we'd like her to live in Canada where we can take care of her." To Fry, that's "being involved in people's lives on a bigger scale."

Sindi Hawkins has had three occupations. She joked, "I've just gone down and down. First I was a nurse; that was great. Then I was a lawyer. Now I'm a politician." Hawkins regretted that our society hasn't cultivated a sense of public service, and felt that people don't appreciate that politicians provide a service. "They think we're all in the hog trough, we're all just out to get what we can off the public." And it's worse in BC than in Saskatchewan, where she grew up. "I looked up to the mayor, city councillors, MLAs, the premier. 'Wow, Tommy Douglas!' We've lost some of that shine." In her three occupations, she sees a common thread of serving people, and she would call herself "a humble servant to other people."

Many women thought of themselves as community activists, advocates, problem solvers, community workers, volunteers or even artists. One said, "I create things." Another said, "I worked for my fellow citizens with my fellow citizens." But Libby Davies said not all politicians are community activists. "An activist is always trying to engage with the system around her and take on some of the issues. I see myself as a politician who's tried to do that."

For those willing to risk what's left of their reputations by openly claiming to practice this questionable profession, there is missionary work to be done. They believe that ducking the negative perceptions means we will never make progress against an unfair prejudice. "I was proud to be a politician and I wouldn't blink when I said it," asserted Penny Priddy. "I did not feel I had to apologize, had to say I was a nurse so I wouldn't have to say politician." Priddy was recently part of a group that didn't know

Hedy Fry works politically much as she worked as a medical doctor, mitigating what she can to make things more bearable. It's "being involved in people's lives on a bigger scale." *Courtesy Hedy Fry's office.*

her very well but spent a lot of time together over four months. They talked about what they'd learned about each other. "Every single person said, 'You sure changed my mind about politicians. I thought you'd be arrogant and unwilling to listen to anybody else and self-important . . .' And the list went on." The exercise reaffirmed for Priddy what the public thinks when they hear "politician." "But if we apologize for being politicians, if we act defensively or make jokes about it, all we do is reaffirm for the public that that is what politicians are about."

Joy MacPhail and Joan Sawicki also offer a positive attitude about being a politician. MacPhail said, "There's a generic sense that all politicians are corrupted and bad, lazy and all that, but one to one, when you're in the community, people honour a politician. I'm very proud to be a politician." That was how she defined herself from her election onward. And Sawicki reported, "People come to know you and think 'Hey, you're a pretty good person, and you work hard and you've got integrity.'" It's particularly important for women to say they're politicians, she said.

Penny Priddy, centre. "If we apologize for being politicians, act defensively or make jokes, *we reaffirm negative perceptions the public has of us as professionals." Courtesy Penny Priddy's office.*

Margaret Bridgman has "no qualms whatsoever" about saying she's a politician. People play small P politics every day of their lives. "It's a little bit like when people say 'manipulation.' You always tend to think of manipulation as being negative, but the best behaviour trait is to be able to positively manipulate." It's just traditional to bash a politician, she said, although "lots of professions are more crooked and more demeaning than politics."

"It's up to me to feel proud of what I do or I shouldn't be in it," said Patty Sahota, who answered, "Sure, I would say politician."

Some women replied with forthright confidence. Lynn Stephens answered, "I say I'm a politician a little bit assertively, and if they don't like it, too bad." Unless we "respect our own positions, the public won't respect our positions either," observed Elayne Brenzinger. And Joy Langan lined up three confessions she would make. "When you're called a trade unionist, you are thought to be a gangster. When you're called a feminist, you are too. I would say I'm a feminist social activist with trade union political roots and never be ashamed of any of those occupations."

Because she "knows that things we did were right," Erda Walsh would say she was a politician, "and a damn good one. You get horrible politicians who run for the wrong reasons," she said, "but then you get people who work in hospitals for the wrong reasons, or work in media for the wrong reasons."

April Sanders, who was "very unhappy to have the public think there were no decent people in politics," decided she was going to raise the bar. "I got a lot of people from all levels involved in either the party or in the actual job of being the elected representative, people who hadn't considered politics." She could see they thought, "If she'll do it, then maybe it's not such a bad job." She thought her efforts "changed how people look at politicians in our own little microcosm. I do feel proud about that."

Reasons beyond the politicians themselves, however, work against a positive public recognition. Susan Brice saw an attitude change. "There's a general unease throughout the province, the nation—around the globe—which started twenty years ago, and probably has another twenty years to play out. Who knows? People are very uncomfortable about what lies ahead. Things that you could bank on are no longer there. People are saying, 'Somebody should be in charge.' 'Who's responsible?'

'They're not fixing it.'" The final blame falls on the people in decision making, so "you get your Bill Vander Zalms, your Glen Clarks—who become little poster boys promising solutions."

People used to be able to rely on family life, and the church was there. If you had an education, you were guaranteed employment. Because people are angry and uncertain, Brice said, politicians have become the whipping boys for their disappointments. "If you can maintain hope—the hope that really drove this nation in the 1940s and 1950s—that's what will make it better for my children." MacPhail also blamed public uncertainty. "People feel they are helpless about having to turn over a third to half their pay to the government. So they react. They assume the worst."

Lynn Hunter: "It's an honourable profession, and we've got to say so out loud if we want to return power—some of which has been lost—to our assemblies." *Courtesy New Democratic Party.*

Lynn Hunter blamed the public reaction partly on "the diminishment of democracy" as a result of the Free Trade Agreement. "Politicians don't have the power they did before, and it seems like a hollow victory to go to an assembly and be sort of a figurehead when the real power is elsewhere—in corporations." But we won't have people willing to try to return power to elected representatives unless we recognize "it's an honourable profession, and we've got to say it out loud."

Whittred cautioned people to expect only the possible. It's damaging to have "unrealistic expectations of what almost any institution can actually deliver." She cited health care and education, where "we believe that we can do everything. Well, we can't." Nor can government meet the needs of every single group. "When expectations aren't met, well then, of course politicians have a poor reputation."

Judi Tyabji Wilson developed a theory to take this idea one step further. "The problem," she said, "is they're waiting for the messiah, so the media say, 'Oh look! Hosanna, hosanna over here!' Right? And so everybody rushes over here, and then three months later, well, he's not the messiah or she's not the messiah, and so they want to kill him or her." Or at least throw the failure out. "People are so used to putting it out, just chuck it out, get another one."

Cull agreed. "People are looking for heroes, saviours," she said, "so they imbue the next elected person, who hasn't been tried, with all their hopes and wishes and dreams, and they believe those heroes will rescue them from the spot they're in now. That's just a recipe for disappointment. When that person turns out to have feet of clay, they're very disappointed. They're very hard on them, want rid of them, and they start looking for a new hero. I don't know how we break that cycle. In BC it seems worse, maybe because we go for twenty years and then turf a government out and expect the world will be rebuilt in seven days. It doesn't work that way."

Eileen Dailly served six terms as MLA after being school trustee and board chair. "You must maintain a sense of humour." *Image I-32450 courtesy of Royal BC Museum, BC Archives.*

THE CALLING

WE NEED YOU

Given the state of public response, why on earth would women want to participate in electoral politics?

"Stereotype, sustained by patriarchy, pictures women as servants, nurturers, motherly organizers who often give way to their emotions," wrote Calgary Reform MP Jan Brown in the summer of 1994. "Politics represents an overwhelming challenge for women. Not only are they struggling to rid themselves of a stereotypical social role, but they also have to re-establish themselves in a new environment; one that is quite foreign from the world in which they were initially socialized as children."[65]

"I think people who do well in politics often come in because they love the political game," said April Sanders. "They're political junkies, brought up through the system either by their families or by their own circumstances." In the long run that sustains them better than being recruited from a mainly nonpolitical life.

Some participants are brought in by a particular party leader. Some thought politics is important, volunteered at an election and stayed on. Only about half a dozen of the women I interviewed had to buy a membership in order to run. Pat Carney, for example, had belonged to no party, but the federal Tories said, "The Liberals have Iona Campagnolo, the NDP has Pauline Jewett, we need you." Amused by that and recognizing her lifelong interest in things political, through no particular partisan lens, she agreed to join the Progressive Conservative Party and stand for a federal nomination in Vancouver Centre.

Affirmative action has fans and critics, but it worked for Sophia Leung. Leung had tried unsuccessfully for a federal Liberal nomination in the 1993 election and for a provincial Liberal nomination in 1996. "I was raised in a political family. My father had been elected congressman in China in the 1940s, and I had strong convictions and a dedication to help the community and help make changes," she said. But after two losses, she felt that she'd tried and had enough. Boundary changes for the 1997 election produced a new riding in Leung's area, and her leader asked her to run. She looked at the lineup of already a dozen potential candidates, thought seriously, and then said, Yes! I will accept the challenge. "The Prime Minister was very clear. He'd like to encourage more women. And you know, sometimes women have difficulty [getting] nominated."

Leung felt that missing the nomination fight was a minor part of her achievement. "The rest I had to earn." In some ways, she said, being so chosen gave her a boost at the polls because people thought she must have some sought-after qualities, but as for the nomination fight, "I don't feel anyone made a sacrifice for me."

Controversy ensued, both outside and inside the Liberal Party. Some thought Leung was favoured, and the usual objections toward affirmative action were made. Tory Pat Carney was "against hand-picked nominees because they go in there knowing they owe their allegiance to the boss, and they're handicapped because they've been privileged by gender and race. I think you have to go in and get your knuckles skinned and fight like everybody else."

Judi Tyabji Wilson would agree, but not Sheila Orr. "I remember Judi phoned me and said, 'Don't you think that's awful [Leung's appointment]?' And I said, 'No, I don't think it's awful. I think it's high time we started saying, okay, if we can't win working with that system, then let's change the system.' It's two thousand years we've been waiting around." Orr agreed such candidates "have to do it on merit," but she didn't want them "done in on gender."

Hedy Fry, then president of the BC Medical Association, was targeted to run as a federal Liberal and could have had an appointment in 1993 for Vancouver Centre. She declined. "I was running against Kim Campbell, and we decided it was not a good idea for me to be appointed to run against a prime minister." Fry had never been appointed to anything. "I had always earned my stripes and thought, if I can't win a nomination, what the heck use am I?"

More than a third of the women who have been members came from political families where politics was served up with meals. Many had family ancestors who had run for or held office. This was particularly true of visible minority women, most of whom were not born in Canada, but throughout the group there are examples of fathers or grandfathers or uncles holding office, and mothers or aunts or grandmothers who were active and impatient. But no BC woman member has a female ancestor who held elected government office in BC, and Tilly Rolston, a

Tory and Socred for Vancouver–Point Grey in the 1940s and 1950s, is the only BC elected woman who has an elected BC member among her descendants. Her grandson, Peter, was elected NDP MLA for Dewdney for the 1972–75 term.

Kids in political families learn early why politics is important and get used to being known in their community as activists. They go door-to-door and stuff pamphlets in mailboxes or inside storm doors. They fold and fill envelopes, and when stamps and envelopes still needed licking, they licked stamps and cut their tongues on envelopes. Now they help the computer operators. Their mothers railed at their fathers for never being around for family gatherings,

The Rolston family included two MLAs, Tilly Rolston in the 1940s and '50s and her grandson Peter in the 1970s. The former was described as "a graceful street fighter." *Photo courtesy the Rolston family.*

always missing the kids' band concerts because there was an election planning meeting, spending more time with those political scoundrels than they did with their own flesh and blood, and using the family's hard-earned cash for . . . for what? Their fathers complained that there was never a cookie in the house even though trays of goodies went out the door for political fundraisers, and they stomped around in a grumpy mood when supper was late because of mom's political meeting. Didn't she know he had a committee meeting at seven? Everybody stayed out late on election night to hoot and holler if they won, commiserate and plan the next election if they lost.

My own childhood was like that. Riddles at our house were often about political names and oddly titled ridings. When my kids named our cat Clod because he seemed heavy-footed, my mother changed that to Claude, as in Quebec's Claude Ryan, so they could practise bilingual pronunciation with a name they should know. My dad ran for the Diefenbaker Tories in the 1945 federal election. My husband was campaign manager for a federal Liberal in the Trudeaumania campaign. When I ran, I chose the NDP, as did my sons. My youngest son ran for a provincial seat in Ontario when I was in my second term as MLA for Kootenay. My middle son ran for a BC federal seat in the 1997 election. The Trudeau Liberal and I were the only electoral winners in the whole bunch, but few political moves get past the eye of some member of my family; they all have an opinion.

"Family dinner-table talk was always politics or religion," said Peter Rolston. Before his grandmother ran for elected office, she had been extensively active in women's organizations. As her husband's health failed, however, so did the family fortunes. Peter said, "She needed a return for what she spent her time at. She must have seen politics as an opportunity to do what she liked and be paid [a modest stipend] for it." Peter remembered visiting Rolston one Easter with a same-aged cousin. They were about ten, and Rolston lived at the Empress Hotel, with long halls, gables, carpets, and all the special effects of such a luxury hotel. Rolston was "a lot of fun," and always entertained her grandchildren royally.

Eileen Dailly and her brother became interested in politics during the Depression when their dad lost his job because of the government's political decision. Losing his job for something over which he had no control and being denied recourse brought the whole family to "see the importance of politics in ordinary lives," said Dailly. "We joined the CCF Youth movement, and my brother went into municipal politics," staying there for many years, while she spent six terms as an MLA after serving as trustee and then chair on the school board.

Val Meredith's dad was a cabinet minister in Alberta for about two decades, and both Sindi Hawkins and Lynn Stephens, who sat as BC Liberal MLAs, had fathers active in the Saskatchewan NDP. Hawkins preferred the centrist policies of the Liberals. Stephens's family always talked politics, and her father knew T. C. Douglas, but she couldn't support the NDP in BC. "In BC the NDP is labour-dominated and reflects class distinctions. In Saskatchewan, NDP is just helping neighbours." Stephens was the eldest of seven children. Two are NDP, but her next sister won a nomination for the Liberals in the 2002 Saskatchewan election. Another sister was her campaign manager, and a brother and sister-in-law were volunteer managers in the same campaign.

Stephens's defection was not overlooked. "My mother said she wouldn't support me with money. I thought she was joking or being contrary, so I asked for her cheque after I gathered ones from my siblings. She said, 'I love you so much, but you're in the wrong party.' But she contributed in my next two campaigns."

Joan Sawicki felt that in a way she was taking her father's place by running for a nomination in 1986. He firmly believed that people could change things for the better only through the democratic system, so Sawicki worked inside the NDP. "My father had passed away, and in 1985 I had a powerful sense that he had worked all his life for social democratic principles and that somehow it was my responsibility to pick up the ball and run with it." The family's political pedigree was a great help to Sawicki when she decided to seek a nomination. "I had done my homework with the long-term members because I was born into this party and I knew how to do that, and I knew its importance." Getting both the voting and the emotional support of those members helped Sawicki a lot. Her mother and two sisters also offered help. "In retrospect, I didn't let them support me very much because politics was a big issue in our family. There were lots of fights between my mother and my father about the time he spent on politics. My mother was sort of there with him because that's what wives did at that time, but she resented it strongly."

Family influence was not always directly political. Kim Campbell felt that it was her mother's faith that she and her sister could do anything they wanted that got her into politics, more than any political influence of a number of distant relatives who had once been elected. Agnes Kripps's Ukrainian background meant that in her family, "talk at home was always about freedom of the Ukraine and how precious our freedom was in Canada—and of continuous, devoted community volunteer service. It was a process."

Iona Campagnolo never forgot childhood experiences in Prince Rupert, even though they were not directly connected to her family. "When I was a little kid, ten years old, the Japanese were taken from our community. The aboriginal kids were taken from our community to residential schools. That made a very big impression on me." And it led her to a life in public service.

Immigrants and their children have demonstrated a laudable willingness to serve in Canadian assemblies. Born in Trinidad, Hedy Fry immigrated to Canada in 1970. Before the 1993 election, Prime Minister Jean Chrétien called her several times to ask her to run for the Liberals. "The third time the prime minister said something very important to me, which I will never forget and which makes me guess him quite a judge of character. He said, 'When did you come to this country?' I said, '1970.' He said, 'It's been good to you, yes?' And I said, 'Yes.' And he said, 'Are you going to put something back?' And guess what? My father always used to say, 'You have a talent—use it. Always put something back.'"

Those were the last days of the Mulroney government, she pointed out, with high mortgage rates, people losing their homes and extremely high unemployment. "I was seeing patients with ulcers and high

Hedy Fry, an immigrant from Trinidad, says "If you have a talent, use it. Always put something back." *Courtesy Hedy Fry's office.*

blood pressure, with all kinds of problems purely because of those realities. And while I could help Joe or Josephine, I thought, 'Hey, if I were a politician, maybe I could help a whole bunch of Joes or Josephines.'" Instead of knocking on government's door asking for infant seat belts or reduced emissions, she could actually be in the place where she could get that done. Fry ran for office and was elected, the first of five times in Vancouver Centre. She is the only Trinidad-born MP in the Canadian Parliament. In 2006 she entered the federal Liberal leadership race but resigned before the final vote when she ran out of financial resources.

Ida Chong was the first MLA in BC of Chinese descent who was Canadian-born. "Being raised in my culture—you cannot ever shake it off." She showed an interest in politics in high school, but resisted a teacher's advice to go into political science because it wasn't practical enough. Instead she became a certified general accountant, but later decided to run municipally. After her partner agreed, she approached her parents. If they had said no, "I would have respected them enough to withdraw—or else suffered a lot!" Her mother wondered, "Why would you do that and bring all that attention on yourself? Why would you want anybody knowing your business—who you are, how old you are, how you live, where you work, what you do? Why would you want people to watch the decisions you make?" But her father said, "You're running for what, councillor? Why don't you run for Mayor?" With her father's agreement, Chong ran for Saanich council and sat on the Capital Regional District before she took Oak Bay–Gordon Head in 1996 and again in 2001 and 2005. Chong said before people vote for her they often want to know how well she speaks English. "Somebody phoned me up one time and said he'd got my brochure. 'You're a cute little thing. Your credentials are good. You live in the community, you've got a house in Saanich, a business, everything's great.' I said, 'Do you have questions?' He said, 'No, I just needed to hear your voice. Thanks very much.'"

Rosemary Brown, born in Jamaica, launched a political career in the tradition of her politically active family and because she felt discriminated against in Canada. Political involvement is a natural thing for immigrants, she believed. In 2002 she said, "The massive number of immigrants now going into politics indicates that they finally are beginning to understand where the decisions are being made, the decisions that either close the door in their faces or open the opportunities for them. So they want to be there when the issues are being discussed and the decisions being made." She thought they want to change the way their community is being treated through government or legislation, not for any sense of power. "Not very often today do you see people going into politics for self-interest because it's so much easier to own a corporation. Be a dot-com billionaire if you want to get things done. There is a limited amount of power in politics." Brown sat for four terms, from 1972 to 1986.

Sindi Hawkins had disappointed her father "on the front end by not being a boy—you know Indian families." Her two older sisters were stars, but she dropped out of school for a year before she went back and got a nursing diploma, "the fastest way to a job." Then she got her law degree. She knew her dad would be the hard one to crack when she wanted her family's support in running for election. "When I phoned, he said 'I know you'll win. You've done everything you said you'd do.'" She ran and won in Okanagan West in 1996 and won twice more in Kelowna–Mission.

Jenny Kwan, who was born in Hong Kong and came here as a baby, said, "My family thought I was crazy, as do most families with politicians in their lives." But they were supportive and "worked maybe even harder than me to get me elected, and it's neat for me to see my parents, who don't speak English very well, being very involved in the process." Her mother has to take three buses to work every day, and as she rides she talks Cantonese to others about her daughter and her political goals. Kwan's parents are now involved in a Neighbourhood Watch project because of the connections they made through her political activities.

Jenny Kwan's family thought she was crazy to go into provincial politics, but they worked "maybe even harder than me to get me elected," and they were drawn into neighbourhood activities. *Photo courtesy Jenny Kwan's office.*

Kwan has represented Vancouver–Mount Pleasant since 1996.

Patty Sahota's dad, who was involved politically in India after partition, was hesitant. "They'll build you up and they'll break you down," he told her. He also warned her to remain humble. "After all, it's public service." Sahota was elected in Burnaby Edmonds in 2001 for one term.

Anna Terrana, who was born in Italy, called her mother in Italy to tell her that she was going to run for election. "Anna, don't do it! They'll kill you!" "But Mother,'" I said, "'this is Canada. Nobody is killed over a position in politics.' After that she was so very thrilled to have a daughter who was in politics." Terrana won Vancouver East federally in 1993 for a single term.

The Free Trade Agreement was the "one issue that stood out" for Judi Tyabji Wilson, an immigrant from India, when she chose to run for the Liberals in the Okanagan. "My family has always been very close to agriculture; my dad came to BC because of the wine industry." Tyabji read the Free Trade Agreement, recognized some of its implications—particularly on the environment—and decided to run, first in a 1988 by-election in Boundary–Similkameen. She didn't win election until 1991, when she ran in Okanagan East and became the first Indo-Canadian woman elected to the BC legislature. She sat only one term.

The Training Grounds

Only one BC woman, Mary Ellen Smith, was elected to an assembly without major party financial support and the organization that make election campaigns lively and extensive. Members need more than party backing, though. They must be acceptable and attractive to voters, who seek a member they can talk to, someone they believe can make their point in the assembly and probably someone they know, even if only a little bit. The training ground for MLAs and MPs is politics as practised by municipal councils, boards and nonpolitical organizations in communities.

Smith chose to run as an Independent People's candidate in 1918 when she was the first BC woman to run provincially. Well-known as an active Liberal, she was endorsed by the Liberal Party in the election. She was also a life member of the National Council of Women and had been an original member of the Vancouver Women's Forum, president of the Vancouver Women's Canadian Club, charter member and president of the Nanaimo Women's Hospital Auxiliary, president of the Women's Work at the Methodist Church in Nanaimo, regent of the Imperial Order of the Daughters of the Empire and ... the list goes on and on, concluding with organizer and fundraiser for the Returned Soldiers' Club. As well, she had been a leader in the campaign to win the franchise for women.

Like Smith, five other women who served in the first half of the twentieth century were long-time members and leaders of women's organizations. Helen Smith, Dorothy Steeves, Laura Jamieson, Tilly Rolston and Nancy Hodges served such organizations as the Council of Women, the Suffrage League of Canada, the Pioneer Political Equality League, the Women's Christian Temperance Union, University Women's clubs, the Women's League for Peace and Freedom, Business and Professional Women's clubs, branches of the Canadian Club, the BC Civil Liberties Association and the Young Women's Christian Association.

The women members who came after them were increasingly more active in school boards, municipal councils and professional and community organizations. "Councils are where women earn their political stripes," Pat Carney said. Serving on local boards and councils sensitizes women to the problems of electoral politics. It hones their skills for working with people whether they like them or not, which—psychologists tell us—is harder for females than for males, and they learn the difficulties of making a decision as opposed to espousing a cause. Nearly half of BC's women MLAs and about a quarter of our women MPs were in municipal politics. Kim Campbell chaired the Vancouver school board, for example, and Rita Johnston served on Surrey council.

Mary Ellen Smith, our first woman member, was a leader in the campaign for woman suffrage and ran at the first opportunity: a 1918 by-election in Vancouver. She replaced her husband as MLA and was the first woman in the British Commonwealth appointed to a cabinet. *City of Vancouver Archives, Port N29.*

Personal interests may direct a woman's choice of municipal office but they don't dictate her success. Grace McCarthy owned a number of flower shops in Vancouver in the 1960s. "I was minding my own business—I had my own business—when the editor of a little local newspaper walked into my shop one day and said, 'We want to run you for parks board. There's a vacancy coming up, and we need good people. You know all about flowers and plants.' I didn't use any of that information, by the way. Not one whit." Far more to the point, she had previously chaired a board of trade, the first woman in BC to do so.

Many women didn't enter local politics as a stepping stone to provincial or federal politics but seized the opportunity when it arose. Penny

Priddy was chair of the Surrey school board when redistribution opened a new Surrey seat for the 1991 election. She had been a party member since 1987, but it had never occurred to her to run provincially until people started asking her to think about it. After a lot of thought and consultation, she decided that with a good team, she could probably do it. "So by timing and happenstance, as opposed to long-term planning," she won the nomination for Surrey–Newton. "I had to compete with a man who had been in the party longer than I, had been a Surrey council-lor, and I think it had never occurred to him he would have to compete for a nomination." Priddy launched her provincial career by defeating Premier Rita Johnston, who had also moved to the new riding.

Shirley Bond had a passion for politics all her life. She started when her kids were in kindergarten in Prince George and her interest led her to become a school trustee. "I was nonpartisan on school board," she said, but in the 1990s she was attracted to Gordon Campbell's leadership. In the Liberal Party, although she had not been a member, "the tent was big enough to include everyone." She decided to run in 2001 and had a "very hard-fought, very grassroots" nomination fight. "It was one of the most exciting days of my life when I beat a prominent businessman for the nomination," she said. Bond won the seat in Prince George–Mount Robson that had been vacated by Lois Boone.

For some women, the year they ran was just the year that they felt, "It's time." Time to speak out, increase their political efforts, support the need for more women in elected office or step up and do the job better than other potential candidates. Eight of them specifically observed that they looked at the competition for nominations and felt, "I could do it better."

What really got Jan Pullinger into politics was her awareness of feminism and women's issues coming to the fore. Legally separated from her husband, Pullinger wanted to revert to her maiden name but still had to have his permission. During her repeated applications and protests, an exasperated bureaucrat noted that the rules were the same for men and women. Pullinger heard the issue; she got it. "He didn't seem to have noticed that only women change their names. That was when I became a feminist. I got it."

It became clear to Pullinger that the rules are here to preserve the status quo "with a handful of white men at the top and everybody else at the bottom, women always below the men. We needed a politi-cal change."

Pullinger was in Victoria working on her master's degree in Canadian studies when the MLA in Nanaimo resigned. "I knew it was now or never." Her son was fourteen, and she had a support network in place in Nanaimo, so she could manage it. She'd just won a twenty-thousand-dollar fellowship, which she had to give back before she knew whether she'd win the seat. "That was hard." But her phone rang constantly, and she perceived a lot of support. Pullinger had to resist pressure to back off because a woman who had tried for the nomination in the previous election wanted the nomination too. She won the Nanaimo seat in the by-election and Cowichan–Ladysmith in two general elections.

Disagreement with other parties' policies encouraged some to run. Brenda Locke didn't see NDP programs as good for the province and "didn't want to see a lot of debt and passing problems on to my kids." Then Gordon Campbell "captured my imagination in terms of the future of the province." Before the Surrey–Green Timbers nominating meeting for the 2001 election, two other candidates dropped out, so she had no race for the nomination. "The riding was viewed as a pretty tough win," but Locke knocked over incumbent Sue Hammell, a cabinet member, who later took back the seat.

Similarly, Val Roddick said she "just had to" do something. "Specifically I felt very strongly about the way things were running in the province and that we weren't getting things done and people were losing." Recruited as president of the Riding Association to find a candidate to replace MLA Fred Gingell, who had announced that he would not run again, she went to the very first campaign school for women "to just learn a few things about how I should go about this." When a group of people approached her to run after Gingell died while in office, Roddick decided to do it. "I didn't expect to win. I just thought it would be worthwhile going through the program." After explaining how she had been activated by dislike for government policy, she asked me—a member of the government that drove her to run—a question of her own. "What got you in?" When I replied that it was the same thing—anger at the programs of the sitting government—she paused and then observed, "I guess that's why we have party politics."

The so-called restraint program of the Socred government led by Bill Bennett after the 1983 election specifically propelled four women to office in 1986, 1989 and 1991. I share that category with other New Democrats Lois Boone, Elizabeth Cull and Barbara Copping. Boone

Author Anne Edwards was drawn into provincial politics when she joined the picket line at East Kootenay Community College to protest the Restraint program of the early 1980s. Here she visits another picket line in Cranbrook. *Photo courtesy Anne Edwards.*

had been elected to school board in 1981. "That was all I intended—until restraint." In 1986 she was strongly encouraged to run in Prince George North and won the seat as the first woman MLA from the North.

My own life-long interest in politics did not include membership in a party after I returned to work as a journalist in the early 1970s. Still freelancing when I moved to the College of the Rockies as an instructor, I stayed away from party politics. But after the government implemented its restraint program, a group of New Democrats asked me to run. I bought a party membership and said I'd think it over. I had gone on a picket line for the first time in my life when college workers walked out at the beginning of the Solidarity strike against the restraint program. Having done that, I decided I might as well go all the way, and I did, winning Kootenay in the 1986 general election to become the first woman MLA for the region.

Cull described her recruitment. "I can thank [former Premier] Bill Bennett for my political career." More generally, she observed, "Since high school I have always been one who led the charge," but as a career civil servant Cull had put her political beliefs in a closet. In retrospect she believed she would have run provincially or federally at some time. She was already on her local school board. But in 1989 she told herself "there's no sense hiding my politics anymore if I'm going to lose my job anyway. I won't be a deputy minister that way." She was nominated and won a by-election in Oak Bay–Gordon Head, retaking the seat in 1991.

Copping had been working at BCIT, where as a doctor she had started the health program in 1974. "When Bennett's restraint program came in the 1980s, I became very political in order to see my program survive. During that time all the student services were being threatened, and I saw most of them cut, except the health services—counselling, athletics, all that kind of thing." She was on the school board and "after the restraint years, my interest was up." In 1991 she won a very difficult nomination fight in Port Moody–Burnaby Mountain and went on to win the election.

April Sanders is also a doctor, and government treatment of doctors became her issue. "I wasn't brought into politics by the love of the game, but by loathing," she said. When she graduated, Sanders was angry about Social Credit policies that limited where new doctors could practise. "I went through medical school and was then informed that I didn't have the right to practise wherever I chose." That was her "first sting." Then her anger switched to the NDP when the 1991 NDP government cancelled a pension plan agreement which had been engaged by the BC Medical Association and the previous government just before the election. She ran in 1996 and won Okanagan -Vernon. When I interviewed her after she had served a term as a Liberal and was back in practice, her medical office was closed because she and other BC doctors were protesting Liberal policies toward doctors, which included the shredding of a contract. "The irony does not escape me," she commented dryly.

Elayne Brenzinger's pivotal issue arose when she was working as executive director of a facility for special needs children; the provincial government changed the rules and she disagreed with the changes. To do something about this she took twenty-one families to Victoria to make their point. The opposition Liberals received the group warmly and gave them a room in which the media could interview them. They got a meeting with the minister, but according to Brenzinger, nothing changed. The attention-catching coverage of the trek—a radio report aired every hour as they crossed on the ferry, and there was huge newspaper and television coverage—got Brenzinger in touch with Christy Clark of the Liberals. Clark, in charge of finding women candidates for the 2001 election, asked Brenzinger to run for the party in Surrey–Whalley. Brenzinger twice said no, partly because she feared she couldn't do it—couldn't stand on a platform to speak publicly, for one thing. "Then something tweaked in my mind, and I said, 'I can do this'. . . . and when I found there was support to help along, I decided that was what I wanted to do."

Before accepting, Brenzinger "interviewed" Gordon Campbell: "I was basically interested in what he was like in person, what were his values." She had thought of him as "the businessman," but found a "very warm, caring person, very concerned about children and families and women—completely opposite of what I expected." Thinking this was a man she could work for, she joined the party. She had no competition for the nomination. The incumbent was Joan Smallwood, a minister in successive NDP cabinets and three-time MLA for the constituency, but Brenzinger won. A couple of years later she left the Liberal caucus, however, citing disagreement with Campbell as leader. She joined a new party and lost in the next election.

Government forest policies, particularly on forest renewal, prompted Joyce Murray to buy a membership in the Liberal Party in 1998. Before the year was out, someone suggested she run in the next provincial election. "I did consider it, but didn't feel it was a fit." In the spring of 2000, however, she attended a campaign school for women just to find out what it involved. Then "I felt there might be a fit between my management experience, my interest in good environmental policy and my background in my city. I had lived here and raised three kids in the schools, and I felt that I could be an effective representative for New Westminster, the longest consecutively-held NDP riding in the province." Murray did upset the long-held NDP supremacy and sat in cabinet for one term. She was defeated in New Westminster in the next provincial election and in the federal election that followed, but she ran in a 2008 by-election in Vancouver Quadra where she won and became an MP.

Daphne Jennings's political career began with the proposed Charlottetown Accord. She found several of its clauses unacceptable, so she waged a personal war on it. After she wrote a letter to the editor which was too long to run, she had it printed at a local shop and distributed it in people's mailboxes "for miles around my place." She went to local MP

Joy Langan's office to tell her she was "not representing the people fairly" because she was not bringing forward arguments against the accord as well as in favour of it. By the time the referendum was defeated, Jennings was hooked. She went looking for a political party, found Reform and joined. In 1993 she ran in Mission–Coquitlam when she was asked and set out "to represent people, never mind the parties." On voting day she beat out Langan.

With a "passion for education," Linda Reid was a strongly committed and politically active teacher. When government manuals and binders came across her desk in the late 1980s, she would wonder when was the last time these people saw a child. "Some things were not workable. Some of it was Bill Vander Zalm rewriting educational policy on Sunday morning by himself. It was a hodgepodge approach to education." Fellow teachers urged her to go beyond the BC Teachers' Federation into provincial politics, and she decided to try for a Liberal nomination in her home riding, Richmond East.

Reid faced no contest. For one thing Vander Zalm was the incumbent, still the premier and a formidable opponent. As well, no Liberal had won election to the BC house since 1979. "Many suggested I run in another riding instead of being sacrificed to the sitting premier," but she felt it important to run where she lived. By the time of the 1991 election, Vander Zalm had resigned the premiership in disgrace, the Liberals were reviving and the Socreds were crumbling. Reid took the seat and has represented the riding ever since.

Cull too faced no competition to be NDP nominee in 1989 for the by-election in Oak Bay–Gordon Head, a traditionally Social Credit riding. She opposed Susan Brice, another powerful woman who ran for the seat left vacant by Brian Smith, a cabinet minister in successive Socred governments. Brice had followed Smith to Oak Bay council and as mayor of Oak Bay, and she was felt to be a strong candidate to succeed him again. Although Cull would be seen to be a good candidate—a highly articulate, clearly committed school trustee—the seat was no cinch. "Oak Bay had a meeting and decided to put me up," Cull said.

Brice herself could see that this would be a difficult election for her as a Socred. "I knew it was a very, very tough time, but I knew that if I ducked it, I would regret it." If she didn't win, she hoped "it would make the leadership of the Social Credit Party realize what was happening." Cull won the by-election and the next election.

By 1996—since Cull was by this time a strong member, a good constituency MLA and a minister who had held such powerful cabinet positions as Health and Finance—Oak Bay–Gordon Head was not such an attractive place for the Liberal Party, which many former Socreds in the riding supported. The Liberals named no candidate until the electoral term was more than four years old. Ida Chong said, "I was not a Liberal. This was definitely a matter of recruitment. By late August or early September, it was quite clear that an election would be called. The Liberals were desperate for a candidate, so I got another round of phone calls." She asked why they were phoning her, not even a party member, and they said she would be a good candidate. "You think things out, you make reasoned and balanced decisions, you're accessible and easy to talk to, and you are ready to talk about what you care about, all your passions."

Still reluctant, Chong did ask for a ticket to hear Gordon Campbell talk to a group of Victoria women. "A ticket was delivered to me within hours." Campbell "said all the right things," so she agreed to run, and the Liberals sold her a party membership. Although Chong won the nomination, she was uncomfortable running against Cull. "I felt awkward because it seemed as though I was going against her personally, although that's not how it was." On voting day, she edged Cull out and has held the riding ever since.

Another woman strongly pressured to run was Simma Holt, a writer with the *Vancouver Sun*. She told Liberal friends, who were trying to persuade her, that she didn't like Pierre Trudeau. Finally she met him, they shared a joke and she felt she could work with him. Had she not been fifty-two and "tiring a bit of fighting the war against men in the journalism field," she might not have agreed to run in 1974. "I had no interest in politics," she said with particular emphasis. "The only beat I never had in my life was politics." Nevertheless, she had noticed that government was "giving grants to hippies to take care of hippies and drug users, and I was angry at the abuse." She thought, "Nothing on earth is more important." She mused later, "It's funny, I really didn't intend to get so deep in politics, but all my books are political." Holt ran and won Vancouver–Kingsway.

After being a business and economics newspaper columnist, Pat Carney ran a consulting business in the North, dealing mainly with the petroleum industry. When the Progressive Conservative Party asked her to run in 1984, she agreed and was nominated in Vancouver Centre. The election call took so long, however, that she decided she could no longer afford to be without income and resigned the candidacy. Only days later the election was called and she reversed her decision, awkward as that was publicly. She did not win that election in 1979, but her campaign contributed to her win nine months later when Prime Minister Joe Clark's Progressive Conservative government collapsed, forcing another election.

A decade earlier, Iona Campagnolo had been working as a Liberal for some years before running for the federal nomination in Skeena. "There was no nomination fight," she said. "Nobody wanted it. It was a losing riding. The manager of the radio station where I was sales manager intended to run. I was going to be his campaign manager." A week before the nomination meeting, he told Campagnolo his wife was ill and he couldn't be the candidate. "You run, and I'll be the campaign manager." She agreed, knowing "there were women all over the country just dying for a nomination." Although that was the only election Campagnolo won, she continued to serve the national party as president.

"The politics of the time" demanded Lynn Stephens's participation in an opposition party and led her to be president of the Langley Liberal

Val Meredith at the centre of a group of Reform MPs dressed to tour Kimberley's Sullivan mine in 1999, just before it closed. A founding member of Reform, Meredith felt compelled to carry the banner in 1993, was elected and stayed for eleven years. *Photo courtesy Val Meredith.*

Constituency Association. Thus in 1991 she was in a spot where she was "it." "I realized if you complain, you have to serve," said Stephens. "I didn't intend to run, but there was nobody else." She knocked off cabinet minister Carol Gran as the Socred government went down and stayed until 2005.

Val Meredith was instrumental in creating the Reform Party. "I was at the founding convention of the Reform Party of Canada, Halloween 1987, in Winnipeg." When a federal election was called in 1988, "there weren't that many people involved in the party, so I allowed my name to be on the ballot." She didn't win and tried to find a replacement for the 1993 election "as I thought I had retired from politics." Meredith had already served seven years on council in Slave Lake, Alberta, three of them as mayor. In 1993 she sought advice from "the volunteers, the people, my mentors and business people in the community as to whether I should put my name on the ballot," and they convinced her that she was known as the Reform Party representative in the area. "I sort of felt compelled to continue what I had started." She was elected and served eleven years as MP of Surrey–White Rock–Langley.

Driving her neighbour to a meeting drew Margaret Bridgman into the Reform Party. "He was an elderly chap and didn't want to drive. I thought, Well, I might as well stay; he's only going to be an hour or so. I listened to Preston Manning, and I joined."

By 1993 she was president of the Surrey North constituency. Away on holiday, she got back on a Sunday to hear that the candidate, who had been in place for a year, had resigned because of ill health. The writ was dropped on Monday. "A couple of people were, well, not really that interested." Recognizing that "the people have to have somebody to vote for," Bridgman put her name up. It was an easy campaign. "One of the chaps had a pickup truck and built some kind of stand out of two-by-fours on the back, and with ordinary light bulbs, wrote the word 'Reform.' And he just drove around town with this thing flashing 'Reform.'" The party paid his gas costs.

"That year it was almost as if, it was like a disease or something. I mean it was Reform all over the province. If you had a Reform sign on your car, people tooted—this kind of stuff. So when the actual writ was dropped, lots of people came out." Bridgman had not held political office before. People didn't know her publicly or through organizations, so it was strictly a party win. She joked, "Somebody said you could have put a pig up there and they would have got in."

When I asked Bridgman about her campaign manager, she replied, "I went over and talked with this friend of mine the night I won the nomination. And I told him that I had lost my presence of mind that afternoon, and would he be my campaign manager? And he said, 'Why are you asking me?' I said, 'Well, first of all, I don't know anybody else to ask, and second, if I could lose my presence of mind, so can you.' Then I said, 'Have another scotch,' because you know we were sitting there having scotch. And he said, 'I've never done it before,' and I said, 'Neither have I; let's just call it an experience and take it for a ride and see where we go.' And so he did, and he sort of pulled it together really well, actually."

Bridgman's whole campaign cost about twelve thousand dollars. "I think it was the cheapest campaign . . . in the records. And I won. So I'm standing there and thinking, 'Now what do I do?' You know I'm supposed to be at work tomorrow. And the fellow I was working with, Bill, started laughing. And that's how I got into it."

POLITICAL PAIRS

Marriage to another politician lends a rare flavour to a woman's electoral career. BC has had a dozen women who were elected provincially or federally and were married to men of similar achievement. There were wives who took over their husbands' seats when they died and wives who forged a separate path, and they range in time from Mary Ellen Smith, who won her husband's seat in 1918 after his death, to Katrine Conroy who won her husband's seat in 2005 after her husband had retired. As well, there were wives who were members while their husbands worked in the backrooms.

Smith's husband, Ralph, had had a long career as Liberal MLA and MP before he became MLA for Vancouver City and then finance minister after the 1916 election. He died a year later. Smith depended on decades of organizational activism to win nomination as the Independent People's candidate—endorsed by the Liberals. Although at least one Vancouver women's group publicly opposed her, she looked so like a winner that the *Province* commented two days before the election, "If Mrs. Smith wins, many Vancouver husbands will owe their wives new hats and gloves and chocolates. Such 'inside' wagers are frequent."[66] Smith took nearly 59 percent of the vote and went on to win Vancouver City in 1920 and 1924 as a Liberal. She became a beacon in many western democracies as the first woman in the world to have won the seat her husband had held before he died.

Nearly forty years later Lois Haggen took her husband Rupert's seat after he had won three elections for the CCF in Grand Forks–Greenwood. He suffered a stroke after the 1953 election and died during his term. "At first," said Alice Glanville, a friend and supporter, "he would go into the legislature, but that became more and more of a chore." As a result his wife did much of his constituency and legislative work for him. She would even drive him to Victoria, where he stayed at home while she worked out of his office. He died before the 1956 election, so Haggen ran in the riding and took it with a commanding vote. Glanville remembered no nominating convention. "They persuaded her to run in his place." Haggen was re-elected in 1960 and 1963 and spent her three terms with rural electrification a major goal. The city of Grand Forks made her freeman of the city after her political career, and she continued to work and lead many community and provincial organizations until her death in 1994.

Buda Brown and her husband Donald Cameron Brown were both MLAs, but under different party names. Donald had been elected in 1945 and 1949 in Vancouver–Burrard as a Conservative candidate for the Coalition, but he was defeated by the Social Credit candidate when he ran in 1952. Buda Brown, who ran unsuccessfully as a Tory in the 1953 federal election, ran successfully for the legislature in 1956 as a Socred in Point Grey and was re-elected in 1960 in Vancouver–Point Grey. She died while in office in 1962 at the age of sixty-eight.

Just as Brown was re-elected, Margaret Hobbs's husband George, familiarly known as Tiny, ran provincially and won in Revelstoke. He died after little more than a year in office, and a by-election was called in 1962. Bill King, who was to become MLA for that constituency for a decade in the 1970s, recalled the party caucus meeting in Revelstoke after Tiny's death. "Margaret and I were being looked at as candidates. The consensus was that Margaret had an excellent chance of winning the riding, and also that it would be good for her, so recently widowed, to be confronted with the challenge of continuing her husband's political career. She'd been very much involved at the constituency level and was experienced in the whole political structure. She ran and won, but lost the following year." Hobbs had been a member of many community organizations, and on a personal level was known for her neighbourly acts of kindness. Both she and Tiny had been active for years in the CCF, and she was well informed on the Columbia River Treaty, having assembled an enormous file on it since the beginning of negotiations. In her short year "she proposed Bill 32 in 1963, an act limiting spending by any party in an election to fifty thousand dollars and demanding publication of sources of campaign funds."

Grace MacInnis, the first woman elected as an MP in BC, was the daughter of J. S. Woodsworth, founder of the CCF. While she was in Ottawa working as secretary to her father and the CCF caucus after the 1935 election, she met and married MP Angus MacInnis and moved to BC, where she became an MLA for Vancouver–Burrard from 1941 to 1945. She kept running both provincially and federally and working as a party organizer, Speaker and coordinator, at the same time working with Angus, who served five terms

as an MP before he retired due to illness in 1955. She nursed him until his death in 1964. Because of her activities and her personal public presence, it is diffi-cult to say she "took over her husband's seat," but a year after Angus died she ran federally and won in Vancouver–Kingsway. She served another two terms before retiring, one of them as the only woman in Parliament.

In her lifetime she was invested as an Officer of the Order of Canada and presented—in her home because of her ill-ness—with the Order of British Columbia. She received eight honourary LL.D. degrees and many

Grace MacInnis was the first BC woman MP. Daughter and wife of federal politicians, she had served one term in the legislature before she won federally in Vancouver Kingsway in 1965 and served three terms. *Courtesy New Democratic Party.*

honourary memberships, testimonials and awards from local and na-tional groups including Japanese and Jewish Canadians, the Labour Congress and tenants' associations. She was the first woman to be made freeman of the city of Vancouver, and as part of Vancouver's centennial celebrations in 1986, she received the Distinguished Pioneer Award, of which only a hundred were awarded.

Camille Mather, a strong peace activist before she entered electoral politics and now our oldest living woman former MLA, ran and was elected as the CCF member for Delta South before her husband Barry was elected as an MP for Delta. Mather said her political career paralleled that of her husband, who had been a columnist for the *Vancouver Sun*. "I relied on Barry's well-known name in all my elections." Mather ran as the incumbent in the 1963 election but was defeated and never ran again for politics, although she was asked. "We both thought it a poor idea. We'd probably both lose because people would think we were taking money out of the pockets of the people." It's an old-fashioned idea, but one that still persists: women who work—if their husbands are making a good living—must not take a job that could go to a man who may need to support a family.

Daisy Webster was well known in CCF-NDP ranks along with her husband, Arnold, who was the MP for Vancouver–Burrard for four terms from 1935, then MLA for Vancouver East and provincial leader from 1953 to 1956. Webster had been a CWAC during World War II and later served as a member of the Social Planning and Review Council of BC. She had been a provincial inspector for home economics in schools and had contributed so much to her community, notably through the Vancouver Council of Women, that in 1986 she became, with MacInnis, one of the hundred people awarded Distinguished Pioneer Awards. Persuaded to run in 1972 by "insistent" party leader Dave Barrett and her parents, long-time party supporters, she took Vancouver South, although she retired after one term. Perhaps her best-known issue was the provision of adequate public washrooms, a cause she championed at the urging of her leader, but one that she made popular and for which she pushed through legislation affecting every community in BC.

Judi Tyabji was elected in Okanagan East as a Liberal when Gordon Wilson led the party, and they carried on a very public courtship after the Liberals took over as official opposition in the provincial house in 1991. Tyabji's first marriage was "not really a marriage," she told me. Based on traditional Indo-Canadian practice, "it wasn't a very nice relationship, and I think I was looking for an escape route." The affair, however, helped lead to Wilson being deposed as party leader They later married. After her defeat at the polls in 1996, she served a term as city councillor in Powell River. She has written two books about provincial politicians and now works as a consultant with Wilson, also retired from politics.

Jan Pullinger, elected in a by-election in 1989 for the NDP in Nanaimo, became a friend of the other MLA for Nanaimo, Dale Lovick. She was re-elected in 1991 for Cowichan–Ladysmith, as Lovick was in Nanaimo, and they married in 1994.

Many within the two constituencies were upset when the two were living together but unmarried. "They'd drive from Parksville to Duncan to tell me off." After they married, many were upset that Pullinger did not take Lovick's name. "I was harassed about my name." But when someone said she should have the same name as her husband, she would take the opportunity to say, "Hmmm, I see your point. But I suggested that to Dale and he refused to change." Many were also upset that Pullinger continued as an MLA—running and winning again in 1996. "For two years they might not come out and say it, but they suggested that I shouldn't be taking up a job that some young man could have and—in the newspapers or to my face—demanding to know why. It was outrageous." The media "were unable to write about either of us without including the other and adding a chippy comment about the 'fact' that we would be getting two 'million dollar-gold plated' pensions. As if!" Pullinger called it "an everyday, energy-draining experience."

Gretchen Mann Brewin grew up in a strong CCF family, the Manns of Toronto. "My dad ran six times for the CCF in Ontario," she told me. Brewin remembered the talk at the dinner table, the round of political visitors to the Mann household, participating in elections and going every summer as a family to a camp run by the CCF on co-operative principles. The man she married belonged to another stalwart CCF family, the Brewins. Andrew Brewin, also a founder of the party, became a prominent MP and was followed in Parliament by his son John, Gretchen's husband. Gretchen Brewin, with four children, answered the call when the party and organized labour were looking for school board candidates in Toronto. When she moved to Victoria, she became a city councillor and then mayor for two terms. She also ran federally without success but won provincially in 1991 and 1996. "John was enormously helpful and keen that I do it." They are now divorced.

"My mate, father of my son, husband of eleven years, was very active in politics," Joy MacPhail said of Gerry Scott. "That's why we ended up marrying each other. Not only did we have a common background—United Church kids—but we also had a fascination and love for politics." MacPhail said her parents, two sisters and one brother all expected her to run for election. "I had been fascinated with politics from my late teens on. I remember writing to Michael Pitfield, who was Pierre Trudeau's principal secretary, and asking him what I needed to do in order to get his job. I was swept up in Trudeaumania at the time." MacPhail's son Jack was born during the 1988 election when Scott was running against John Turner for the federal seat of Vancouver Centre. Jack was three when MacPhail was elected to the legislature for Vancouver–Hastings in 1991. She ran and won in the next two elections and became interim leader of the party in 2001. Having decided not to run for leadership, however, she retired in 2005. She and Scott, a two-time secretary of the provincial NDP, divorced in 1992.

Gretchen Mann Brewin had been a school trustee in Toronto before moving to Victoria, where she served as a councilor and then mayor. She served two terms in the legislature, during which time she was the third BC woman Speaker. *Courtesy New Democratic Party.*

Christy Clark's dad was an activist in both the Liberal Party and the BC Teachers' Federation. He had run unsuccessfully for the Liberals three times in the 1960s and 1970s. "When I went into politics, Dad was delighted, because politics was so much a part of his life. Mom was suspicious." Clark told of her father being out at meetings, organizing, doing political work as long as she could remember and of her mother's occasional impatience at the demands politics makes on families. In good family tradition, Clark married Mark Marissen, a political strategist she met at university in Ottawa. He and her brother, another keen political activist, were key to her campaigns. Clark said of her husband, "He's not a front-room kind of guy. He's quite happy to leave that to me and be an armchair quarterback."

Clark was recruited in Ottawa by Gordon Campbell, who phoned and "bugged" her to run in Port Moody–Burnaby Mountain. "When someone like him phones and asks you to serve in public office, it's an offer you don't take lightly." Her Liberal connections gave her an ability to raise money through that network, but she got a tough challenge to her candidacy. Looking back, she saw that she came back to BC with "a time disconnect" and was from a part of Burnaby that wasn't even in the riding. "They hadn't met me, but I showed up at their riding association meeting and said, 'Hi. I want to be your candidate.' It must have been a little jarring." Clark won a tight race in 1996, and took the seat again in 2001.

For decades, Shannon and Leonard O'Neill's house in Salmon Arm was the gathering place, the billeting place and the sympathy centre for CCF-NDP members and travelling organizers. In 1990, after Leonard's death, O'Neill was on the search committee when it was looking for a candidate. A friend who was also an activist and who "used to nudge me over the edge" got O'Neill to agree that "we can't just not have a candidate. So if nobody else will do it . . . " O'Neill said, "Everybody stopped looking, I guess, because we never did find anybody else." After one term, with her son suffering from a severe illness, O'Neill withdrew again to the organizational side of her party.

"What got me into politics more than anything else was my husband," said Sharon Hayes, who took Port Moody–Coquitlam federally for the Reform Party in 1993. He was a political activist, so after they joined the Reform Party she suggested he run for the nomination. But he wanted her to go for it because "I'd probably do a better job than he would." Hayes won and was re-elected in 1997, but resigned shortly after because of her husband's ill health. She explained that her election "really did make a huge change in our home life—huge. I had been basically the homemaker, so it threw onto the family all these things that they probably had taken for granted."

Even though she came home most weekends, she had appointments and meetings to go to. "My husband went through somewhat of a depression." He had been "the energizer for the campaign—the guy that says, 'Okay let's go!'" and had literally worn out a pair of shoes. Then to see his wife leave and "get swallowed in a black hole, and he's left there, people coming to him, calling him Mr. Sharon Hayes." As well, in the two years before that, his mother and father died. It was also a difficult time for Hayes, "to have that exhaustion, and a husband who was a very different person than I'd known before. He was very successful in the career that he had chosen." Until her election Hayes had been a stay-at-home mom, putting most of her efforts "around my own family and probably my church activities." Hayes has no regrets about her retirement.

Libby Davies's father was "always involved in the Labour Party in Britain, and when we first arrived in Vancouver, the first thing he did was sign up in a provincial election campaign in Point Grey." Her father worked at First United Church at Hastings and Gore, so Davies became involved in that neighbourhood, where she met Bruce Eriksen through the Downtown Eastside Residents Association. They married and both served in municipal politics until his death nearly twenty years later. In 1996, when she was approached to run federally in Vancouver East, Bruce was dying of cancer, "but he was the one who encouraged me the most," Davies said. "I think in some ways he knew that it would be another door opening for me personally."

In the 2004 federal election, Conservative Nina Grewal won election in Fleetwood–Port Kells, the riding next to Newton–North Delta

Nina Grewal was one part of a number of BC political couples. She and husband Gurmant were the first married couple elected simultaneously to the Commons. The media made a fuss about both getting capital allowances. *Patrick Tam/FlungingPictures.com*

where her Conservative husband Gurmant had already been MP for a term. They were the first MP married couple in Canada. Other politicians, the media and some of the public responded by questioning whether they deserved independent capital city allowances since they would be living together—as though other MPs had never shared Ottawa digs.

Grewal was soon embroiled in a news uproar, however, when her husband was found to have taped conversations with Liberals who, he said, had offered "political rewards" if he and his wife would vote with their minority government. She made no comment about the whole situation, saying she was not a part of her husband's negotiations. Grewal had the visible support of the Conservative women MPs in June 2005 when they left a caucus meeting by the back door while the men left by the front door where the media were waiting. "We left together," Ontario Tory MP Diane Finley said later, to

Katrine and husband Ed Conroy represented the constituency around Castlegar–Trail—he before the 2001 Liberal sweep of seats, she after. Before running, Conroy was one of BC's first woman steam engineers. *Photo courtesy Patrick Tam/FlungingPictures.com*

show "we're solidly with Nina." Another colleague, Alberta MP Rona Ambrose, said, "They just assume that because he's her husband she was complicit. It's a bit sexist really."[67] Grewal never did comment, although her husband left Ottawa on sick leave and then declined to run in the 2006 election, in which she ran again and won.

Katrine and Ed Conroy were both involved in politics in their community before Ed ran and won Rossland–Trail in 1991 and held it for two terms. In 2001 he lost to a local mayor in a Liberal sweep. In 2005 Katrine Conroy took back the constituency, now called West Kootenay–Boundary. One of BC's first women steam engineers before she followed a career in community services, she became NDP caucus whip after her election.

THE FACE OF FEMINISM
IN BC

In the early years of last century, many feminists saw women's involvement in politics as a new broom "that would sweep away corruption,
neglect, and brutal greed."[68] They were maternal feminists. Social feminists believe women should be granted equal rights whether or not they
follow a higher morality. They would say, "A feminist is somebody who
believes that women are systematically oppressed—treated unfairly—
and who works to remove that oppression."[69] Active feminists of the
1970s and 1980s were far more likely to be social feminists than maternal feminists.

Rosemary Brown had a lifelong commitment to feminism. "Basically, that's all there is. Race is important too, but feminism is more basic." Born in Jamaica, she grew up in a family of women activists. When
she came to Canada, she suffered discrimination because she was black
and because she was a woman, and for the rest of her life she devoted
herself to eliminating both kinds of discrimination. A strong, articulate
woman, she was seen as a leader in helping to weave a Canadian web of
equality for all. Socialists see their politics as exercises in equality, and
Brown often said her feminism was her socialism. An MLA from 1972
to 1986, she had been a leader in the community before that time, and
she was a leader nationally and internationally until her death in 2003.
To many women, Brown was the face of feminism in BC.

Equal pay for women, she said, was a BC feminist issue. "It's always been our issue, and it's one every woman should be able to defend,
not just in the visceral sense that it's the right thing to do, but in terms of
history and economics and analysis and all of those kinds of things—you
should be there.

"I mean, that's the crux of all politics: that we've never been paid for the work that we do. That's why when we divorce, we end up poor; when we are old, we end up poor; when we are single parents, we end up poor. That's why when we are unmarried, we end up poor. The whole argument about 'the corporation can't afford it, the government can't afford it'—what you're saying is that women should continue to subsidize the economy. That is patently unfair. So you take our labour at a cheap rate, and then you get upset with us when you have to pay a pension because we are poor, which is because you haven't paid us properly to start with."

Rosemary Brown said "the crux of all politics" was that "women have never been paid for the work that they do." Every woman "should be there" to argue that point from every angle.

In the 1960s, Brown was a founding member of the Vancouver Status of Women and directed its Ombudservice for women, the first in Canada. She was first elected from a slate put forward by the Status of Women Council to run in the 1972 provincial election, served four terms in the legislature and then devoted herself to national and international interests of women and blacks. She was the first to hold the chair in women's studies at Simon Fraser University. "For feminists," said Brown, "the whole point of moving into power arenas is to revolutionize them, rather than to use them as a stepping stone to personal and private advancement."[70]

Many women—and men—will avoid publicly calling themselves feminists, largely because of the man-hating, aggressive and flamboyant public image feminists had in the 1970s. Many of them explain by saying they are not bra burners, a term that holds on despite the fact that it is decades since anybody publicly burned a bra for equality.

Shirley Bond made a typical comment for those who do not call themselves feminists. "I absolutely believe that women should be treated equally and fairly and that they are as skilled as men, and we deserve all the same opportunities as men, but I really would not describe myself as a feminist." Bond viewed feminism as "the more radical end of the spectrum, and while I am aggressive and I think outside the box, I find no need to express myself at work as a feminist. I actually love being a wife and a mother."

As Margaret Bridgman put it, "I don't believe in differentiation because of sex and I've believed that way since I was twenty. I don't think women have equal rights. I think they should have equal rights. We've probably got as many fools in our women side as the men have chauvinists." She wanted people to be judged on their intelligence and behaviour in a group, "and it doesn't matter whether you're male or female."

Over the years, local newspapers and national magazines have polled women to see if they call themselves feminists. The strongest women in the country have waffled. In my interviews, women who didn't like the word "feminist" called themselves "humanists," "personists," "equalists" or even "a product of the women's movement." For Sindi Hawkins, the term was too limiting. "My values are more than being a feminist." One of BC's former ministers of women's equality sees such reluctance as peevish. Sue Hammell said, "I've been a feminist a long, long time, and I find it almost amusing when people can't say it and describe it. If you carry those values, say what they are."

Sydney Sharpe, in her book about Canadian political women, *The Gilded Ghetto*, pointed out that "a poll conducted in 1993 showed that only one-third of Canadian women call themselves feminists, but 80 percent of all Canadians, women and men, agree that the women's movement has been good for society and that more should be done to achieve its goals. . . . One thing is clear: many women who believe in some feminist goals do not care to call themselves feminists because the word has become too ideological and pejorative."[71] Sharpe ascribed their reluctance largely to what she sees as "the fact that the label can seriously hinder relations with spouses, friends, and employers."[72]

In 1991 Penny Priddy, an avowed feminist, established the first women's equality ministry in Canada. She was not the first to have responsibility for women's issues, but she was the first with a full-fledged ministry to do it. Its establishment capped two decades of serious wrangling inside the New Democratic Party about whether it was needed. The party had resolved twice in convention that there should be an independent ministry, but opponents wanted women's issues to be resolved across the board in all the existing ministries, not in a separate ministry. Premier Dave Barrett's refusal to establish one in his 1972–75 government was a boil that pained the party despite that government's positive record on issues of interest to women.

Priddy came to office believing that a feminist analysis was one of the requirements for her as minister. "You begin," she said, "on the premise that women should have equal opportunity and access and recognize that it's not there, no matter what it looks like on the surface. Analysis means you look at each problem and see how it affects women's lives." It requires a subtlety different from that of twenty years ago to see unequal impacts even though things appear equal. "Nothing is gender neutral," she said. Feminist politicians must make solutions fit their goal, recognizing that women's equality is not any government's only agenda. As minister she sought equality solutions "that fit in with the government policy that gets accomplished." While that isn't always possible, "You have to see that the case for women is on the table every time a decision is made."

For example, she recalled, "I hadn't been minister very long when Cassiar went down." The Cassiar asbestos mine had closed in the face of recognition that widespread use of asbestos in building materials was damaging people's health, but Cassiar was a one-industry town, built just for that mine. "There were meetings about what we should do about Cassiar. My deputy and I said to each other, 'What about the women in that community?'" A cabinet committee had been struck, but the women's equality minister was not on that committee, "and nobody could figure out why we wanted to be. We knew many of those miners had partners who worked in the town. We also knew that in times of economic stress there is greater incidence of child abuse, spousal abuse, and so on." Priddy got on the committee and "actually put some resources in."

Priddy encouraged every member of caucus to apply a "gender lens" to issues. She observed later, "Not everybody paid attention—I know that. We did training in all the ministries. Some ministries legitimately tried to use it, so when a cabinet presentation came forward, headings actually said 'The Effect on the Economy,' 'The Effect on the Environment' and 'The Effect on Women.'" However, it was difficult for some ministers to direct staff to consider the effect on women of a measure for which they wanted cabinet approval because they had no experience in estimating effects on women, and they did not want another hurdle to getting approval. Deputy ministers hardly knew what to say."

Although Priddy did not reach all of her goals as women's minister, she had the strong support of women's groups in the province. Ten years later, when the women's ministry in BC was demoted to being a ministry of state, she could claim to have initiated many of the improvements that her government had achieved. The minimum wage had become the highest in Canada; 65 percent of minimum wage earners are women. BC had a senior's supplement; 24 percent of senior women live in poverty. The BC Child Care Program provided centres and a subsidy to help low- and middle-income parents.

Mary Ellen Smith seldom sat still and enjoyed a moment's peace. After her political career, she was one of the first woman to represent Canada on an international body, the International Labour Organization, appointed 1929. *City of Vancouver Archives, Port N-31.*

Pay equity applied to both the public sector where women made 90 percent of what men do and the private sector where women made 73 percent of what men do. And by 2000 the number of women in executive positions in the civil service had moved from 10.9 percent to 33.5 percent.

Not all women were as committed as Brown or Priddy, but most agreed that women do not have equal treatment or equal access to jobs or perks or respect. They said women are not equal in pay or in good jobs or in appointments to positions, not considered as good as men when it comes to some of the important jobs, such as doctoring or being a politician, not always considered equal by the general public—but they are equal.

Ida Chong wondered how to describe a feminist. "Someone who believes you should be able to be all that you can, and do all that you can?" Women who denied being feminist often said feminists were women who, in the guise of demanding equality, demand special treatment. But

Elizabeth Cull laid out a positive statement of purpose. "Feminism is realizing that there are systemic relationships in the world that tend to ignore women. As a feminist, my purpose is to change those balances so women get a greater say."

Hedy Fry said, "We have mediocre men in positions of power, but a woman has to be bright, intelligent, committed—have every one of the pieces ticked off. So until we can get mediocre women in positions of power we will not have achieved equality."

People do not operate at the same level of commitment in every circumstance, but feminist or not, most women work toward equality goals at some level. Highly committed, Cathy McGregor said, "I see feminism as an approach you take to everything. You're concerned with gender issues and leadership roles that women could play all the time. You look for ways of being sure that women are involved. You challenge views that are clearly male-dominated and you should always have the courage to say, 'That's wrong because it doesn't address the differences between men and women, and it needs to.'"

Some women members enthusiastically take up issues. They rally. They petition. They write letters to the editor and send delegations to power wielders. They are the ones who make the epithet bra burner hang on even though it carries all the distortions that come with controversial ideas. They may be what Betty Hinton called "extreme people . . . who are difficult for the public to embrace." While recognizing that these women built the foundation for better women's equality in the latter half of the twentieth century, Grace McCarthy observed, "The burning of the bras and all those flag-waving things, the placard-carrying things, didn't get them very far, I don't think. It might have made a statement and got people thinking, but it gave women a sharper edge than was their due."

But Mary Ellen Smith, Helen Smith, Dorothy Steeves, and Laura Jamieson—the first four women elected to the legislature—supported woman suffrage before it was a fact, worked for better conditions for women and made no bones about their dissatisfaction with how women were treated in the public realm. Even in 1941, when Tilly Rolston was first elected, the *Daily Colonist* called her "the constant champion of the harried housewife."

The media is too often timid. After the January 28, 1988, date of the Supreme Court decision to keep medical committees out of abortion choices, Darlene Marzari wanted the anniversary to be recognized and celebrated as Bertha Wilson Day in honour of the Supreme Court judge who wrote the decision, but the *Province* didn't even print her letter advocating the idea.

A curious attack came in the early 1990s when Judy Rebick, the well-known national women's activist and journalist, targeted the women in Parliament saying they had not done enough for women and she refused to support any of them for re-election. The BC women she denounced included Progressive Conservatives Kim Campbell and Mary Collins, and New Democrats Dawn Black, Joy Langan, Lynn Hunter and Margaret Mitchell, even though all of them had spoken up and worked hard for women's equality rights. Mitchell, for example, had donated her office to those who demanded an equality clause for women in the Charter of Rights and who would otherwise have had no place but their kitchens to work until the vote was taken months after constitutional reform talks began.

Unpopular measures to achieve gender equality do not always bring immediate reward, but they can make it easier for others to follow. Resistance to men-only clubs—which still exist, with dogged defenders—has motivated many protests by women. Pat Carney, when federal energy minister, would not meet at the all-male Petroleum Club in Calgary; she invited oil magnates to meet her in her club, the YWCA. Her resistance wasn't just to prevent the old boys from having their cigars and port together. The ban against women, she said, "was an actual barrier to the advancement of women, who couldn't hold certain jobs in the oil industry because they couldn't have breakfast at the club where the deals are made."

Mitchell regularly challenged House of Commons puerile locker-room attitudes. In May 1982, in her plea for more transition houses for battered wives and children, she referred to the finding of a house standing committee that one in five men in Canada regularly beats his wife. She unintentionally became what she referred to as "a bit of a national presence as women's critic." "Male MPs from both sides of the Commons guffawed and made snide remarks," "snickered" and "laughed uproariously," reported the *Vancouver Sun*.[73] Mitchell recalled that "I couldn't even speak, the noise was so loud. I was quite shocked, and said so." In a procedural motion the next day, Mitchell proposed that the Commons apologize for "the shameful and disgusting display of discrimination and ignorance by members who degraded this House yesterday with their

Margaret Mitchell was shocked by the "shameful display of discrimination and ignorance" by members of the Commons which erupted when she reported a committee's findings that one in five Canadian men beat their wives. *Photo courtesy Margaret Mitchell.*

performance." The motion, which needed unanimous approval to get on the agenda, did not receive it. Nor did a similar motion by Liberal Marcel Roy, male chair of the committee that issued the report.

A year later, in February 1983, under a headline saying "Trudeau, MPs Laugh at Talk about Poverty," the *Sun* reported that Liberal MPs "hooted and hollered as New Democratic Party MP Margaret Mitchell tried to discuss the plight of those living below the so-called poverty line." The debate concerned figures showing three to four million people living in "extreme poverty;" Mitchell knew that most people living in poverty are women and children.

Many women encourage political action, although feminism is not their primary area of interest. Agnes Kripps's long-time public cause was support for Canadians who had immigrated from the Ukraine, but as an MLA speaking to a national convention of Ukrainian women, she encouraged them to step out publicly. "I told those ladies, 'Don't just lick stamps. Don't just stuff envelopes. Get out and get involved.'"

Jackie Pement didn't think of herself as a feminist first. As alternate director of her regional district, though, she saw unfair treatment of a woman employee and decided she was too old to worry about hurting feelings. "As alternate you're not supposed to say too much, but I just let them have it over fairness and how they were treating this employee. It was a male-female thing. The guy was using his authority and it wasn't good. And the guys on the RD—directors, mostly men—were taking the male side of it. The problem is it's not going to change unless you do say something."

Susan Brice felt the existing model often missed compromise solutions that people could have found. "You sat around a table and everybody took their stand. At the end of the day, somebody called the question, and everybody voted and the yeas got it, and the nays didn't, and that was it."

Brice preferred the process and inclusion of a consensus model. She praised the synergy of work on the Capital Regional District when she sat on the board as mayor of Saanich, Gretchen Brewin sat as mayor of Victoria and Norma Sealey sat as mayor of Sidney. Brice and Brewin in particular strove for consensus and never clashed. "We didn't always agree—we had different political positions—but we were able to do things." The CRD introduced a blue box program that people had said couldn't happen, for example. "The people who came together were all problem solvers." But she added that when she was the only woman in a group, she risked being marginalized for any unusual approach. "It's certainly not the moment to have a group encounter session."

Women members often initiate and carry out programs for women who have already drawn public sympathy. Although Canadians have not always recognized opposition to violence against women as a reasonable or humanitarian cause, this is now an excellent example of an issue where good programs improve the lot of women without making the women who espouse it seem as radical as Mitchell did in 1982.

On December 6, 1989, when a Montreal man who claimed he hated feminists shot to death fourteen women at a school of engineering, the issue of violence against women drew wide support. As federal minister responsible for women's affairs, Mary Collins set up a commission, though she had great difficulty getting funding; her government colleagues were not as ready as the public for practical action. The resulting report and the dogged determination of Dawn Black, who put forward a private member's bill, kept the issue in the public eye and helped Collins to get her commission and to have her work recognized.

As minister of state for women's equality, Lynn Stephens protected funding for transition houses, safe homes, second-stage housing and counselling programs for women and children who had witnessed abuse. Her colleague Sheila Orr applauded her for focussing "resources to provide services for vulnerable women most at risk." Stephens was working inside a government that had significantly cut funding to other women's programs.

Many women members help individual women in straitened circumstances, even though the discriminatory machines grind on, and many members see equality as a cost to society that may not be affordable to their government. They offer help, great or small, outside the governmental system. Orr set up a nonpartisan, nonpolitical program in her constituency office to give people, often women, the kind of support that friends and relatives used to offer. "We supply help, we supply furniture, we supply second-hand clothing; we get excited when one of our moms or dads gets a job. A dear lady comes every Friday morning for her *TV Guide,*" which gives the staff a chance to check that she's all right.

Gillian Trumper, in her long public life, has worked with a number of women's groups, but described herself as a more hands-on person who might "prefer to sit down and work with them one-on-one." She felt it was harder "to get down to it with women who've got real issues" than to "get out there and protest."

Even strong feminist women recognize that sometimes, if you don't play the game, you don't get on the field. They use the usual political skills for their progress. "You have to learn to play hockey," said Darlene Marzari. Jan Pullinger made a point of being belligerent rather than being run over, and Christy Clark was considered a strong player, hard to best in the give-and-take of the adversarial system. Joy MacPhail skillfully led her two-woman caucus in a house otherwise taken up with sneering, yelling, desk-thumping government members. Had she not played the game the way it was set up for the men of the past—and played it superbly—many think she would have been mowed down and fed to the cattle.

Val Meredith thought she was elected on her merit as the first woman mayor of Slave Lake, Alberta, before she came to BC. She did not expect special privilege, which is expected by women who "want to be in politics but don't want to have to play the game the same as a guy." Val Roddick felt similarly. "If you want to do it, you do it, and I don't think whether you're a man or a woman has anything to do with it."

Some women quietly feel equal—but different. They are happy to have men make the decisions, announce them and defend them, but they feel that they contribute by being at the meetings where decisions are made. Brenda Locke said, "I want us to gain equality, but I want us as women to maintain who we are as women. I still want to contribute to policy and dialogue, all of those things where it is very important to have diversity."

But for Daphne Jennings, being a feminist would preclude being womanly. "No, I'm definitely not a feminist. I am proud to be a woman. I like to be treated like a lady. I hope I act like a lady. I think feminists took a wrong turn and sometimes they threw out more than they gained."

Carol Gran thought women present a stronger case when they include their children. "It looks self-serving when you stand up and go on and on and on about abortion—it makes women look hard and cruel. If you had a child on each arm and said, 'We need protection,' how much more power could you get?"

Sharon Hayes's work in advocacy for families brought her "nose to nose against most feminists, who to my mind were more interested in women being unfettered than in looking at the best ways that women can express themselves in society." Feminists seemed to her to be "women wanting power for power's sake. And I don't agree with that."

Several women objected to feminists "who want more than equality." Anna Terrana said, "If a feminist is the person who hates men or takes for women more than for men, well then, I'm not a feminist because I still think we're all the same." Patty Sahota, the youngest of the political women, would deny that interpretation. "It's not even true. We just want equality, equal access." And Camille Mather, the oldest, agreed. "I just think there should be equality and opportunities in the workplace. But I don't think that women are better than men or men better than women. Some men are more intelligent and some are more crooked. Some women are more intelligent and some are not completely honest." Kim Campbell addressed the same disjunction when she said, "I'm a feminist. I'm not homophobic."

Elayne Brenzinger did not relate to talk of gender discrimination at all. "I personally haven't had that experience. I wouldn't tolerate it from my husband, first of all—or from anyone—not to accept me as an equal. I don't run into it."

DEATH-DEFYING ANTICS

"I don't think the skills of a British Columbia politician are transfer-able to other provincial jurisdictions," Christy Clark told me when I asked her if being in BC contributed to her decision to run for election. "I was born and raised here, imbued with this particular political culture, and I don't think it's the same skill set."

BC politics is a rowdy game which requires a strong ego, a highly competitive spirit and a strong sense of direction. The polarization and circus atmosphere add a clarity that can be lost in more sedate political worlds, because while polarization may cause uncomfortable conflict and confrontation, it does create clear-edged issues. In my own case, the gov-ernment restraint program of the early 1980s outraged me, but I knew who created it and who opposed it, and my own personal opposition to it caused me to run for office. In other places such a controversial program might have been proposed by one party and resisted by another party, which advocated a different method of carrying it out. In BC, when the government embarks on such an ideological program, the opposition fights it all the way screaming, that was wrong!

BC's rambunctious nature struck Jan Pullinger as negative. "The death-defying antics of BC politics is certainly a deterrent to women—it is so vicious here." Karen Sanford specifically referred to the legislature in Victoria after the 2001 election: "Anybody watching what's happen-ing at the moment down there with seventy-seven jeering, sneering [Liberal] MLAs against the two [NDP] women who are there would not be encouraged to run."

But Joan Smallwood remarked, "Because we are known to be a politically volatile group, we are also politically interesting, and I think that encourages a lot of women to run. Politics works when it's noisy, and BC's a noisy place." Penny Priddy believed we have a greater sense of individuality here, which she called "the sense of goofy." That's just fine, "because when you're goofy you can be far more risk-taking. Static is the last thing that British Columbia politics is." And Hedy Fry, with her Ottawa experience, suggested that we are just trying to be heard. In our big family, BC sits at "the farthest end of the table," and if we want to be heard, we have to bang on the table with a spoon. "The people sitting closest to the head of the table get heard all the time."

Many BC women members see politics in Ontario and the Maritime provinces as yesterday's pudding. Families there vote generation after generation for the traditional parties—Liberal or Conservative—which seldom face a successful challenge from new populist parties as they have in BC, the Prairie provinces and Quebec. In the latter half of the twentieth century, British Columbia, Saskatchewan and Manitoba have all had CCF-NDP governments more than once. Alberta elected Social Credit governments for decades, and Quebec has been governed by the Union Nationale and the Parti Québécois. BC women believe that, in Ontario and the Maritimes, the long apprenticeship they would have had to serve in established parties might have kept them from running. Judi Tyabji Wilson said, "I would have probably done the same things—fundraising and acting as a party operative—but I'm certain I wouldn't have run for office nor been elected as an ethnic, twenty-six-year-old, pregnant woman." BC has a freer, more open attitude, and "we're in an emerging political regime, so there are still openings for that sort of populist. But in Ontario, they have a very established thing. It would have taken me another ten years."

Sharon Hayes said, "I don't have the right pedigree" to run in Ontario, and Evelyn Gillespie never felt the political interest in Alberta or Ontario that she developed in BC. "If I were in Ontario," began Val Meredith, " . . . well, for one thing, I wouldn't be in Ontario." And Lynn Hunter wondered where she would have found a good fit in another province. "You have to be somewhat of a radical in order to gain political office in British Columbia—radical left or radical right."

Darlene Marzari, one of about a half-dozen elected BC women who spent part of their childhood in Ontario, said she ran for election precisely because she moved to BC. "When I came to BC it was a young place, and I was a young person. I had great passion and enthusiasm and great ideas that needed to be exercised." BC gave Marzari what she called her "language for social discourse." Previously, as a student in London, her studies involved writing "great yet-to-be-published tracts on policy and the development of housing policy in England."

Her field work, on the other hand, took her "into east London, where I worked with a group of girls and came to understand that nothing I did with those girls in terms of making them happy, alive, alert, thoughtful and moving toward post-secondary education—which is not something that even crossed their minds—would work except to change the fact that they were living in poverty and that their mothers were beaten. One of the mothers died while I was there. It flipped my world. I experienced that dichotomy between the theoretical policy side, where you write the great papers, and my work experience, where lives were in complete disruption. I lived in two worlds, which, surprisingly, has never changed."

When Marzari came to Vancouver, she chose the new community work model at UBC's school of social work. The program led the rest of the country in experimenting with community work "and dare I say, political analysis." Then she worked for the city of Vancouver as one of its first social planners and organized eastside neighbourhoods to successfully resist expropriation of the Chinese community in the heart of the city. Still "moving in two worlds," she was able to piece together an understanding of how society works, how it could work, and that

Carole James, middle, is the first woman party leader in BC to be elected to the legislature. Jenny Kwan, left, and Joy MacPhail, right, carried the load as opposition in the 2001-2005 legislature. Other women leaders were not elected once they became party leaders. *Courtesy Carole James' office.*

poverty was a social issue to be recognized by government, not a private problem to be alleviated by social workers. "Oh, how radical! I started to understand that including the community made good common sense. That there was such a thing as bad and good." Bad economic policies, for example, may be just "weird economic rhetoric, with subsidies based on which constituency has the most powerful person. There was something to fight."

"Would I have run for office somewhere else? I don't think so. Had I stayed in Ontario, I would have become a good social worker, always wondering why there was good and evil, and wondering why I was simply managing rather than solving, why I was part of the problem and not the solution. In BC I came up against the evil; it was here in the form of post-war planning gone wrong, threatening to demolish a whole neighbourhood of people that had helped build this city."

Elizabeth Cull thought she would have been a politician wherever she lived, but she conceded that "coming to BC from Ontario was a shock. British Columbians didn't see themselves as Canadians first. Now I'm just as regional as anyone else." Cull believed this difference was continental. "Maybe people with a wacky mindset gravitate to the West, hit the ocean, and don't have enough money to go back."

Women responded slowly but steadily to their political opportunities in BC, leading the rest of the country in several important ways. The suffragist surge that carried Mary Ellen Smith to election in 1918 ebbed and undulated, returning to full flow only in the 1970s and 1980s with the second phase of feminism, which happened in spades in BC. A new core of consciousness rippled into the public mind, and more people recognized that past discrimination against half of the population had robbed our public bodies of women's enthusiasms, skills and knowledge.

In the 1970s the numbers of women political candidates billowed. Over the years the count of elected women has risen steadily with a few notable jumps. Provincially the number of women in the house hovered at three or less until 1972, moved to six for four elections, and has resolved at around nineteen as the century turned. The federal progression, with fewer seats available, has moved from one or two until 1980 to five or six from 1988, and now we have nine women MPs. If the pattern continues—sitting at a plateau for several elections, and then doubling—the next doubling could put BC at 50 percent female representation (see Table 1, page 174).

TABLE 1: BC WOMEN ELECTED IN GENERAL ELECTIONS

BC Legislature				
Election Year	**Women Candidates**	**Women Elected**	**Total number of MLAs**	**% MLAs that were women**
1920	3	1	47	2.1
1924	7	1	48	2.08
1928	4	0	48	0
1933	11	1	47	2.1
1937	13	2	48	4.16
1941	12	5	48	10.42
1945	13	2	48	4.16
1949	12	2	48	4.16
1952	12	3	48	6.25
1953	23	1	48	2.08
1956	15	2	52	3.85
1960	13	3	52	5.77
1963	13	1	52	1.92
1966	14	4	55	7.27
1969	10	5	55	9.09
1972	25	6	55	10.9
1975	27	6	55	10.9
1979	26	6	57	10.53
1983	30	6	57	10.53
1986	45	9	69	13.04
1991	85	19	75	25.33
1996	128	20	75	26.67
2001	102	19	79	24.05
2005	101	17	79	21.52

Note: the tables do not reflect women elected in by-elections.

Canadian Parliament

Election Year	Women Candidates	Women Elected	BC Seats	% BC MPs that were women
1921	0	0	13	0
1925	1	0	14	0
1926	0	0	14	0
1930	0	0	14	0
1935	1	0	16	0
1940	1	0	16	0
1945	1	0	16	0
1949	2	0	18	0
1953	7	0	22	0
1957	2	0	22	0
9958	1	0	22	0
1962	2	0	22	0
1963	9	0	22	0
1965	5	1	22	4.54
1968	3	1	23	4.34
1972	4	1	23	4.34
1974	10	2	23	8.69
1979	16	2	28	7.14
1980	19	3	28	10.71
1984	25	4	28	14.28
1988	43	6	32	18.75
1993	76	6	32	18.75
1997	60	5	34	14.71
2000	60	5	34	14.71
2004	66	5	36	13.88
2006	46	9	36	25

TABLE 2: CANADIAN ASSEMBLIES OPEN TO WOMEN

Prov/ Terr	A. Right to Stand	B. First Ran	Interval from A	1st Elected[4]	Interval from B	Won 10%	Years from A
BC	1917	1918	1	1918 (1)	0	1972	55
AB	1916	1917	1	1917 (2)	0	1986	70
SK	1916	1919	3	1919 (1)	0	1995	79
MB	1916	1920	4	1920 (1)	0	1977	61
ON	1919	1943	24	1943 (2)	24	1985	66
QU	1940	1948	8	1962 (1)	22	1985	45
NB	1934	1935	1	1967 (1)	33	1987	53
NS	1917	1920	3	1960 (1)	43	1997	80
PEI	1922	1951	29	1970 (1)	48	1989	67
NF[1]	1925	1930	5	1930 (1)	5	1991	66
YU	1919	1925	6	1967 (1)	48	1967	48
NWT[2]	1975	1975	0	1975 (1)	0	1983	8
NUN	1999	1999	0	1999 (2)	0	1999	0
CAN[3]	1920	1921	2	1921 (1)	2	1989	69

1. Women had to be 25, although men could vote at 21. Equality came in 1948 when Newfoundland joined Confederation.
2. One woman sat in the seventh NWT Council, 1970–75, but NWT did not have its own assembly until 1975,
3. Women closely related to soldiers or serving in the military could vote in federal elections from 1917 but could not stand for election.
4. Figures in parentheses in "1st elected" row indicate how many women were first elected in that year.

The number of women who run and win in elections depends on recognized factors. They should be nominated in a winnable seat, for example, a constituency that has proven receptive to their party. Because the major parties must put a candidate in every seat, there will always be an opening for a New Democrat in a strong Liberal or Conservative riding such as West Vancouver or Peace River or for a Liberal or Tory in NDP-friendly Vancouver East or Nanaimo. Seats in such ridings have been won by candidates of nonprevailing parties under special circumstances. When Liberal Joyce Murray ran in New Westminster in 2001—in the landslide election that buried all but two of the NDP—she was the first other-than-NDP candidate to take New Westminster since the 1949 election. Women must also be given safe ridings, however, if we are to increase the numbers.

Volatility in the electoral world helps to bring more women into politics by shaking loose incumbents and testing voters' party loyalties. When governments are stable the incumbents, mostly men, seldom face a challenge for the nomination—and even more seldom face a successful challenge. When change is in the air, incumbents often retire and leave room for new candidates. The impact of the volatility attending such elections was evident in 1991, when the BC electorate was ready to change from its Social Credit government and incumbents had vacated many seats. The number of women candidates doubled, as did the number of women elected (see Table 1).

Nationwide, BC compares well (see Table 2). The western provinces had all elected at least one woman by 1920, and the other provinces trailed along in sporadic bursts of enthusiasm—if one may use that word. Although Ontarians elected Agnes Macphail as the first woman MP in the country in 1921, it took twenty-four years from the time women got the franchise and the right to run for the Ontario provincial assembly until the first woman ran.

It's interesting to note Prince Edward Island women gained the right to run in 1922, but no woman ran until 1951 and none won until 1970. Nevertheless PEI was the first province in Canada to elect a woman premier. Catherine Callbeck, first elected provincially in 1974, was elected as premier on March 29, 1993 in the first provincial race where the three major parties were led by women. She did this two years after Rita Johnston in BC became the first woman premier. The difference was that Johnston had been selected by the Social Credit legislative caucus, not the electorate.

Moving to even 10 percent women members of the respective houses has proved a slow process, but BC women led the way in the provincial assembly. In the 1941 general election, voters approved five women—10 percent of the total—but after that BC did not elect ten percent women again until 1972. In 1991, when nineteen women were elected to an assembly of seventy-five members, BC became the first Canadian assembly to elect women to 25 percent of its seats. It did even better in 1996, when nearly 27 percent of its members were women. Two by-elections during that term returned women, raising the percentage to 29, but an increase in the size of the legislature and a drop to seventeen women elected in 2005 brought the number down again to less than 22 percent.

The number of women candidates has generally followed the same curve as the number of women members, with about 20 percent of the women candidates winning election. At this rate of success, two hundred women would have to run to give women forty seats, half of the seventy-nine seats in the legislature. The legislature will increase to eighty-five members in 2009, of course. So far no election has tempted quite 150 women candidates.

British Columbia women reached 10 percent of BC's federal seats in 1980, fifteen years after we first elected a woman to Parliament. In 1988 and 1993, BC elected six women or 18.8 percent of its federal seats, and thus met the federal average of 18.75 percent. In 2006 nine BC women won election, making up 25 percent of the total provincial contingent.

In Canada's 2004 federal election, Equal Voice—a national organization formed to help reach gender-equal representation in Parliament—encouraged the four major parties to aim for "104 in 2004" or one-third of the 308 seats. It was clear as soon as nominations closed that it would not meet its goal, and the final count gave women 21.1 percent of the 308 seats.

Rosemary Speirs, chair of Equal Voice, said, "The percentage of women elected yesterday in each party reflects the priority given by party leaders to women's equality. The NDP did best at 26.3 percent, the Bloc Québécois with 25.9 percent, Liberals at 25.1 percent—and the Conservatives at token levels of representation with 12 percent women." Worldwide, Speirs added, "Women in Wales recently gained 50 percent of their Assembly, and women in Sweden are 45 percent, and in Rwanda 48.5 percent. Canada ranks way down the list—36th in the country rankings by the number of women in our last Parliament."[74]

We can count the women elected but we may never know for sure how many BC women have run for election to the legislature or Parliament. Neither the provincial nor the federal government requires candidates to list whether they are male or female or state their occupations, which could give a clue: no man, until maybe the last decade, would list his occupation as homemaker. Many people, several libraries and the few political parties who answer their mail helped me deal with names such as Chris, Pat, Kim, Kelly and Terry, so that only a dozen or so names were left in real doubt out of about 837 women—close enough for the purposes of broad discussion.

Vancouver women were the first in the province to run and win legislative seats, and their monopoly held until 1941 when Victoria elected Nancy Hodges. Interior voters sent Lois Haggen of Grand Forks to Victoria in 1956, and in 1960 anti-nuclear activist Camille Mather of Delta became the first woman elected from the Lower Mainland outside Vancouver. Three interior women won election in the 1960s, expanding women's reach across the south of the province. Karen Sanford in 1972 established women's presence on Vancouver Island north of Victoria, but it took until 1986 for Lois Boone to win a Prince George seat in the North and for me to win in the Kootenays. Constituencies in Peace River and Cariboo have yet to elect a woman. Since 1991, when the number of women in the legislature began to hover around twenty per assembly, the distribution of the women members has stayed quite stable. About half have been from Vancouver and the Lower Mainland; four or five from Vancouver Island, two or three of them from Victoria; two to four from the Southern Interior and one or two from the North.

The first BC woman MP, Grace MacInnis, was from Vancouver, and except for Iona Campagnolo, elected in 1974 for Prince Rupert, the Vancouver monopoly lasted until 1988 when Lower Mainland women began to win election. Still, twelve of BC's twenty-five women MPs have been from Vancouver and seven from the Lower Mainland, but only four from Vancouver Island and one each from the Interior and the North.

Is there a clear profile of these BC elected women? Do they have a consistent age range, marital or parental pattern or occupational bent? What I found from my questions to women members is that the average BC woman elected as an MLA or MP was in her late forties when she was elected and will be in her mid-fifties when she leaves elected office. She has been married and has children, was born in Canada and has a loose or no affiliation with an organized religion. She is likely to have been in business or in the field of education or other community work. She has nearly a one in three chance of having been in municipal politics, and about a fifty-fifty chance of being a recognized professional. If she is no longer a sitting member, it is likely that she was defeated in her last election, and if she was an MLA, she has a very good chance of having been in cabinet.

Lois Boone, the first woman elected MLA from BC's north, fired the pistol starting a Canadian Legion-sponsored track event in Prince George. *Photo courtesy Lois Boone.*

A Different Approach

A SOLUTION BEATS
A VICTORY

A sociologist at a meeting that I once attended explained the differ If you go to a playground with a little boy and a soccer ball, she said, the boy will kick it around a bit. If another little boy comes, the two will compete for the ball, playing like one-man teams. If a third little boy comes on the scene, each boy will ally with another as it suits his game. If working as a team will beat one boy, the other two will do it, but if that single boy gets control of the ball and needs the help of another, he can choose either of the other boys. What they want to do is score a goal.

Go to a playground with a little girl and a soccer ball, and she may kick it a bit. If another little girl comes along, the two will talk together before they figure out what game they will play. If a third little girl asks to join the game, they will re-choose the game and the rules before they resume playing. If they are going to be competitors, they want to know it is only because of the rules of the game, and the game is one they all chose. This pattern is not universal, of course, but it does speak to the different approaches women and men take in politics.

"There's absolutely no similarity between women's usual way of working and the way men operate in politics," said Margaret Lord. "You can't be a woman in the legislature. You can't operate in the space that most women operate in—looking for consensus, working together with people, finding the solution to problems through discussions. Even within the NDP, considered to be a party that offers lots of process, it just doesn't work that way. It's all a huge game of high stakes: who can shout the loudest, who's got the biggest stick, who's got the ticket to lose or gain. Until it changes, women will never be equal to men in politics."

Precedents for consensual decision making exist in recent discussions and negotiations with First Nations, said Iona Campagnolo, who represented northwestern BC. "The aboriginal tradition of long-house decisions and matrilineal and matriarchal patterns contribute to what BC is doing to get to group decisions which are not on a military construct."

But there is a cost to this. "Trying to work collectively often leads to the critique that women can't even make a decision on their own," said Penny Priddy. "It's not a fair one, but there is a timeline, and there's a point when you've just got to say, 'Thanks for your advice, and I'll make the decision now.' I'm a feminist and a New Democrat. I can get you process from now till the third millennium. But I'm also a nurse, and if somebody's bleeding to death in front of me, I only have a limited amount of time to ask them their preferred treatment methodology before I just shove my fist into the artery."

There are women who jump right into the fray. Tilly Rolston, first elected in 1941, was once described as "a graceful street fighter" because she adapted well to the adversarial approach that characterizes the parliamentary system. According to her family, she "had a robust sense of humour, gave as good as she got, and rose above jibes and hecklers." Her grandson Peter and his wife Louise, who wrote a biography of her, told me that "she was not a particularly reflective woman; she was combative."

Most of the women I interviewed early in the twenty-first century, however, said they liked to work collaboratively, seek consensus, and be well versed before they addressed a problem or an issue, so they could reach a solution without a fight. Gretchen Mann Brewin tried to avoid "I win, you lose" conclusions, working to a course of action that a number of people "own." She observed, "It is so true that the notion of having power is some kind of a turn-on for guys the way it is not for women." In politics a man may choose a solution he thinks will work, make it his own, and appeal to his network to support him, often in exchange for a similar favour in the future. A win is recorded on his scorecard, usually publicly, and he assumes the solution fits the problem.

April Sanders noted that working women have little recreational time compared to working men. "A lot of politics, in my experience, was done in the pub, on a golf course, in a locker room. Men naturally form gregarious units where they have tremendous amounts of free time and can deal on very superficial levels to get jobs done." Women, "who are much more isolated and have many more responsibilities to occupy their time, tend to be solution-oriented as opposed to getting something done." They will take longer and make decisions on what needs to be done.

Sanders described how she dealt with the old boys' network. "Men have a much more significant web that is very difficult for women to penetrate. My solution was not to rail against it but to pilot fish it." Having convinced the leaders of the old boys' club locally that she should be the candidate, she let them convince the other members of the web. "It would never have occurred to me to fight the old boys' system," but if she had, "it certainly wouldn't be through organizing women's groups and transition houses and support groups, who traditionally have no funding and no alliances beyond their social group." The difference between how men and women do politics and the money involved, she said, is huge.

Carol Gran identified one of her methods as a male way of doing politics: she would go straight to the premier. That was logical, because with his support, it didn't matter what other members of cabinet or caucus thought anyway. "That is a fact. There's only one vote in cabinet." Gran had tried, when she went into cabinet, to "let my stuff go, and

Iona Campagnolo, BC's first woman Lieutenant-Governor, had been an MP. "If I had grown a thick skin," she said, "I would have considered myself a total failure." Carole James, Official Opposition Leader, is on the left. Photo courtesy *PatrickTam/FlungingPictures.com*

succeed or not on the merit of the proposal and their trust in me. And I lost a lot of times."

Even Margaret Lord, who found the system soul-destroying, finally came to use the direct-to-power system. She was open and responsive to the groups in her riding, but "in Victoria there would be a whole different game." She had to learn the game. "I'd say to myself, 'You've got to go in there and you've got to be tough.' I'd say to the minister, 'If you get this done and this done, I'll go along with you on that.'" Although she was able to accomplish a few more things, "I really, really resented that you had to act like a man to do your job as an MLA."

Brewin also objected to doing her work by playing on the "generosity" of the power elite. "Personal diplomacy and consensus suited me better than nagging at ministers, nagging at the premier because you wanted something done, watching who the premier hung out with and how those structures all worked."

The combative nature of the assembly creates another problem for women, who in the broader world are socialized more strongly than men to avoid abusing others and protected more than men from harsh treatment, verbal or physical. Abuse is not too strong a word to use about the treatment of politicians by other politicians, the media and the public. One needs only to read, watch and listen to media coverage or bring up an issue in the coffee room at work. An unwritten understanding allows the public to despise, oppose and loudly insult politicians. The media is acidly critical, and other politicians hone their skills to wound and savage members of other parties. Should political women just grow a thick skin?

"If I had grown a thick skin," Campagnolo said, "I would have considered myself a total failure. Everything hurt, but you're usually working so hard you haven't got time to think about it anyway. The day you can't feel the pain, you've got to get out. You're no use to anyone." Other women think the abuse is foreign to good public policy and good government, and that it goes far beyond civil behaviour. They are not so philosophical about tolerating the current climate.

Question period stands as the prime example of the most immediate and fierce political hostility and is often characterized as a cockfight, but question period is only the most compressed and media-covered part of legislative debate. Every single hour they spend in the house, members are adversaries. While most of the aggression displayed in an assembly is political and partisan, a detour into the personal is never ruled out in these bloody wars and can reach depths that would not be countenanced in another workplace. When members talk to the media outside the chamber, they must win the battle of the scrum, and a personal attack works well. Because few in the public pay close attention to policy detail, poking a stick in the other guy's eye is understood better than poking holes in arguments, proposals and policies. Interest groups join the game to reach their audience. Both female and male ministers know that if they haven't been harangued today, they will be excoriated tomorrow.

Even if you understood the system and used it to your advantage, as did Sanders, that advantage had its other side. Often, said Sanders, "it was basically sublimating the things you needed as a female in order to work, to survive and be healthy, whether that was admitting you cared if you saw your family on the weekend or whether the decision you were making about funding was really wrong and would hurt people. The worst kind of things that make politics work in Canada are contrary to the female spirit and cause a lot of angst for the women involved. And I certainly experienced that."

Brewin said bluntly, "I don't like fighting with people. I'm probably not a good fighter." Daphne Jennings had a personal strategy. "I walked every morning to the House. I'd get to the bottom of the steps and I'd just say a prayer: 'Lord, help me to accept whatever is said to me. Help me to treat people decently.' Because there were some pretty rude things said to people."

Given that consensus is so prized by women, why is it so elusive? Susan Brice noted that "Men are a little more nervous than women about allowing things to float out there a bit and then have it evolve. Most men will say, 'Well, that's it. We can't talk about this all night.'" Brice saw that allowing things to evolve is "an absolutely critical part of the whole thing," and every group has its own process. "I am not overly process-oriented, but too often I've thought I had the right solution, only to find it wasn't warmly embraced, and then to realize that as the group worked on it, we ended up with a far better solution."

Christy Clark observed, "Women listen a lot more intently." And the ones she worked with were prepared to change their minds based on new information. They were not aggressive in making their opinions known "because part of being prepared to change your mind on new information is not being too entrenched in one position."

Margaret Bridgman noticed that "women don't jump in with a sink-or-swim concept. We tend to say, 'Okay, what are the options? If that's the best solution, what is the second-best solution?' Men will say, 'Oh, to hell with the second-best solution; we don't need to waste time.'" Women know mistakes "could take six months to turn around."

Nobody worried that Joy MacPhail couldn't take care of herself in political battles, and she admitted, "It sounds funny coming from me, because I'm known as a yappy, feisty fighter, but in politics women will join together to avoid confrontation and try to figure out a consensus." Feisty as she was, she too would rather advocate in a non-confrontational mode. But men, "in the exercise of state power, will raise the testosterone level to the highest pitch. They will try to have one solution, and arrange to be the one who proposed that solution."

Christy Clark says women listen a lot more intently and are prepared to change their minds if there is new information. Here she chats with former BC Premier Ujjal Dosanjh, now a Liberal MP. Photo courtesy *PatrickTam/FlungingPictures.com*

Margaret Mitchell touched on one characteristic that goes far to explain why men are less interested in group decisions. "You don't get to control the same way when you work as part of a collective." But a group decision gives a woman satisfaction that the group is onside, knows the rules and is playing by them.

Women research meticulously. "I research an issue to death and then I go listen to a lot of people, and I send out questionnaires to my constituents," said Betty Hinton about how she deals with issues. She and her staff go through all the completed questionnaires. She calls people. She has advisory boards "because I don't pretend to understand every issue, and there are people out there who are living it day in, day out. They can give me a perspective that I haven't got. And I read volumes."

Similarly, Sindi Hawkins said, as "a people person and a lawyer, I don't make decisions on the fly. I like to get the facts and weigh the arguments. There's always someone who won't be happy. Who's going to be affected? What are the implications? I try to research it myself to make a decision I can defend—that's the ideal."

The women interviewed felt they worked harder at research than the men because they are uncomfortable speaking publicly when they know little about a subject and its implications. For women, library research and asking questions of informed and interested people supports both their defence against aggressiveness—they are less vulnerable when they know facts—and their preference for group involvement. "When you're a female politician," said Erda Walsh, "you know you are going to have to prove that your idea is really good. A man doesn't do that because he assumes that everybody is going to listen to him anyway."

Pauline Jewett, a political science professor before she entered politics, was a stickler for precision and detail. Her research assistant Stephen Lee said, "She absolutely demanded to understand things and to be informed, and to be knowledgeable and to have the research done." She wanted to know more and have better research than anybody else, even when "anybody else" was the Government of Canada. She was often as well prepared as ministers, said Lee, who also observed hers was "not the normal behaviour pattern for, in the end, a more or less backbencher, in a more or less third or fourth party in the House. And yet she took all of that enormously seriously, which made her very effective."

Simma Holt also had her previous professional life to build on. A long-time reporter, she needed research when she reported out on a parliamentary committee on corrections. "Basically, I did most of it," she said. "I wanted little quotes. I wanted that report on corrections to be like a book." Holt was proud that the report "was accepted unanimously in the House of Commons and used as a reference on corrections throughout the free world."

Sharon Hayes helped initiate a family committee within the Reform caucus in Ottawa and then chaired it. "That was work," she said. "That was researching issues, presenting cases, making the effort to present the other side and saying, 'Okay, you're looking at an issue, its broad effects on a lot of things. Have you thought about where the Canadian family fits into the issue?'" It was a task that needed to be done, "and so I did it." Hayes felt her work was typical of the way women work. "I won't say men won't put effort into it, but it's at the level of presentation rather than the background digging."

Listening to people is equally intense research. Libby Davies said, "When I work in my riding, I visit people in the hotels and rooming houses or down at the Woodward's squat. To me that's the reality of what I'm dealing with, and it's the contact with those individual constituents that gives me a sense of purpose." Gillian Trumper said, "I spend a lot of time, not so much doing all the upfront political stuff but going into groups, talking to people as individuals rather than massed in a meeting," where she might hear only one group with one specific interest.

Getting around her own biases without losing her principles was important to MacPhail. "I have my biases, but there cannot be winners at the expense of losers. You need as much information as possible to make good decisions, and investing in consultation and in getting as many points of view as possible has paid off in the long run."

Margaret Bridgman went beyond party policy to take direction from her constituents. If a groundswell on an issue went against the Reform platform, she would tell her constituents how to prepare a petition, which she would present in Parliament. She had a town hall meeting on the abortion issue. "A bunch of special interest groups were there, 150 people, and I said, 'Just introduce me. I'm sitting right there on that chair, and I'm listening. We'll have sort of a straw vote here at the end. And I'll

Pauline Jewitt, a successful academic before she became a BC MP, was "a stickler for precision" and as foreign affairs and constitutional critic demanded "better research than anybody else," said her assistant Stephen Lee. Here she talks to federal leader Ed Broadbent, right. *Courtesy New Democratic Party.*

get to know how everybody feels, but convince each other because I'm going with the flow.' And I sat down."

Brice said, "I learned fairly early on that you seldom argue anyone into changing their point of view, but you find common ground or a way to express things so that people will go a certain route they otherwise wouldn't have." Brice described it as being "persuasive and not argumentative."

But is gathering so much information and so many opinions useful in the hierarchical, military structure of politics? Evelyn Gillespie was convinced that the efficiency of consensus is worth all the difficulty to get it. "Given the experience I've had, I would do a lot more at the community level to encourage consensus building. It's really not good enough to have one group coming with a single interest; a coalition with that interest is really powerful." Linda Reid also described herself as "a process person. I have clear expectations about building camaraderie, bringing people on side, ensuring we are crafting good, inclusive decisions." Dawn Black said women "look for results rather than just the confrontation." She thought committees were where members accomplished things.

"Women recognize that they need and want a support circle for their work," observed Penny Priddy, "whereas men don't need to process it out in the same way." And Darlene Marzari, who was always nurturing the people she worked with, said she herself couldn't survive without nurturing. "I always looked for support. And it's simply not there inside an army structure. Don't expect it. I constantly went back to the people—that was my nourishment—and put what they said into a policy framework. Just being with these people for whom I was advocating, talking to them, kept me sane."

Kim Campbell said, "My goal always in public life was to remember that real flesh and blood human beings had to live with what I did. For example, if you're making criminal law, it will make people criminals. That's a big responsibility." Campbell found great comfort and energy in talking to voters. "You get a lot of affection from people. People are courageous. In the '93 campaign, meeting people is what got me up every morning. Meeting only the press would have killed me."

RESPECTING EACH OTHER

Our governments are made up of ordinary people, many women that I interviewed told me, the kind we meet every day in our communities. As neighbours they respect the opinions of their peers and can fairly represent them in an assembly.

"The democratic process is about representation, and who better to represent someone than a neighbour?" said Evelyn Gillespie, who always tried to have people think of her as a neighbour. "I live in this community. You can come and talk to me when I'm gardening or in my pyjamas. I am no better, no worse, than you are. I don't have special knowledge, but I'll do the work that's required to accept this responsibility."

"We have a system of government where we choose our governors—the people who make the laws on our behalf—from our family, our friends and our neighbours," Sue Hammell said, "not a military dictatorship." Ordinary people have all the blemishes and flaws that everybody else in our society has. As an elected representative, she said, "I'm only as good as the people around me." She added a joke to illustrate her point. "This guy is watching Parliament, and the fellow beside him says, 'Gawd, there's a lot of horses' asses in there.' And the first guy says, 'Well, there's a lot of horses' asses in this country, and they deserve to be represented too.'"

Although members insult members of other parties in public, yell at them in the chamber and dispute with them in committee, overall they believe that they virtually all came with sincerity, even the politicians they don't agree with. Lois Boone said. "I may not like what they do, and I may not agree with their position—all that kind of stuff—but most of them aren't liars and cheaters."

"When you start to think about it, 99.9 percent of us who seek office don't have ulterior motives," said Rita Johnston, "Unless there's some proof, I get quite annoyed when I hear some of the nasty comments. I think, 'You don't know what you're talking about.' The media really help to spawn that, making us look like a bunch of bandits. And really, the NDP was great at making us look like we were a bunch of bandits. That's politics, I guess."

Sindi Hawkins thought politicians are despised by voters because "what they see is ribbon cutting, mass events, travelling in jets all over the province. What they don't see is the preparation we do for committees, the meetings we do, staying in lousy hotel rooms, never being home . . ." She interrupted her list to exclaim, "The amount I hate travelling now!" Then she added, "The public perceives that we don't work."

Barb Copping talked about how she changed her opinion during her one term. "I went into the system with a great amount of disrespect for the opposition. But at least they were people who had philosophies, whether you agreed with them or not, and ran and tried to do something about it." She gets upset at the general apathy of people who, with so

"Elected representatives are only as good as the people around them," says Sue Hammell, who would encourage the public to get interested and contribute to the political process. Photo courtesy *PatrickTam/FlungingPictures.com*

much going on, won't bother to read beyond the headlines and research the issues affecting everybody's lives, including their own. "So I came out with more respect for politicians—and I'm talking all politicians, anybody that ran for office. They're hard-working. They go into it believing that they will make a difference for the better, and I do think it is an honourable profession."

But a single politician who attracts distrust can destroy trust in all politicians. "There are examples of politicians who make terrible decisions for their own political interest and not for any sort of public interest," Libby Davies noted. "And when people realize this, they feel pretty burned." The unpopular Brian Mulroney has spawned a cynicism that is reinforced by the media, she said. Politicians have bad reputations "because there have been some pretty bad politicians," said Lynn Stephens. "Brian Mulroney is at the top of my list." And Margaret Mitchell said, "When I was there, there wasn't the same kind of nastiness toward politicians, and I guess we've got Mulroney to thank for a lot of that. During his period they really beat politicians up."

"Some politicians do get involved in corruption," said Daphne Jennings. "We know the dishonesty is there. But I don't think it's the majority." Gillespie was more generous. "There are some bad apples in the box, but I can't say I ever ran across anybody who was crooked." "I don't think we have a larger percentage of unscrupulous people than any other profession," said Linda Reid.

Nevertheless, the women that I interviewed admitted some guilt in damaging the reputation of politicians just by participating in an adversarial system. "That in itself is almost a self-perpetuating thing," said Katherine Whittred. "It's our job to bring other politicians into disfavour." Lois Boone agreed. "As politicians, we spend our entire lives trying to discredit the other person, and the media picks up on it—that's part of it, trying to find some dirt on somebody."

The idea that members of other parties are scoundrels is repeated and repeated, until people think all politicians are in there to feather their own nests, observed Mary Collins, but "that's the furthest thing in anybody's mind that I know of." Since her political career, Collins has been working abroad, particularly in Russia. "It is true in other places. When Russians learn you're a former politician, they just assume you must be enormously wealthy because that's the only reason people go into politics there."

Christy Clark said politicians "kick the crap out of each other all the time. We are all of us collectively responsible for denigrating our own profession. That is a product of the media's appetite for scandal, which in turn is fed by the public appetite for entertaining details. I think the sales of *People* magazine and the viewership of *Entertainment Tonight* and the appetite for scandals of the *Vancouver Sun* and the quality of politicians who run for public office are all linked. Because I think public literacy is diminishing about politics, and it's a vicious circle."

Learning to make things look simple because complexity won't get across in a ten- to thirty-second television sound bite involves reverting to time-tested methods: make every disagreement a fight and call the other party's champion a name that encapsulates what's bad about their team and what's good about ours. Politicians learn to ignore all the policy thinking that led them to their position because it can't be communicated in the time available to define us versus them.

"A lot of people think televising Parliament was the death knell," observed Kim Campbell. "John Turner described question period as bullshit theatre, and it is, but it's an important part of the democratic process." Still, as a kind of a game it undermines the seriousness of what politicians do, the seriousness of "most of the people I know who were elected to various levels of government."

Gillespie said, "What could be more embarrassing than having a school group come to visit during question period?"

Margaret Bridgman mentioned another aspect of adversarial politics. "You get good politicians who have to defend bad ones because they're party members. So while you're doing that to me, I know damn well you don't believe it, and I don't believe it, and so what does that do to your credibility? Here you are spinning me this—how much else are you spinning me?"

The urgent need to be elected does have an effect, said Joan Sawicki. "We promise what we can't deliver because people want to hear it, and we have to say it so they'll vote for us." Or the party takes a stance a member has opposed. Jackie Pement said, "I can remember saying I think so-and-so—and then being in the situation where I had to say something that had been softened or worse." That's where the bottom line comes up against personal integrity—how far can a politician stretch?

Val Meredith said, "We all know examples of where we've said one thing and done something else." She blames a poor outcome on poor communication, because "there's usually a reason for changing your mind." We should give voters information to include them in our decision making if we want them to get involved in politics, "to feel it's important to get out and vote."

Cathy McGregor faced a dilemma over the privatization of the Coquihalla highway. "Somebody came up and said, 'Is your government considering privatizing the Coquihalla?' I lied and said, 'No, they're not.' It had gone all the way through Treasury Board, and I knew that they were considering it. I thought it would be a stupid decision, and I fought it all the way." As an honest politician, she should have been able to admit some people were pushing that agenda, and she was opposing it because "that's wrong and here are the reasons why." The principle of cabinet solidarity prevented that, and McGregor concluded that not only the media but the whole British parliamentary system encourages dissimulation.

Gillespie also blames groups advocating less government. If less government is best, then "government has no value. Taxes are simply the exploitation of people. All tax money is abused. Nobody cares—politicians don't care. The prime minister's a crook. They say it over and over again." There are many at fault, she concludes. "If we want people to respect politicians as a group, politics as a profession—or even a passing occupation—maybe we feel a little bit of guilt about it ourselves. We know that it's a pretty special place to be. If we know that, we have to treat each other with respect."

Women in an assembly seldom find a work group that is all-female or even one that is led by a woman. The partisan barriers set up by the structure of our assemblies act like ranges of mountains, keeping people from working together. Some women try to work co-operatively, however, not competitively in the usual way of the assembly, and to foster positive acquaintance across party lines.

When there is communication between members of different parties, Margaret Lord "found camaraderie with women because we were women. We had common ground. You could start a conversation with Judi Tyabji Wilson by saying, 'How are the kids?' and then go wherever the conversation took you. I couldn't start a conversation with [her husband] Gordon Wilson by saying, 'How are the kids?'"

The common bond, our role as mothers and daughters, provides the bridge just as it does in our communities. "Whether women are right-wing or left-wing," observed Darlene Marzari, "the reality of women's life—the fibre of the community—is built around how women knit it together. So real issues, the issues of caring for elders, caring for the vulnerable, caring for children," the ones that women share, can be brought to the table only when all the women members co-operate to assure they are no longer considered minority interests.

Dawn Black reflected, "I think my greatest success was working with women in other political parties to achieve things for women." Black spearheaded the campaign for a private member's bill declaring December 6 a national day of remembrance for the women who died in the Montreal Massacre. "That was a big success, and I still feel really positive about it," she said. Mary Collins, who was minister responsible for the status of women at the time, also cited the Day of Remembrance as one of the achievements she cherished. It was "Dawn's original idea. I was able to get government support, so we were able to do it."

On December 6, 1989, a twenty–five-year–old man went on a shooting rampage at l'École Polytechnique de Montréal, killing fourteen woman engineering students. He had failed to achieve entrance to the school of engineering, and for forty-five minutes he roamed three floors of the Polytechnique screaming that he hated feminists. Except for four men who attempted to resist him, he shot only women, the fourteen who died and another twelve who survived. He then turned the gun on himself. A search of his body turned up a letter saying how he hated feminists and included what was presumed to be a hit list of another fifteen Montreal women.

The event became a symbol of the horror of male violence directed at women. Black's private member's bill and her unflagging organizational support, along with Collins's efforts in the key women's ministry, led to broader recognition and the proclamation in 1991 of a National Day of Remembrance and Action on Violence Against Women. It brought men as well as women to the task. The subsequent white ribbon campaign was begun by men wanting to change male attitudes that lead to violence against women. The culmination of their activities was a huge number of people striving for concrete change.

Another proud achievement for Black was the federal committee report "Breast Cancer: Unanswered Questions." "For me, politics was always personal," said Black. When a good friend in her thirties was diagnosed with breast cancer, she was pregnant for the third time. To be treated for her particularly aggressive form of cancer, she had to have an abortion, adding that loss and sadness to the stress and physical ordeal of her cancer treatment. "That incident got me looking at the whole issue of breast cancer." Research disclosed that the federal government's only commitment to breast cancer research was $850,000, and she thought, "Migawd, people pay more than that for a house in Vancouver," and started working on the issue in Ottawa.

Black sat on the Standing Committee of the House on Health, Welfare, Social Affairs, Seniors and the Status of Women, and was a member of the subcommittee on the status of women, so she suggested a study. "I didn't really have to convince them," she said, "all women, from all the parties." Tabled in June of 1992, the report convinced the government to increase funding to twenty-five million dollars over the next five years. As well, women in the Ottawa regions started following the committee, sitting in on the hearings. Black connected with

Dawn Black often worked with women across party lines. She activated the campaign to establish a Day of Mourning after the Montreal Massacre and was the spark plug of a committee report that prompted significant funding increases by government for breast cancer. Photo courtesy *PatrickTam/ FlungingPictures.com*

them, and they started a breast cancer action group in Ottawa. The subcommittee achieved both of its goals: to raise consciousness and to increase funding. "But in retrospect what was really positive was the fact that women in all parties were working on these issues and working together."

When Black became aware that stalking of women by men—former husbands or lovers, admirers—was a major problem in Canada, she wrote to municipalities across the country for feedback. In Surrey, councillor Judy Villeneuve took it up with the Union of BC Municipalities. "I directed a private member's bill. Judy got support all across the province and across the country, and through the municipalities, pushed the federal government." The government responded to "all that support for my private member's bill across the country" and legislated against stalking.

Black saw clearly a general need for women to co-operate across party lines. A New Democrat, she worked with Tory minister Mary Collins, Pierette Venne, a Tory MP from Quebec who moved to the Bloc Québécois in 1991, and Mary Clancy, Liberal, to form an association for women MPs. Collins was gratified that this group of women "worked together as colleagues from all parties on issues." She recalled that "Mary Clancy and I and Dawn—there were all kinds of things we worked on together, cross-boundary."

Black described the genesis of the committee. "There was an incident in Parliament where one of the Tories called Howard McCurdy 'nigger.' And around the same time I'd been called a 'harlot' or something in the House—or 'fishwife'—I don't know." A group of women asked the speaker for a committee to deal with "these homophobic, sexist and racist remarks that were floating. And to give [Speaker] John Fraser credit, he let us set up this committee under his office. I think it all fell apart after we left, but it did raise some consciousness, and certainly it made these guys know they were going to get slapped if they said these things. Even if it didn't change the way they thought, it made them shut up." Black said of her work with women in Parliament, "I got support on various issues from government ministers Barbara McDougall and from

Mary Collins at a meeting of the Parliamentary Committee on Equality Rights. MP Sheila Finestone, later a senator, is second from left, next to Collins, and MP Pauline Browes is fifth from left. As minister responsible for the Status of Women, Mary Collins initiated a federal panel on violence against women. *Photo courtesy Mary Collins.*

Mary Collins—I got a lot of support from Mary."

Collins, who was the minister responsible for the status of women from 1990 to 1993—just after the Montreal massacre had become a major agenda item—was able to initiate a federal panel on violence against women. She worked with women's organizations across the country and with colleagues in every province "to really start to get a public focus on the issue." She had the encouragement of the police, and she needed all the support and encouragement she could get. "As minister for status of women, you don't have a big budget. You have to influence many other people to get things done." Collins found many people who didn't want to do it, or do anything. "But I had a lot of pressure from the school teachers in Ontario, who helped me prepare an examination of what the issues were across the country and get together some kind of a strategic plan to deal with it." Out of that panel's advice came legislation on stalking—encouraged by Black and her campaign—and a number of other programs as well as funding. It also acted as a clearing house for information.

Joy Langan, herself the recipient of a breast implant, launched a women's campaign against the sale of Meme breast implants, which had proven a danger over time to the health of women who had them. "I put in a private member's bill, but it was never drawn." (Private members' bills in the House of Commons are put in a bin, and a draw determines which ones will be debated.) However, she had some support from the Liberals and a woman from the Bloc and great support from NDP women members, some researchers, a couple of doctors and a couple of former employees of the federal health protection branch. She received some plain brown envelopes, but still she had trouble getting press until she finally figured it out: "The male editors didn't think it was news." To concentrate on women reporters, she had a coffee and muffin session for them at the press club across the street from the Hill, made contacts and kept them updated. "That was a turning point."

Langan raised questions day after day in the House through a succession of health ministers, and she brought three women to Ottawa—one from Quebec, one from Vancouver and one from Calgary—who had endured horrendous side effects from Meme breast implants. "We met with Benoît Bouchard, the health minister [at the time]. They told him of the horrid consequences of the implant." But their real life experiences were anecdotal evidence to him and his ministry because they were not included in scientific studies. So he dismissed them. "We chastised him in a press conference afterwards, and he phoned me the next day to apologize."

When the group was debriefing in Langan's office later, "we began to relay experiences with the medical and political system and caught ourselves saying, 'I know, I know,' and in the case of our colleague from Quebec, 'Je sais, je sais.' We decided we had to start a network of women across the country and bingo!, we had a name: 'I know/Je sais'—meaning, they may not believe us, but we know." They held meetings in Montreal, Toronto, Edmonton and Vancouver, with experts presenting information. Pharmaceutical companies, who along with plastic surgeons strongly supported continuing the implants, called the experts quacks. Nevertheless, there were more than a hundred women at the Vancouver meeting.

"In Vancouver we became active at the Women's Hospital in a breast implant information group. Unfortunately, the doctor in charge of the program at Women's . . . insisted that the advisory committee for this group be 'representative,' so we had at least two plastic surgeons on it, and they blocked a lot of stuff. However, we plodded on and made contacts and got women out to the meetings about class actions, et cetera.

"Before I was un-elected, Benoît Bouchard announced a moratorium on the sale of breast implants and took Meme implants off the market. It was a great victory. The group sort of disbanded after that, and I have lost track of Marcella from Quebec. I keep in touch with Linda from Vancouver, though our friend in Calgary has succumbed to her cancer. The bad news is that promotion of breast implants is now alive and well again, and the rules have been relaxed." On October 20, 2006, Health Canada announced it had lifted the sales ban on silicone breast implants despite resistance by scientific experts.

Support from women of another party meant a lot to Iona Campagnolo on one occasion in particular. "I remember when I was fighting all the wars on anti-choice. Groups were coming at me from every corner." Only in Thunder Bay did anyone offer support. "There was a huge rally, anti-choicers blocking my way at the airport, blocking my way at the hotel, blocking my way everywhere." Campagnolo would ask her taxi driver to take her luggage to the back while she walked through the crowd. "Walking through this gauntlet of abuse, people staring and swearing—all of those words. I never did see a Christian. Then suddenly this group of about ten women with roses came along; they were mainly New Democrat women, and they came and stood beside me, and they walked beside me into the hotel. I was never so—oh, I was thrilled! It was a tender moment, I can tell you."

In the BC legislature, a bill to allow the distribution of unused restaurant food to food banks was an inter-party issue, and that fact was nearly its downfall. Members from both sides of the house have different viewpoints on the morality of having food banks, but the major barriers to the bill were those the system itself puts in place to stop co-operation across the floor. Despite healthy support on both sides for the substance of the bill, Liberal Ida Chong and New Democrat Gretchen Mann Brewin had to wrangle and manoeuvre to get the legislation passed.

When Chong was elected in Victoria in 1996, a Victoria city councillor encouraged her as a member of the opposition to introduce a private member's bill allowing food banks to get unused restaurant food. A colleague had introduced such a bill the previous year, so she talked to him and consulted with her party's research department. When she learned that six other provinces had introduced similar legislation, she put it on the order paper. It didn't get anywhere before the session was prorogued in the spring. "All that fall, people asked me my biggest disappointment. It was this bill. Since it had support on both sides of the house, why wouldn't the government let it move ahead?" She announced publicly that she would bring the bill back in 1997. At that point Brewin, a government member, told her that the government had drafted the legislation, which made Chong wonder why her bill could not have gone ahead. Well, that's not the way it works, said Brewin. "But that's not fair. I've spoken about it," said Chong, who had a database of more than two hundred people to whom she wrote letters asking them to send a message to their own MLA. She was moving it forward more than her colleague had done the previous year.

"At the end of March or early April, although Gretchen had indicated that I shouldn't, I put it on the order paper—until I was sure the government would bring the legislation in. I asked for assurance in writing, but Gretchen said, 'Of course we can't give you anything in writing.' 'Then why tell me you have something? We're all in agreement, why don't we get this through?'"

Chong knew no party would write such a letter and that Brewin was also frustrated, but she also knew that if circumstances led to closing the session, the bill would die. But ten days later Brewin called across the floor, "Ida, our bill is coming up." "It came from the attorney general, and except for about three sentences, it was my bill. I take credit that if I hadn't pushed, it might have taken longer."

Brewin also mentioned the food bank bill as one of her achievements. "There was a piece of legislation that helped in communities, finding a way food banks could accept food from restaurants and hotels—even though the NDP hated the whole notion of food banks. It took a long time to do simply because the opposition was interested in pushing it." What's wrong with that? No government wants "to totally respond to what the opposition suggests because somehow you lose face, lose the drive, power—I don't know what you lose, but I guess it was tainted."

Although she called it "Gretchen's bill," Cathy McGregor, also a government member, discussed the bill when I asked her what changes she would recommend in the legislative system. "It was one-page legislation. It was good public policy, and it was being called for publicly. But the power brokers wouldn't let it on the agenda. Why? Because the Libs wanted it. We had to wait until the next session, when we would announce it as part of our package, and then it's our initiative, and blah, blah, blah."

A number of former women politicians have, after their resignations, co-chaired the Women's Campaign School, a nonpartisan BC organization that works to get more women into politics at every level. Former chair Penny Priddy said, "We have found that women from different political parties can actually work together and can get something accomplished." The school, which has held annual gatherings since 1999—for anyone interested in the electoral process, running or just helping in campaigns—has expanded beyond BC and is giving the same workshop in other provinces. A score or more of BC's members and former members, both federal and provincial, have chaired and otherwise supported it, and many of its students have since run and been elected.

You Be the Leader

A notice went out on July 30, 2003, on an electronic mailing list created and managed by the Canadian Women Voters Congress. The subject line was "Unknown declares for NDP leadership."

> Greetings to all the politically active women in BC!
> Last year, I attended the Women's Campaign School in Vancouver, since then I have been waiting for an opportunity to be of service to the people of BC. I have decided to offer my vision, integrity and commitment, and seek the leadership of the New Democratic Party!
> To become an official candidate, I require at least one hundred signatures from NDP members in good standing to support my campaign. I would appreciate hearing from anyone who would consider signing my nomination documents!
> A brief bio is available at http://xxxxxxxx.com/xxxxx /, and I would be happy to email a full CV or chat with anyone wanting more information about me.
> Thank you for your support!
> Romana Frey

What marvellous freshness and naïveté it showed! I was unable to reach Frey to talk, but I wonder what prompted a woman so enthusiastic and untested to offer herself in a war that creates armoured shells around many politically experienced, skilled and savvy women and draws immediate aversion from most women members.

Rosemary Brown said in her memoir *Being Brown,* "I know that myth has it that all politicians dream of one day being the top boss, dictator, prime minister, president, king or queen. But whenever I had thought of NDP leaders, it had always been with amazement that anyone would want to compete for the job of leading a group of people I perceived to be fractious and cantankerous, albeit dedicated and committed to very strongly held views. The challenge of holding the multiple and diverse parts of this group together through a shared vision of justice for all seemed to me nothing short of Herculean. I had always admired the leaders, but never envied them."[75] When Brown ran for the leadership of the federal NDP in 1975, she did it to make the point that women's equality went beyond asking the men already in office to treat us equally and included the possibility of women taking positions of power themselves in order to effect change.

More than a decade later in her book *Toeing the Lines: Women and Party Politics in English Canada*, Sylvia Bashevkin remarked on Brown's loss, Flora MacDonald's failure to win the federal Tory leadership in 1976 and the number of times women had run but failed to win provincial leaderships. She wrote that these events reflected "a fundamental unease with the prospect of a female party leader."[76] That unease has been confronted but not defeated.

Four women members of the BC legislature have become provincial party leaders in the last fifteen years. Rita Johnston in 1991, Grace McCarthy in 1993, and Joy MacPhail in 2001 moved from MLAs to BC party leaders, named to their positions between elections by their caucus or party but never elected as leader. Carole James became a provincial leader in 2003 and was elected MLA in 2005. Of the three women MPs who became federal leaders of House parties, all within the past twenty years, one was from BC: Kim Campbell, named leader in 1993. But the attitudes of the 1970s and 1980s, to which Bashevkin referred, have not disappeared as we move into the twenty-first century. Women leaders still generate unease, although we no longer think such women out-and-out freakish even if few women want the job.

Johnston and Campbell were both defeated after their predecessors had totally destroyed any chance of their party being re-elected to government. McCarthy tried a rescue mission for her party in BC without success. MacPhail became interim leader after her predecessor stepped in at the end of a term and was defeated in circumstances similar to those of Johnston and Campbell. She declined her opportunities to run for the position officially, although she held the interim position for two and a half years in a caucus of two, which increased to three in a late-term by-election.

Linda Reid, Joan Smallwood and Hedy Fry all contested party leaderships unsuccessfully. Many other women members—including Iona Campagnolo, Pauline Jewett, Pat Carney, Elizabeth Cull, Jackie Pement and Penny Priddy—have been encouraged to do it and considered it but didn't run. Although women lead many important community organizations—local, provincial and national—and do a good job of it, three-quarters of BC's women MLAs and MPs do not want to lead a political party. Only a dozen or so expressed any interest at all or entertained anything more than an outside chance of being persuaded to run for leadership, and then only if the need arose in unusual circumstances. In fact most were emphatic about their stance. "No. Never," said one member. Another, asked if she had ever considered it, said, "Not once. Not once."

Audrey McLaughlin and Alexa McDonough were the longest-serving Canadian women leaders, having led the federal NDP about six and seven years respectively from 1989 to 2003. They took the opportunity to try some of the approaches more welcoming to women, organizing their caucuses to seek consensus. But in the assemblies and in the politics that surrounded them, they operated within a pyramidal, confrontational system where expectations for leaders favoured, just as they always had, the drama of aggression.

Male politicos and media commentators expressed their pleasure when the federal NDP chose Jack Layton to succeed McDonough. Not a few reasserted their idea of politics as a cockfight and rushed onto the air or into print to blame the two women for trying over the past dozen years to change the game. Rex Murphy said, "Mr. Layton may be the first [NDP] leader since Ed Broadbent who is actually a real politician; who is as comfortable with the game of politics and all its messy arts of scrum, stunt and press conference, as any other real politician anywhere. Mr. Layton is the outward and visible sign that the NDP will not be singing hymns in a largely deserted church in the next election, but buzzing about the country, actually trying to win votes and challenging the credibility of Paul Martin as prime minister. . . . The NDP has returned to politics understood as a search for votes, rather than as a forum for ostentatious piety."[77]

Warren Kinsella, Liberal Party functionary, wasted no time joining the chorus from Ottawa, first on his website, then in a press interview. Despite the fact that Layton had no parliamentary experience, only civic, and both McLaughlin and McDonough were MPs, the latter after leading her provincial party as an MLA for fourteen years, Kinsella said, "Layton is an experienced politician who[m] we have to take seriously. . . . [He] clearly has skills that his two immediate predecessors didn't have."[78]

Adam Radwanski, in the *Ottawa Citizen,* recognized that Layton had shortcomings. He reported that to many folks "he comes off as too glib, too smug, too insincere. They think he's all sizzle and no steak." However, Radwanski felt those shortcomings were not as serious as those of McLaughlin and McDonough—failure to rouse the media to attention. He assigned no blame to the media, only to the women. "The worst possible fate for a politician is to fall off the radar. But that's exactly where the previous two NDP leaders spent most of their time. Few voters particularly disliked either Audrey McLaughlin or Alexa McDonough. But that's because they had no idea who they were. With Mr. Layton, that won't be a problem."[79]

Obviously the way that most women work toward solutions does not suit the male media, who could not detect political thinking unless it were served up in "scrum, stunt and press conference." Women see the conundrum. Compete on your own ground and you are not heard. It is assumed you are preaching, and that your discussion of complexities is piety. Do politics the way it's always been done, sharpened by our modern technology—compete as an aspirant to manhood—and you are seen as a shrill, pushy, unattractive woman. Until you begin to shriek and do it the right way, the media ignores you. Neither alternative is appealing.

But the media's response to women seeking and holding leadership is far from the only reason that few women harbour any desire to lead a political party. Lois Boone, a northern MLA, said, "It takes too much commitment and far too much out of your personal life. You couldn't be leader without living in the Lower Mainland or you'd never be home. Look at the hair on people who have become premier! Glen [Clark] went grey in two months."

Pat Carney wouldn't want to be leader "because you can't live in British Columbia and be leader of a federal political party." She wasn't willing to move to Ottawa for either her journalistic or political career. "I would never go as far as to say I'm a British Columbian first and a Canadian next, but I'm near to that. My people were here, my kinsmen, before Confederation, so I have that sense of distance."

Beyond geography, there is the workload. "I've seen our leader work," said Victoria's Ida Chong, "and the physical stamina that he has for the work that's required of him." Besides the stamina, leaders have to be building a party year-round—not an easy thing. "So exciting as it may be, you must feel you were destined to do it, and I don't think that path was laid out for me."

"I have goals, but no fire in the belly to become leader," said Lynn Stephens, and Sophia Leung remarked, "I'm not seeking power or control. I just really want to make changes. It's that simple." Defining the issue more specifically, Cathy McGregor said, "I strongly believe I have many leadership qualities, and I like to play a lead role in organizations I belong to, but I don't necessarily need to be at the top of a hierarchy as long as I feel I am making a difference—that I'm part of a team . . . that I have a role as a leader, not the leader." Jan Pullinger called it leading from a centrarchy.

Bonnie McKinnon said flatly, "No. When I look back at being an MLA, the abuse people pile upon you, and the press just bang-bang-banging at you constantly, and for the leader it's even worse. Why would anyone want that? To me it's a very thankless job." "It doesn't suit my temperament," said Eileen Dailly. She takes everything very seriously and worries about doing things correctly. "That would be too much of a strain for me." And the gender difference registered with Joy Langan,

A path to the leadership of a party? "I don't think it was laid out for me," says Ida Chong. "You must feel you were destined to do it." Here she talks with George Chow in Victoria. *Photo courtesy Patrick Tam/FlungingPictures.com*

who said, "Once I saw the abuse that Audrey [McLaughlin] took, not only from her political enemies but also from her caucus, I wouldn't be a woman leader of a party for all the money in the world."

Iona Campagnolo had a close brush with running as federal Liberal leader. Defeated after her first term as an MP, she became the president of the federal Liberal Party through tempestuous times. "There were quite a few who wanted me to run," said Campagnolo. "Nick Turner from Alberta raised a lot of money, and Gordon Gibson Sr. raised money here. [He} came out in his booming voice: 'I'm going out in the boat tonight, and I'm not coming back till I have a million dollars on the line for you.' 'Gordon, I'm not running.' 'Yes, you are!' To Joey Smallwood I had to say 'No, no, no. I'm not going to run, because I won't win; John Turner will win. And I don't have the education.' I don't think anyone should be leader who hasn't got an appropriate economic and liberal arts education." As well, she felt her French wasn't good enough, and she didn't want to be the token woman candidate.

Somebody launched a rose campaign. "They sent me one rose every hour for days and days. All you could see were red roses." She phoned her mentors and said, "Give back the money, I'm not going to run." Campagnolo had seen at least two prominent Liberal leadership candidates whose debts in a lost cause lasted at least fifteen years. "I know because I raised money for those men over and over and over again, and I didn't want to be an old woman paying back debts." While she did consider running from time to time, she is comfortable with her decision. "You don't have to be a leader to lead."

Pauline Jewett once considered running for the leadership of the provincial NDP, according to her former assistant Stephen Lee. "When Dave Barrett stepped down there was a kind of an open field with several leading candidates." Lee and others thought Jewett would be the perfect middle candidate, "given her federal experience, her profile in the party, her vice-presidency of the federal party and her stature in the disarmament movement. She was the kind of person who could break a deadlock, and she was from New Westminster." She finally agreed, but she needed what Lee called a "vision shift." She would have to disengage from federal affairs, her central interest, and from international affairs, and see herself as a possible premier of BC. By the time she made that vision shift, "people who would have supported her were already committed."

Penny Priddy was asked to consider running for leadership, but before answering she looked back at her experience as a cabinet minister. "I knew how much time I put in. I worked hard, as did everybody. I was a new grandmother. I had breast cancer—although I don't think the breast cancer would have been a factor if I'd really wanted the leadership. But I have a marriage of thirty-six years that I'm very much attached to. I didn't want to work every single waking minute and not have time to do some of the other things that kept me a healthy and adequately sane person most of the time."

"For a short while," Elizabeth Cull thought about running for the provincial NDP leadership when Mike Harcourt announced he was stepping down. "I thought about it seriously. I had lots of support, and I thought I had something to offer, something very different in leadership potential than Glen Clark." Cull had held the health and finance portfolios, "both good experience. I didn't think Glen would lead the kind of progressive left party I'd want to work in, and if he were leader, I didn't think I'd get re-elected." So she decided to do it. But by next morning she didn't feel good about the decision. "I let it go a few days and found I didn't really want to. Unless you have a burning desire to be leader, you shouldn't run."

Jackie Pement thought of running in that same leadership race. "I thought about it because I wasn't happy with who was running. I thought, 'Why not? Why shouldn't I stir the pot?' As we got closer to it, I thought, 'That's a lot of work and a lot of people involvement for me to just stir the pot,' and I thought, 'No, this is a bad idea.' It's the only time I thought about it. If I'm satisfied with the leadership, I'm happy to be part of the group."

But for some women, the way leadership was exercised within the system held them back. "I see leadership as a shared responsibility," said Evelyn Gillespie, "but that's not the way we practise leadership in this party, and certainly not in this province." Instead everyone wants to pin all the faults on the leader—maybe all the successes too—but she added, "Without a sense of shared responsibility around leadership, I'm not interested at all."

Libby Davies, on the other hand, thought she might be able to change the way leaders operate when she was asked to run as a possible successor to Alexa McDonough of the federal NDP. "For months I kept on saying, 'Oh no, no, I'd never do that.'" But then she had a conversation with a woman who said the NDP is not ready for a woman leader, despite the fact the party had elected two.

Davies was challenged by the idea of trying to present a different kind of campaign and trying to run caucus in a different way. "Alexa's style of leadership was much more around consensus building, but somehow that's not allowed in our caucus." Davies tried to think of new ways to do it. "It made me examine a lot of questions about what political leadership is and how gender is still a very unrecognized or unacknowledged part of the debate around leadership. We have very entrenched models, where the leader lays down the law, and you like it or you lump it. When McDonough tried to develop consensus, that was always read as being weak." By the time she thought it through, it was too late for Davies to run. "But the exercise made me face some questions that I have not been willing to answer myself as a woman who has been involved now politically for more than thirty years."

In 2002 Hedy Fry felt Canada was not ready for a woman leader. "In theory, yes; in practice, no," she told me. "I'm really serious. I don't think that Canadians are mature enough to vote for a woman. They still pigeonhole women. They have a double standard with regard to female politicians who are dealt with far more ruthlessly by the media and by others than male politicians." What is seen as assertiveness in a man—being arrogant and sure of himself—is considered having royal jelly. If a woman is assertive, she's "arrogant, a bitch, shrill, pushy and too ambitious." Fry got to know and respect Audrey McLaughlin, and thought she and Alexa McDonough were bright, articulate women, but people tended "not to give them the kind of attention that they would give to, say, the male leader of the Bloc Québécois, or the male leader of the Tory party, which is even smaller than the NDP right now [2002]."

Fry overcame her reservations by May 2006 when she entered the federal Liberal leadership race to replace Paul Martin after the Conservatives won election. Having defeated Kim Campbell in her riding in 1993, she said, "I defeated one Conservative leader, and I can't wait to defeat another." Although she was "in it to win," she was forced to abandon her quest before the early delegate selection, saying she had to "acknowledge that we do not have the resources to continue in this race."[80]

POWER TO, NOT POWER OVER

When Rosemary Brown ran for the leadership of the New Democratic Party in 1975, she was the first woman in Canada to bid for leadership of a sitting federal party. Her campaign was born in feminism, run on feminist principles and started and sustained by the Women's Rights Committees of the party. The NDP had funded a women's convention in Winnipeg in 1973 as a lead-up to the United Nations' International Women's Year in 1975. Because a federal leadership convention was also planned for that year, the 132-woman convention resolved to run a woman who supported women's rights as a candidate. "The motion originally was that we run a feminist candidate," said activist Hilda Thomas, but this F-word was not yet widely acceptable, so the motion was amended to suit the moderates. Although the convention strongly supported Grace MacInnis, she just as strongly declined. She never labelled herself a feminist and suggested they seek the best candidate, male or female. A committee was struck to find the candidate.

Meanwhile, Brown decided not to seek the candidacy. Her family was young (fifteen, thirteen and seven years old in 1974), leadership demands severely stress marriages and she didn't speak French. As well, advisors agreed that if she won the nomination the fact she was a black woman could make race the central issue. Thus, Brown joined in the search for a woman candidate to replace David Lewis as federal leader. The coincidence of International Women's Year in 1975 made the search symbolic for women outside as well as within the party.

Although the search proceeded across Canada, it soon came back to Brown because, as Thomas put it, "she had a pretty good profile right across the country. She was known by a whole spectrum of women who recognized Rosemary as someone to pay attention to." Her support also included men, which boded well for airing the message that was the central goal of their campaign: there was no place in the party for sexism if the party was to achieve its social programs.

Brown told me, "The whole point in running for leadership was that the New Democratic Party was not taking the debate around gender seriously. It wasn't showing up in their policy development, it wasn't showing up in the kind of legislation they were implementing in the provinces where they had power." More than a win, the committee wanted these issues brought up at the convention and debated right across the country. "My responsibility was to make sure that women's issues were always considered and that the party was always jacked up on the fact that it was in favour of equality for everyone." She says in her book, "We rejected as self-defeating the task of grooming a man, no matter how willing he might be, to assume the job of making a political party more accountable to women."[81]

Brown had never before "run to lose," as she put it, although she could see the rationale. Before accepting the challenge she talked with "everybody." When she was finally convinced that her family would be fine, that she could do the job admirably, and also that she wouldn't win, she responded to the sense of duty her foremothers had instilled in her. She accepted the nomination in February 1975, a full six weeks before any other candidate entered the race.

The feminist campaign had five rules: (1) There would be no star-personality orientation. (2) Brown would stay in until her name was dropped because of the vote; she would be no one's stalking horse. (3) There would be no deals. (4) All decisions would be arrived at collectively. (5) All issues would be based on feminism and socialism.

Collective decision making is difficult, say those who have actually tried it. What goes into it? "Time, frustration, aggravation, turmoil and joy," said Brown, but what comes out is a hugely supportive joint sense in both victory and loss. Her team never gave up on rule four, proving that a committee can run an efficient campaign.

The BC Women's Rights Committee primarily ran the campaign, with the federal committee more like an auxiliary, Brown recounted. "The BC WRC was fierce. It was a lion." The more radical elements in the party became part of it because "when you talk equality you get into a lot of other issues besides gender." Environmentalists, people working for gay and lesbian rights and people who saw the NDP as the party which dealt with the real left issues such as poverty and equality: all joined in. "So it was an amazing group of people that we ended up with."

Supporters raised more than the campaign's cost, even though huge numbers of donations came in five-dollar, ten-dollar and twenty-dollar denominations. Many seniors sent two-dollar bills, and some donors identified themselves as old suffragettes. The committee sold a poster designed by children. They had craft sales, raffles, auctions, musical events and a festival. Women of all parties and visible minority people from home and abroad supported the campaign, a fact that bolstered Brown's sense of having done the right thing.

The media was welcome to attend nearly all Brown's campaign strategy meetings, and she believed that those who reported the convention moved from a "superficial ignorance of the will and power of feminists to a grudging admiration and respect for our commitment, integrity, wisdom and ability." And as Brown approached the convention in Winnipeg, she knew "the national debate on feminism had occurred, the consciousness raising had happened, the shift towards full equality was taking place."[82] The establishment within the party had grudgingly espoused many of the team's feminist demands, hoping to disarm her campaign.

Brown came second to Ed Broadbent in the voting, getting 46 percent of the vote on the final ballot. "I was fighting against the establishment every inch of the way. Tommy Douglas was adamant that what we were doing was destructive. David Lewis was convinced to the end that I was the most dangerous threat the party had ever faced. It was unbelievable! Unbelievable! It went to the fourth ballot. Being on the floor of the convention and looking at the panic on the faces of those guys—as they raced around that floor wishing they could make me disappear—as I sat there and quietly prayed that I'd lose." Laughing, she repeated, "It was quite an experience."

Brown learned later from Lewis that the establishment's fear arose from her many supporters with an axe to grind. One media report, which Brown characterized as accurate, described her as a "pain in the neck to the power brokers of the party . . . who wanted a nice comfortable contest between Ed Broadbent, Lorne Nystrom and John Harney."

Fourteen years later Audrey McLaughlin became leader of the federal New Democratic Party, the first woman in North America to lead a major political party. She saw power in consensus, she said, as opposed to the simple demand for loyalty that characterizes male leadership. "Women see power as power to, not power over." McLaughlin led for six years before resigning, but six years after leaving the post, she said, "Our culture still sees women as not quite as intelligent as men. There is a lot of talk in the media about being 'tough' and 'ruthless,' not qualities that characterize a lot of women, but most men who get into politics have at least learned to fake them." She hoped that continued efforts by women, in and out of politics, could change the accepted concept of leadership, because this would go a long way toward modifying "the cynicism about politicians that threatens to undermine the democratic process."

Kim Campbell said of McLaughlin, "I had the sense that she never really had her party's full-hearted support, and I think that's very much a gender thing—that you're kind of there on sufferance until you win an election. In a party that is never going to form the government,[83] the second-guessing and the blaming will be worse because what is the measure of success? I thought she was very good in the House."

In 1993 Campbell won leadership of the Progressive Conservative Party and, pressed by time rules, called a federal election almost immediately. Political writer Janine Brodie expressed some of its contradictions when she wrote five years later, 'The 1993 federal election marked a profound change in the text of federal politics as well as its many subtexts, including gender relations and the efficacy of the women's movement. The press heralded the election as a breakthrough for women in Canadian politics because two of the major party leaders were women. News coverage of the election brimmed with stories contemplating male and female leadership styles. We learned that Audrey MacLaughlin, the leader of the New Democratic Party, washed her own dishes while Prime Minister Kim Campbell had square-dancing prowess. . . . At the same time, the federal parties were virtually silent about so-called women's issues."[84]

Campbell, born and bred in BC, veteran of Vancouver school board and the BC legislature, became Canada's first and only woman prime minister on June 25, 1993. She is not one of the women who didn't want to be leader. "Of course I wanted to be leader," she told me. "It's natural for anybody in any organization to want to have the top job." Campbell stressed the fact that her generation of girls was brought up to aspire.

"When I was a little girl, people would say, 'What's your ambition?' I never for a moment thought I shouldn't be ambitious." Her mother's trust that she could do anything and her sense that there was a battle to be fought for girls helped to frame her purpose. She became president of her student council in high school and began to think about politics when she learned that she could move people by talking and was a good organizer.

Advice from a fellow university student about running for office made sense to Campbell: "Don't get involved in a party. Be a star." "It's harder to see party women as candidates than one who is a star. Nobody saw girls as leadership apprentices, but all boys were." After she had chaired the Vancouver school board for two years, Campbell joined the BC Social Credit Party in 1983 to run in a provincial election. She didn't win, but two years later she quit practising law in Vancouver to join Premier Bill Bennett's office as executive director.

Working in the backrooms of politics convinced Campbell that she would rather be in the front room as an elected member. She stepped out in a big way in 1986, running in the leadership contest which replaced Bennett. Campbell came in last of a dozen candidates with fourteen votes, but she uttered the most memorable quotation at the convention: "It is fashionable to speak of leaders in terms of their charisma," she said. "Charisma without substance is a dangerous thing." The comment was aimed directly at Bill Vander Zalm, clearly the sizzle on the Socred steak and the candidate who won the race.

The notoriety Campbell garnered in that leadership race helped her win a provincial seat in 1986 and a federal seat in 1988, when she succeeded Pat Carney in Vancouver Centre. In Ottawa, Campbell held the junior ministry of Indian and northern affairs before she became the first woman justice minister and then the first woman defence minister. When Prime Minister Brian Mulroney announced his retirement in March 1993, Campbell jumped into the leadership race. She had the support of many newcomers to the party, and with them she hoped for a participatory process for reaching policies that would add excitement to the campaign. As powerful cabinet ministers withdrew from the race, however, many of their supporters—long-time party heavyweights— joined Campbell's campaign. Few of them saw a need to reform decision-making processes. She could not reject this important support, but by their backing she suffered perceptions that she offered nothing new to the party or the country. Campbell became the front-runner, and over a four-month campaign, the only way the media found to make their stories interesting was "to find the chinks in my armour," she explained in her book *Time and Chance.*

Campbell recognized that the voters did not trust her party. She thought that "changes in our society had outstripped the ability of our institutions, as we currently operated them, to respond effectively and credibly." She wanted change, but she could not make it happen during her campaign. For one thing, "not enough time was scheduled for women's events. It was as if, for the men on the campaign team, the mere fact of my being a woman was enough to appeal to women. They couldn't conceive of a different way of strategizing a campaign. The women were new, unknown to the many old boys who had gravitated to our campaign, and reluctant to complain to me directly" while she was on the road campaigning.

In 1993 Kim Campbell became leader of the federal Progressive Conservative party and thus she became the first Canadian woman prime minister. She was also the first British Columbian to hold the top government position. *UBC Special Collections 44-1-2808b.*

Campbell thought the media wondered how she "dared to be less than perfect in the face of all this support!" but there were some islands of balanced consideration. Lisiane Gagnon, political columnist for Montreal's *La Presse*, wrote an article titled "Why Isn't Campbell Judged by the Same Yardstick as Male Politicians?" It was a stinging rebuke to *Maclean's* magazine for profiling Campbell as a woman with "burning ambition."[85] Noting that burning ambition as a characteristic for a woman in "egalitarian Canada . . . is deadly," Gagnon asked if the term did not better apply to Jean Charest, Campbell's strongest opponent. He was "willing to spend the next few years in a job that will virtually cut him off from his children . . . . This, to me, is burning ambition," said Gagnon.

"It is a no-win situation. If she tries to convey a different political style, less confrontational and more focussed on 'inclusion and consensus' she will be judged 'flaky' and lacking in leadership. If she tries to play by the traditional rules and lashes out at her opponents, she will be judged 'arrogant'. . . . If a thirty-four-year-old man wins over a forty-six-year-old woman next week at the PC convention, this will not come as a surprise to women of my generation. They are used to being upstaged by younger men when the time comes for promotion."

In this case the forty-six-year-old woman won. In June of 1993 she became the first woman to lead the Progressive Conservative Party, the first woman prime minister and the first British Columbian to be prime minister.[86] It is fair to say that many, many women wished her to do well, whether or not they were Progressive Conservatives, whether or not they liked Campbell's style. But it is also fair to say that many, many women still felt that a woman is naturally not as sure in a position of power as a man, more likely to falter or fuss about decisions, not a foolproof opponent to male critics and certainly not as likely to be accepted as a leader by the majority of the population.

Maclean's had also complained that Campbell was somehow "unstable," a characteristic ascribed partly because she was childless. Campbell resented the implication that her two step-children didn't count. When, less than a decade later, the mostly male establishment and media named Mackenzie King the greatest Canadian prime minister—a man without children, who had never even had a spouse, but took direction from his dead mother and passionately treasured his dog both alive and dead—the irony pierced Campbell's sense of fairness.

She was not one of the two PC MPs who succeeded in the election she called, and she stepped down after having been prime minister for four months and leader of the party for six. Much as she would have liked it to be different, Campbell does not regret her experience. For one thing, she had the opportunity to do the job for at least a short time. She did not blame the system for any problems. "There's a huge amount of flexibility within the system, and it really is a question of leadership and how you make it work," she told me. The subsequent government moved partly toward the organizational shape she used for her cabinet. And, she observed, she is better able to promote the causes that she cares about—including women's equality—as a former prime minister than she would as a former justice or defence minister.

Campbell won in circumstances that are often considered typical for women: the party was at the very bottom of a cycle, and its brass knew they had to offer something different. They offered a clever, experienced woman, but they used her as a pawn and continued to campaign in the old way. Although the severe loss in 1993 could be largely blamed on Brian Mulroney, Campbell was charged with not reviving the party in the six months she led it, not breathing life into the dead horse. Doubters of the health of the party have only to follow its progress for the decade after her leadership to see that Campbell was not alone in failing to have supernatural revival powers.

The third federal woman party leader, Alexa McDonough, had led the Nova Scotia NDP for fourteen years, was well-known across Canada, and had all the qualifications to run for leadership of the federal NDP in 1995 when Audrey McLaughlin retired from the job. The party made a strong statement about women's opportunities when they elected her to succeed another woman, an event that few would have bet on. The possibility that it could happen was one reason McDonough ran. If the party reverted to a male leader, she declared, it wouldn't "be because no woman felt she could even step forward and do it. I was outraged at the idea that two is too many."

McDonough's twenty-three years in politics led her to conclude that power for women will have to be taken; it won't be given. As well, "elected women can't fight and win the battle in isolation, within the parliamentary precinct or a political party. It's going to have to happen in the broader society." She labels the recent decline in force of the women's movement in Canada as a serious barrier for women.

Long-time BC party and union activist Bev Meslo ran for the leadership of the federal NDP when McDonough resigned in 2002. Five men had declared their candidacy. Said Meslo, "Four decades after the Royal Commission on the Status of Women, we were about to hold an election without one woman candidate. It would have been devastating to the NDP." Meslo found some support for her seat-of-the pants campaign across the country, driving an old car, passing an ice cream pail at meetings for donations and hosting an active website. Her campaigning as a feminist raised some issues affecting her work in Vancouver as an advocate and a mediator, but she felt she brought women's issues to attention, and she gained the admiration and affection of many.

In March 2004 another BC woman, Connie Fogal, became the leader of the Canadian Action Party of Canada, nominated by the party's founder and long-time benefactor, Paul Hellyer. Although she had been with the party for years, her inheritance of a party that had just lost its anchor began too soon after her husband's death. She told me in an email, "My personal wish is to be elsewhere with others carrying this load." Even so she has maintained an active presence.

The only other woman who has led a publicly recognized federal party is Elizabeth May of Ontario, who won leadership of the Green Party in late 2006 but has yet to be elected to an assembly.

Premier Mom

Rita Johnston had never thought of being leader "until . . . well, until it came up," but she became the first woman to serve as premier of a Canadian province when her caucus selected her to replace Bill Vander Zalm, who had been forced to resign under a cloud.

Sworn in as premier on February 2, 1991, Johnston's down-to-earth manner along with her ability to get to decisions must have contributed to the caucus's support for her as leader. Sensing her no-nonsense personality, people called her Premier Mom. Over an eight-year political career Johnston had been minister of municipal affairs and transit, then of municipal affairs, recreation and culture, then of transportation and highways while deputy premier.

Before the July 1991 convention, which was called to confirm her leadership, her strongest opponent was the well-known Grace McCarthy. The membership split along ideological lines, with the neo-conservatives—"all those right-wing bigots" in the words of one Socred woman member—moving to Johnston's camp to give her an eighty-vote win.

"When it's that close, you know you've got a split party, and it's tough," Johnston observed. As leader she couldn't stop the bleeding. "If you've got a party that's divided, it almost takes the Pope to pull it together. You're just not going to get anywhere if you are divided. We had people leaving the convention saying they wouldn't vote for us. We had Grace McCarthy making statements in support of the Liberal candidate. You can't pull anything together that way. Loyalty to the party only goes so far for some people, and then, bang."

In September she called an election for October 17, a race her party decidedly lost. The Socred government of forty-eight MLAs was reduced to a rump of seven to the NDP's fifty-one. The Liberals, who had held no seats in the previous house, won seventeen seats and became the official opposition. As they did later with Kim Campbell, people speculated about whether the backroom and big-money supporters of the party had made Johnston the sacrificial lamb, knowing the party could not win the next election anyway. Like Brian Mulroney, Vander Zalm had reduced the party's chances irretrievably by the time he resigned.

Johnston's comments on the matter showed disappointment but acceptance. "I've always believed that if you wanted to make changes in the party, you made them from within. You didn't go out and try to demolish what was there because there would be nothing to rebuild. Grace even tried to rebuild. But now Gordon [Campbell] has most of the Socreds—they have joined the Liberals. He's the party now. It's just a different name. Oh well."

Johnston resigned as leader after her party's election loss. The president of the Social Credit Party took on many of the leader's duties, and Jack Weisgerber became the party's house leader. After some concentrated persuasion, McCarthy agreed to run at the November 1993 convention and was elected leader.

McCarthy, who won her first election as a Socred in 1966, didn't think of running for leadership until 1986—"I didn't have the depth of experience that so many other people had"—but she had made her name on the provincial political scene. After two terms as minister without portfolio in the W. A. C. Bennett administration, she had been defeated when the NDP won government in 1972. A master organizer, McCarthy took on the job of party president and led its rebuilding. She toured the province, rallied the membership, and worked closely with the Bennett family, including Bill Bennett, W. A. C.'s son who had succeeded his father as party leader and then premier after the 1975 election.

"We were very well organized under the Bill Bennett administration," McCarthy told me. "W. A. C. had no organization at all. When I became president in 1973, the list of paid-up members was less than five hundred. There may have been people who said they were Socred, but the actual membership was that small. W. A. C. didn't believe in organization. If you did the job well, people would talk to you. But if he wasn't there, it was either going to collapse and go away because we didn't have any soldiers or we had to build the army. In two years we had eighteen thousand members. You know what that would take."

Re-elected with Bill Bennett in 1975, McCarthy was a powerful cabinet member, holding recreation, tourism, industry, human resources, government services and provincial secretary portfolios and acting as deputy premier until 1983. She was seen as a driving force behind Expo 86, the Trade and Convention Centre, SkyTrain and other Vancouver projects. So after Bill Bennett opened Expo 86 in May of that year, when he announced that he would resign in June, McCarthy was ready. "I was very serious about running at that time." She remembered clearly the difficulty of getting to leadership meetings all over the province "at all hours of the day or night when Expo was on. I would leave my home in the morning, go to some breakfast for Expo, run over to Expo itself and welcome some dignitary or introduce them on the stage, then run back to the car and drive out to Langley for some meeting." She called it a great summer and also one of the worst. As provincial secretary in charge of protocol for Expo, "every visiting fireman was my special case." She kept all the balls in the air, but had little time for the leadership. "If it wasn't a plot, it certainly could have been."

"Then almost a right-wing wave seized the process. Bill Vander Zalm put his name up fairly late, but he's an exceptional campaigner. We were neck and neck for a little while, but with a few machinations at the convention, which, to be honest, I have never been a part of," Vander Zalm won the leadership.

"But when the race was over—and some of the political knives came out in the process—there was no bitterness in me." She said to her husband the next day, "If I had won at my age, I would have killed myself working to put three terms into every one and also find a successor. It's just my nature." So BC had a premier doing a great job, she said. "I think I have my health today because of that."

In the 1991 leadership race McCarthy stood without the benefit of cabinet prestige as she had resigned from Vander Zalm's cabinet in 1988. When she ran for the leadership in 1993, "we were out of government and I fell into the trap of being persuaded that I was the only one who could save the party. Without being egotistical, there was nobody on the horizon, and I ran more for the party's sake than for my own. By then I was very tired of the political process." There was no salary and McCarthy claimed very few expenses. She ran in the Matsqui by-election of 1994 and virtually financed her own campaign, but she lost by forty-two votes to a Liberal newcomer.

McCarthy said that, during the time she was leader, she constantly questioned the wisdom of carrying on as Social Credit and made it clear that she would agree to other approaches to assure the representation of free enterprise views in the legislature. Midway through the Matsqui campaign she discussed this poser with Weisgerber who, as house leader, assured her the caucus was all behind her and that she should carry on with all efforts to win the by-election for the Socreds. Within six days, she read in the newspapers that Weisgerber and two of the other six caucus members had defected to the Reform Party of BC. Within two months, a fourth member had also defected to Reform; another resigned four months later to run in a mayoralty race. Only one stalwart Socred remained in the legislature.

Grace McCarthy first became an MLA in 1966. After a stint as Social Credit party president and five terms as MLA, she contested the party leadership in 1986 when she finally felt she had "the depth of experience" she needed. *UBC Special Collections 35-2-53.*

"Machinations had gone on," she explained, so shortly after the by-election she sat down and wrote out a resignation, called a press conference at the party headquarters and left. "I thought, I've had enough. I don't owe anything to any of these people, so why am I sitting up nights writing out plans, visions for mining, visions for forestry? Phoning friends in business asking, 'If you had this situation, what would you do?'" There were endless meetings, and she tried to keep together a "disgruntled bunch of people who honestly didn't know anything about politics or the process." Instead of helping the party to have credibility, they were destroying it. "So I decided I was better away from it." That was 1994, "and I never looked back. From one day to the next I was out of politics." Her party was by that time essentially non-existent, its place taken by the Liberals.

People throughout the province of all political persuasions have admired Joy MacPhail as leader of the provincial New Democratic Party after 2001 in the legislature, where she and Jenny Kwan were the sole opposition to seventy-seven Liberals. She was never officially leader of her party or of the legislature's official opposition, even though she served for two and a half years as interim leader. With the first all-woman caucus in BC, she stood her ground and won her share of battles against a feisty new Liberal government. Rita Johnston told me in our interview, "I watched those two gals, Joy and Jenny, and I think they're holding their own. They come well prepared, but they haven't a hope. They're so outnumbered that it's not even funny."

Prominent NDP feminist Hilda Thomas was also enthusiastic, although she admitted to not having been a particular MacPhail supporter. "I thought Joy should be wafted up to heaven on the wings of angels! She was asked to do the work of fourteen people, and she did it with style and panache and effectiveness."

MacPhail entered the leadership race when the NDP needed to replace Premier Glen Clark after his resignation in 2000—also under a cloud, in his case criminal charges of which he was later cleared—but she withdrew before the vote. "I was completely devastated by my inability to garner any support from the caucus and to overcome the massive membership sign-up of the Indo-community that Ujjal Dosanjh conducted. . . . While I was able to raise lots and lots of money and had support among young people and women, it was clear I wasn't going to become leader." MacPhail had been cautioned not to run because "you'll just be the next Rita Johnston or Kim Campbell." She said, "I withdrew and threw my support behind Dosanjh. So there's irony in that I'm leader of the party now, while Dosanjh became the next Johnston-Campbell."

When the party won only two seats in the 2001 election, MacPhail was named interim leader. Despite urging by party members, the executive chose not to have a leadership convention until nearly three years later, leaving MacPhail working as interim leader. As well, the legislative speaker chose not to use his considerable powers to go around the understanding that you need four members for a party to be officially recognized in the legislature, so she did not get the administrative support due an official opposition leader. However, from her experience in some of the most difficult portfolios of government—social services, health, education, labour, finance and deputy premier—MacPhail played hardball with the twenty-one ministers and seven parliamentary secretaries in Gordon Campbell's Liberal cabinet. MacPhail took comfort from her work. "I know for a fact that Gordon Campbell doesn't say 'She's just a woman.' Not to me. Not anymore."

Nevertheless, she told me in May 2002, "I consider it a huge honour to be the leader of the opposition and leader of the NDP. I'm going to spend all my time rebuilding the party so we don't go the way the Socreds went, but I don't think I'll run again." Why not? "It sounds weird, but I don't want to be premier. This province is polarized. It requires a new kind of leadership with youthful, new, fresh ideas. So that will have to come from someone else."

When the party announced its leadership convention, MacPhail—with wide public respect for what she had achieved—announced she would not run. With Kwan she had rebuilt the party membership, kept the Liberals at bay in the house and brought the party to virtual equity in the polls with the Liberals.

Common political wisdom says that women get the opportunity to become leaders when there is not a lot of competition for the position within a marginal party or for a major party at the bottom of a curve. Shirley McLoughlin, the first woman party leader in BC, led the Liberals from 1981–83, and Susan Power led the provincial Progressive Conservatives for a year from 2001, both marginal parties at the time. Neither party had elected an MLA between 1975 and 1991, but the Conservatives still have no member in the provincial assembly. The best-known marginal party leader, Adrienne Carr, took the leadership of the BC Green Party in 2000 but announced in the fall of 2006 that she would resign. Lisa Maskell became leader of Western Reform in 2003. Neither party has elected a member, although Carr, whose party held about 10 percent of the provincial vote, participated in the 2005 pre-election leaders' debates. When Carr resigned in 2006, she was replaced a year later by Jane Sterk, a party veteran.

Carole James staked new ground as the first woman leader elected by a revitalized major party heading into an election in which it was expected to compete strongly. In 2005 she led her party back to a significant position as an opposition of thirty-three and also initiated a change in the atmosphere of the legislature. Although James came from a family of activists—"We spent a lot of our childhood on protest lines during the Vietnam War, and we were a safe house for draft dodgers during that war"—and her mother ran provincially for the NDP in 1970, she became a political party member only at thirty-two in 1989, when she joined the NDP.

When her children started school, she became involved with the parent associations and then was persuaded onto the Victoria school board in 1990, where she served as trustee and then chair until 2001. In

1995 she was elected president of the BC School Trustees Association and served an unmatched five years in that position. In 2001 she ran for provincial office but lost.

During the 1990s James discovered that her father was Metis. That discovery changed her sense of self and affected her commitment to many of the children she had fostered and the work she did as a child care administrator. In 2002 she resigned as provincial director of child care policy—"I was making myself physically ill, staying in a position with a government that was so opposed to anything I believed in"—and moved to Prince George where she served as director of child and family services for the Carrier–Sekani tribal council.

Carole James greets two Go Go Grannies sponsored on their Canadian visit by the Stephen Lewis Foundation. The Grannies work with thousands of orphans created by the HIV/AIDS pandemic in Africa. *Courtesy Carole James' office.*

When she won the leadership of the NDP in November of 2003, she moved back to Victoria but opted to stay free of the legislature, rebuilding party support by travelling across the province until the election scheduled for 2005. She did not contest a 2004 by-election in Surrey. "It would have been the right thing for a profile but the wrong thing for the people of the community," she told Gordon Hamilton of the *Vancouver Sun*.[87] She had the competent MacPhail in the legislature, and as Vaughn Palmer inelegantly put it, "James keeps her hands clean outside the house, knowing that MacPhail, and all of her baggage, will be packed off at the next election."[88] But James also benefited from the anxiety of the Liberal government members, who kept complaining about her absence from the legislature. "'Keep mentioning her name,' MacPhail taunted this week," Palmer reported, "as the Liberals shoehorned James into speech after speech."

Being NDP leader was not something James had planned. When MacPhail announced her resignation, party members started calling. "I took some time for serious thought so I could make an informed decision. I talked to the elders I was working with, and I took a weekend away in the woods in the middle of absolutely nowhere to spend more time thinking." By Sunday morning she had decided that she would. "I'd had experiences up north that had shown me in so many ways what the government had done and what the changes were doing to people who were already struggling, already living in poverty. I knew I'd regret it if I didn't."

James went right to work. "It was a time in our party's history when there was a chance to focus on the direction we needed to go to continue the work that Jenny and Joy had done around the province. It was such an exciting opportunity." Her years in public service made her confident that she could bring diverse groups together and organize the changes that the party needed. She had settled on a direction that she took into the campaign. "I was the only woman in the race, and I didn't know if the party was ready for a woman leader. My lack of experience in the legislature was a weakness to some people. So I knew that there would be great challenges, but I went into the race as hard as I could." James won the leadership 395 to 215 on the second ballot in a field of six.

The background she needed to be leader came largely from "the experience of working in those northern communities and knowing the diversity in our province, the needs and the differences and the strengths that are out there."

Even with seven former MLAs tempered in the fierce confrontation of the legislature in her own caucus, and a government party that had run untrammelled during the past session, she was able to broker an agreement with Premier Gordon Campbell that resulted in an accord amongst all members to curtail the abusive mood of the chamber. Asked in 2006 what was her greatest achievement so far, she said, "I would say changing the tone of politics in BC." Her party faced some tough partisan issues in her first session of the legislature. "We took on the issues. We were tough on the government, and yet we were able to keep a civil tone in the legislature." The response on the hustings was not positive, however. "The pundits thought the 2005 election campaign was boring. I think the press hasn't caught up with the new direction of politics. You can be tough without throwing mud at each other."

The parliamentary pyramid leaves her in the apex position, with all its drawbacks as well as its benefits. Although James likes consensus decisions, she maintains a leader's veto. "The important thing is to tell caucus that, to be up front."

And James would like to be premier. "I wouldn't have taken this job on if I hadn't seen that as a goal. The more time I spend in opposition, the more driven I am to win because I see where the opportunities are and when they could do it better."

Two women MLAs have bid for leadership of provincial parties without success. Linda Reid, a Liberal since her high school days and a participant in the BC Youth Parliament—once youth premier—became an MLA in 1991. She had worked with the Liberal Party in campaigns and was part of the small group that helped Gordon Wilson rebuild the Liberal Party to become the official opposition in 1991. When Wilson resigned the leadership, Reid joined the competition that floated Gordon Campbell to the top. "There were six men and Linda," she recalled. "I finished dead centre, the Liberal position."

I asked Reid why she ran in 1993. She said, "It was my party. I had a mission to see that certain issues were debated: health, children's health, childhood development. I think I succeeded famously in that we came to government, and those issues are still getting attention." But marriage and the birth of two children dictates that she won't run again for leadership. "It's way too important to me to not take away any more time than I'm taking now."

Joan Smallwood was one of three rivals to Glen Clark for the leadership of the NDP after the December 1995 resignation of Mike Harcourt. Smallwood had not planned to run. "The office was never where I was going. The issues were. It was about standing up and being counted. I disagreed with the direction that the party and people like Glen were headed. So I just felt bound to run."

Smallwood was blunt about what she learned. "Running for the leadership of the party, especially when you're in government, is coming up against an incredible power bloc. People who supported me were told that if they wanted to work again in the province, they'd better get away from our campaign. There were people in community groups supporting me who had their funding threatened." When challenged on such strong accusations, she insisted, "Absolutely. This was the big leagues, and this was big muscle. We went in thinking that we would show at least twice as well as we did, but people had to back away." I pressed Smallwood for details, but her response was a long silence, then, "There were a lot of deals made. I didn't make a deal."

BC WOMEN WHO RAN FOR LEADERSHIP OF BC OR CANADIAN POLITICAL PARTIES

Date	Name	Action	Date Out
1975	Rosemary Brown	ran for federal NDP leader	
1981	Shirley McLoughlin	BC Liberal leader	1983
1989	Audrey McLaughlin	Federal NDP leader	1995
1991	Rita Johnston	BC Social Credit leader	1991
1993	Kim Campbell	federal Progressive Conservative leader	1993
1993	Grace McCarthy	BC Social Credit leader	1994
1993	Linda Reid	ran for BC Liberals	
1995	Alexa McDonough	Federal NDP leader	2002
1996	Joan Smallwood	ran for BC NDP	
2000	Adrienne Carr	BC Green Party leader	2006
2001	Susan Power	BC Progressive Conservative leader	2002
2001	Joy MacPhail	BC NDP leader (interim)	2003
2002	Bev Meslo	ran for federal NDP leader	
2003	Lisa Maskell	Western Reform leader	
2003	Carole James	BC NDP leader	
2004	Connie Fogal	Canadian Action Party leader	
2006	Elizabeth May	leader Green Party Canada	
2007	Jane Sterk	BC Green Party leader	

Joyce Murray, who was encouraged to run at the Women's Campaign School, advises interested women to decide yes, and then "go out with a yes-I-can attitude." Murray has sat in both the legislature and Parliament. *Photo courtesy Patrick Tam/FlungingPictures.com*

WHERE TO?

Shine in a Dark Place

"I do not want to pull through life like a thread that has no knot," said Nellie McClung, Canadian political pioneer. "I want to leave something behind when I go; some small legacy of truth, some word that will shine in a dark place."[89]

BC women with similar motivation have embroidered a fine mosaic of legislation and social change. They expressed pride in having helped to make things happen in their assemblies, their constituencies and their province and country. All of the women I interviewed were proud of having achieved progress for women, children and other groups of small influence. What also stuck in most of their minds was their success in promoting and getting funding for certain projects or in addressing broadly consequential issues for the country or the province. On a personal level they spoke of keeping in touch with themselves—not selling out to the system—and nurturing family and friends, and they celebrated their faithfulness to collaborative ways of reaching decisions.

Opportunities to foster gender equity have never been hard to find. When Mary Collins became the associate defence minister, the Human Rights Commission ruled within her first week that women must have equal access to all jobs and occupations in the Canadian Forces. "Everybody wanted to appeal it, including the military and my senior minister. And I knew that we couldn't appeal it." Collins believed the resistance was nothing but hot air, so she went about gathering enough support through the PM's office that no appeal was made. "They were just going to have to live with the new equity."

Most women who won equality issues worked with groups of

other women. Sue Hammell, a former BC minister of women's equality, cited the Minerva Foundation as an achievement she treasures. "It's not government-based; it's a community-based foundation whose mandate is to use the economic strength of women to develop their potential, to participate economically, to provide opportunities and training for young women as well as other women, but to focus on young women, and to deal somewhat with issues of safety." She called her contribution "synthesizing the desire of women to start the Minerva Foundation."

Pauline Jewett's former assistant said she would have been proud of her role in getting the constitutional Charter of Rights to recognize sexual equality. Jewett worked with a whole movement of women, but in the House she personally "broke the taboo of pushing that forward."

Using her position as Speaker, Joan Sawicki got action from institutions. "Gender may have actually allowed me to bring about progressive change not otherwise possible. Our being in situations that are traditionally male signals that this is not the status quo." When she assumed the Speaker's office, the institution "expected and braced for something different." In the end they embraced some long-overdue administrative changes that Sawicki—and even the clerks—considered significant.

Similarly, at the Commonwealth Parliamentary Association, where Sawicki was the only woman on a fifteen-member governing body, she used her position to resurrect the languishing Commonwealth Parliamentary Women's Group (CPWG) that had been relegated to holding its business meetings after general meetings while the men were already enjoying cocktails. The women were treated like visitors. The reality of Sawicki being the only woman at the executive table created the embarrassment needed to get the constitution changed to formalize the CPWG and to ensure its work was scheduled into the official agenda at all CPA annual meetings.

"One of the things I did that probably had the greatest impact on the system," said Pat Carney, "was to set up a task force on Barriers to Women in the Public Service," whose report was subtitled *Beneath the Veneer*. When Carney looked at management in her ministries—both energy and international trade—she found no women in the entry levels. "You can't have women deputy ministers unless you have women assistant deputy ministers and directors general, and I found they were not in the system. The figures show this task force did cause systemic change."

Elizabeth Cull prized her initiative of taking the decision out of the hands of hospital boards on whether or not their hospitals would do abortions. As local societies ran the hospitals, anti-abortionists had been taking over the elected boards and blocking access to abortions, contrary to a Supreme Court ruling that abortion should not be denied a woman with a doctor's referral.

BC's first woman minister of education, Tilly Rolston, revised the school tax system to better equalize rural and urban contributions with a formula that remained the basis of school taxation for decades. She was also well-known for getting legislation to allow the colouring of margarine. The butter substitute became popular during World War II when butter was rationed. Her daughter Amy's notes on the family said, "Tilly was responsible for the famous 'Margarine Bill' making BC the first province after Newfoundland [which was not yet a province] to have coloured margarine. Heretofore, due to a regulation enforced [to gratify] the dairy industry, margarine had been white. Now one could mix a yellow coloured tablet into it, a very messy business."

When she made a speech Rolston demonstrated the "messy business" by breaking a bead of bright orange food dye into a pound of oleo margarine, stirring until the glob went beyond streaky orange-yellow-white and finally wrestling it to a uniform medium-bright orange. The demonstration always had the whole audience involved. The product still didn't resemble butter, but at least it no longer looked like lard. Rolston's grandson Peter said his grandmother "had a hard time getting men's support for this one," since they considered it inconsequential.

Eileen Dailly, BC's second woman education minister, said, "I couldn't believe it when I arrived in 1966 that all the pages running around were boys. When I brought it up in one of my first speeches, the laughter was unbelievable—the hooting! Old Bennett called across the floor to me, 'And what are they going to wear?' because the boys wore long pants. It was incredible. We couldn't do a thing about it then, but in 1972 when the NDP came in, one of the first things Speaker Gordon Dowding did was engage girl pages." Dailly also put no-fee kindergartens into the school system, set up regional colleges and established the first First Nations school district. The latter was for the Nisga'a people, and she smiled when she reported that the Nisga'a high school had a "white club."

But Dailly is most renowned for banning the strap in schools, which she called her most satisfying achievement. Disallowing corporal

BC's second education minister, Eileen Dailly, was best known for outlawing the strap in schools, but she also introduced no-fee kindergarten, set up regional colleges and established a First Nations school district—whose students set up a "white club." *Image I-25347 courtesy of Royal BC Musem, BC Archives.*

punishment, she said, "set a whole tone that was in keeping with the philosophy of most of our members and our party that violence breeds violence." It was contradictory to try to teach children not to hit anybody when teachers were hitting them, and Dailly, a former teacher, knew it didn't work. "Most of the kids who were punished either had learning disabilities or came from homes where they were always in trouble, and all they were used to was getting hit. They needed help, not being strapped." The legislation was highly controversial, and Dailly was "proud and pleased that it still stands. Young parents today wouldn't put up with strapping—at least I doubt they would."

But both Dailly and Premier Dave Barrett were surprised by the public reaction. "The hate mail was unbelievable. I was going to be responsible for all the delinquency in British Columbia. Even today I get some older people telling me, 'You did the wrong thing removing that strap.'" The caucus—except for a few members—was behind her, and Barrett gave his complete support. "But even Dave said he had no idea there would be so much mail." BC became the first province in Canada to put a corporal punishment ban into provincial legislation. Later, at an international meeting of education ministers, the chair asked the most controversial measure each minister had experienced. Dailly said, "Removal of the strap." The minister for education in Bavaria, "which many of us think rather Spartan, said, 'You mean to say that in Canada you still use corporal punishment in the schools?'"

Camille Mather faced a house in uproar when she drew attention to the situation at Jericho Hill School. "It was barren and dirty. I don't think the windows had ever been washed—that sort of thing. Lack of care, lack of thought." Despite the mocking uproar that ensued in the chamber, "Something was done: the government committed up to a million dollars for two new buildings."

When Joy MacPhail took over the portfolio of children and families, a storm was brewing over a new adoption act that allowed adopted children to search for their birth parents and vice versa. "It was very controversial," she said, "but it was so important, and we ended up as a government bringing in the most modern law, one that's emulated around the world. It's unheralded by the broader public, but I still run into people whose lives have been changed for the better by that legislation." Margaret Lord, who was parliamentary secretary to MacPhail and active in making that act happen, saw that it made a difference in the lives of a lot of people. "That was the type of thing I don't think any other government is going to tear apart; it needed to be done."

When Grace McCarthy served as social services minister, as the position was then called, she created the Help Line for Children, the first in Canada. "That had never been done before. Then the Canadian government took it on and several jurisdictions in the US."

Seatbelt legislation for children was crucial to Rosemary Brown. "I had worked on the brain-damage ward as a social worker, so I had seen the damage when children were thrown around inside a car. When the legislation was introduced and it didn't include children on the grounds that parents should be free to make that decision, I was very upset." Brown fought this issue as an opposition member and eventually got legislation.

The Grandparents' Rights Amendment Act was one of Linda Reid's proud deeds. "Grandparents had no standing in the courts. Judges didn't even have to acknowledge them. These little darlings are entitled to a relationship with their grandparents whether the parents are divorced or not," said Reid. In opposition, Reid "talked to everybody about it in every corner of the chamber" until the legislation was introduced and passed.

In a private member's bill, Val Meredith tried to get legislation so that government could "designate as dangerous offenders—so they would not be let out—prisoners who are already incarcerated." She pointed out that the party in power "won't pass a private member's bill and give somebody else the credit, but they will take the idea and work it into their own legislation. If you want the change more than the recognition, then you've accomplished something." Government legislation on declaring dangerous offenders was changed, and "the bill included changes to how children's testimony was given and received."

Anita Hagen demanded attention for seniors. "I was the first person I know of in elected office" to insist that issues of older people—social and health policy as it affected them—be discussed in the legislature. As well, she was proud of "some real progress in human rights" under her ministry. To ensure inclusiveness when her government formed the Human Rights Commission, "we established a bottom-up multicultural committee with a well-formulated procedure for nominations to come from the breadth of the multicultural community."

To Hedy Fry, "the last place of legislated inequality in this country" involved homosexuals. She was proud to have been part of "the move to same-sex equality, . . . where same-sex couples are treated under the law the same as heterosexual common-law couples. We first got sexual orientation in the human rights act and then we got to modernization of benefits and immigration."

Inequality of First Nations drew Darlene Marzari to "put natives into the Heritage Conservation Act so spiritual sites were in the act"—even though it became law after she had moved to another ministry. And Jenny Kwan was eloquent about the Nisga'a Treaty, which had been in negotiation since 1909 but became a fact in 2000. "I have never experienced anything quite like that where the caucus came together. At the end of the day, even though it might not have been good for them to support it because their

Anita Hagen greets Ray Worley at a sod-turning for seniors' housing at Queen's Park Care Centre, New Westminster. *Photo courtesy Anita Hagen.*

constituents might have had a different point of view or have thought that aboriginal people don't deserve the negotiations that came with the Treaty, people voted what they thought was right." Joe Gosnell, Chief of the Nis'ga Tribal Council, came to the house and spoke at the bar, telling how his people had come before and been refused, and now history had changed. "For this one moment in time—if I die tomorrow, I have made change."

Caring for constituents is never easy and seldom attention-getting, but Karen Sanford said, "Even though the constituency was huge and it took me weeks to cover it, people still refer to the fact that they could always count on me to do whatever was possible to help them through the bureaucracy or the red tape." Jackie Pement's goal was "better representation" for her constituents. "My personal big issue was getting a voice from the North heard. I feel I did do that." Meredith put a priority on keeping in touch with her constituents and prided herself on her "two-way line of communication between the people I represent and myself—my newsletter."

"A grassroots activist," Libby Davies called herself, and she kept in close touch with the people she represented. As an elected representative for more than thirty years, she had instincts about politics that came from outside her party. "Working with social movements over the years I've watched big gulfs and barriers develop between electoral politics and social movement politics—the NDP as a political institution and other organizations. I feel fairly good about being able to minimize some of those differences and help people find a way to become engaged in the political process." Kim Campbell also broke down barriers, which she saw as "in some ways my greatest success as prime minister."

Sophia Leung said her motto was "serving the community." For one thing, she sat as the only Liberal from the West on the Finance Committee. "A lot of people from the West can't handle the travel. The load is like two committees," partly because BC has proportionately so few MPs.

Involving constituents in decisions felt good. MacPhail remarked, "My greatest achievement in my constituency was moving the PNE—which is a provincial heritage institution—to Surrey," leaving the Vancouver property available for a park. The whole community worked as one, and "I was able to hold back the forces of evil in our provincial government to allow the park to become a reality." The PNE still operates on the Hastings Park property, but the grounds—and the activities of the fair—decreased significantly, leaving room for development of a park on the site.

Marzari too worked whenever she could within a consultative, consensual model. "I stuck with my values about process—I lived them out. The municipal Growth Management Act set up a framework for regional planning in the province. I did it in a participatory way. It could have been imposed. But I had the time—two and one-half years in the job as minister of municipal affairs—to get on with setting up a planning process for settled, urban communities."

Getting a plum for their own constituency gave members a rush too. As Rita Johnston said, "Winning the leadership was probably the greatest highlight, but I guess the most memorable accomplishment was getting SkyTrain out to Whalley." Brenda Locke fought hard to keep the university that her government threatened to close in Surrey. "It was a hard battle to fight—in our caucus as well, but I had the support of Shirley Bond, minister of advanced education, who was proud that she could save this uneconomic project." Lord prized "the six or seven parks and wildlife reserves I was able to convince the government to set aside in my community. When I see them, that's my reward." And Ida Chong worked on "the cemetery owned by the Chinese Benevolent Society—my godfather was involved in that. I had promised him to keep the issue alive and see what could be done." Official ribbon cuttings took place in 2001.

Two municipal politicians remember work they did as mayors. Susan Brice said, "When I came in as mayor there were twenty-four beaches posted unsafe for swimming. By the time I left, there were none. Liquid waste management became my life." Betty Hinton's best achievement was "taking on the provincial government" when she was the mayor and achieving a boundary extension for Logan Lake. "I worked with Rita Johnston, minister of municipal affairs, and we played some pretty hard poker games. She's very good at it. It was an idea that came, I guess, because I think differently than male politicians."

Canada's favourite political topic, health care, was important for several women. Cull is proud she "tried to launch health care reform, but I regret it didn't complete. I still watch and I see current health minister Colin Hansen making some of the same mistakes I made. Ministers need more time." When Collins became minister of health federally, an election was imminent, which meant she held the post only three months. So she focussed, and decided what would make the biggest difference was a commission into tainted blood in the country's blood banks. "There was huge resistance to having a royal commission concurrent with a change of leadership after Prime Minister Brian Mulroney had retired, so I was fighting. I was certainly fighting provincial ministers who weren't all that happy. But I felt it was right, and I established the Kriever commission," which recommended changes that have made Canada's blood supply safer from disease transmission via blood transfusion. Provincially McCarthy was proud to have closed institutions for the mentally handicapped. "Mentally handicapped people no longer are in Tranquille, they no longer are locked up in Woodlands."

Some successes came despite enormous opposition. Daphne Jennings "saved lacrosse as a national sport." Nelson Riis had introduced a private member's bill to make hockey the national sport, and Jennings's caucus wanted to support the Riis bill. "I was the only one fighting for lacrosse, and I thought I was going to lose." Jennings, whose brother-in-law was lacrosse great Jack Bionda, had just ten minutes to speak in a one-hour debate. The Canadian Lacrosse Association backed Jennings and helped frame her speech laying out how much of hockey originated as lacrosse, which had been named in 1859 as Canada's national sport. "I said, 'They're both wonderful sports, but lacrosse should be our national heritage and it is already our Native heritage.'" When a Liberal member proposed a compromise—lacrosse our summer game, hockey our winter game—she got the approval of the association and agreed. "So anyway it won."

Voting hours in BC were controversial for years before Anna Terrana engineered a change that reduced the time difference in reporting election results across Canada. Her private member's bill to change the hours on election day died on the order paper when Parliament was adjourned, so she introduced it a second time. When it was finally drawn and debated, "it went through second reading in forty-five minutes and was put into a government omnibus bill." In consequence voting hours are staggered across the country. "It was a great experience," said Terrana.

Val Roddick simply said, "I really have remained me." Keeping in touch with oneself is difficult when living in the public eye, with opinions and support being asked from all sides at all times—in the virtual war zone—and there is a temptation to do it the easy way by giving simple answers that don't fully reflect one's feelings. As Hagen put it, "Greater than my other accomplishments, I could live with myself during all the time I was in public office." And April Sanders said, "My integrity remained intact. I won't say that that didn't cost me along the way at both the community level and at the party level, but I did not get myself into positions where I asked for support on issues I did not think were right."

"How do you learn about what you're capable of unless you learn to survive your own stupidity?" mused Kim Campbell. "That's probably my greatest success." She was also proud of surviving without becoming a cynic.

Sharon Hayes resigned on a Monday and was home Wednesday watching Parliament on TV when Preston Manning, leader of the Reform Party, "stood and explained why I had resigned and that I had stood up for family. Then Prime Minister Jean Chrétien expressed his appreciation for what I stood for, and he said he appreciated that [her husband] Doug had always sent me the corsage that I wore. And then from the NDP and finally from the Conservatives—a beautiful tribute to my stand for family issues. That was a gift to me across party lines that maybe I left a mark."

Susan Brice said, "I went into municipal politics in 1975—great husband, great kids, good friends. I came out in 1991 with the same great husband, great kids and good friends. I consider that a success in my personal life." And Christy Clark took "some pride in the fact that I have been able to manage the birth of my first child while carrying two cabinet appointments, because that's been much harder than I'd predicted it would be. I know a lot of women have babies while they are working outside the home, but I'm sure that most think their children are their greatest accomplishment, and for me that's true."

I suggested to Rosemary Brown that she might be proud of having been a role model for younger—and older—women. "Yes. Lots of people say they don't want to be. I never had that feeling. I knew that I was not an island unto myself, that a lot of other people were watching me and looking to me to set an example. I'm very honoured to be a role model, but at the same time humbled by the experience."

WASHING THE DISHES, EVERY SINGLE DAY

Nearly all the women I interviewed found satisfaction and real enjoyment in serving as assembly members, but their responses were hedged with warnings to watch out for bugs in the salad. For one thing, although they came to political life brimming with ideas for change and enthusiasm to work on it, they discovered that change is not only hard but slow. If they were to achieve it, they had to learn persistence, focus, perspective and how to listen closely and then communicate ideas to the public.

"Right from the beginning I learned how to have a fairly thick skin," said Val Meredith in summing up her three terms as an MP following a career in municipal politics. "I've learned over the years how to somewhat protect my personal life and that of my friends and family from my public life. That it's a very enjoyable way to contribute to society, that there are some real benefits to it, some real feelings of accomplishment, a sense of community. You get to meet some very, very good people who feel committed to their country and want to participate in the process. So more than anything, I've learned that public service can be a very positive thing if you manage it properly."

Sharon Hayes commented on the gap between ordinary events and the way they are presented to the public. "Everything has been massaged to look like something"—not necessarily something else, but something noteworthy. Penny Priddy said, "I learned that nothing is as easy as it looks, that there is an incredible gap between the perception of what a minister or even a government can do and what they really can do. An even greater perception gap exists about MLAs." To address the problem, members must have a clear, consistent message, because unless they tell people, they may never know even the "really good things" they've done. People can't always figure out what members are saying, maybe because of oversimplification or overcomplication, both of which happen. "The need to be consistent in talking about what you're doing while you're doing it has an importance that I probably hadn't attached to it so strongly before."

Ida Chong said, "School kids once asked me, 'What's the most important quality for a politician to have?' I told them 'The ability to listen. The people tell politicians what to do, so we have to listen.'" Listening to the public led her to greater trust.

But "no matter what you do, you are in for criticism from somebody," Katherine Whittred noted. "Some people say you have to have a bit of a thick skin. Well I guess that's true, but if you can defend what you're doing, that it is sound and right, then you're on solid ground." Change is difficult, and the barriers include inertia, lack of money and people saying they've always done things another way. "You just have to keep hammering ahead."

Wendy McMahon agreed. "The number one thing is to keep on plugging away, keep on raising the issue, keep on it, keep it in front of people." And Erda Walsh said, "If you sat back and assumed that just because you went and saw somebody in Victoria once that you were going to get anything, uh-uh, you're dreaming. I learned that you had to make a pest of yourself." Sheila Orr said that she learned "incredible patience," and Gillian Trumper advised, "You've got to be able to ride with the ups and the downs of things. You can't fold."

If they do achieve a difficult change, politicians soon learn they cannot win an issue and assume it will stay won. A line from the chorus of a song in an old trade union film came back to Joy Langan: "And every generation has to learn it again." Langan said, "I had that reconfirmed from watching politics and learning more about being a working woman, seeing a lot of history and now seeing it repeating itself. We're having to win medicare again nationally. We're having to win the right to maintain control over hydro in BC, for example, and water—we're having to fight those fights again," not just once but twice every generation. Langan believed we're not vigilant enough or good at making sure those who follow us appreciate what they've got. "We don't teach our kids what we've achieved." Joan Smallwood observed that "democracy is delicate. It needs constant rebuilding," and Rosemary Brown said,

"Fighting for equality is like washing the dishes—you've got to keep on it every single day."[90]

Brown found that learning "how much power backbenchers have made my life very exciting." Brown was never offered a cabinet position in the 1972–75 government headed by Premier Dave Barrett, although she was an excellent politician. A powerful ex-cabinet minister told me that this was because she was too focussed on the issues of women, that she saw things in a "narrow, ideological way" that other MLAs didn't share because she thought in terms of "women's rights" instead of being a "whole person." But Brown persistently fought from the backbench for important issues such as changing sexist language in school text-books and getting more women and more people of visible minorities appointed by government to boards and commissions. Her basic instinct told her that fighting for women's share in a society that ignored or of-fended women's rights was important to everyone, not just women.

Being persistent taught Jenny Kwan an important lesson. Kwan, who has sat on both government and opposition sides of the legislature and is young, ethnically different than most British Columbians and a woman, said, "Because I've experienced so many times when someone tries so hard to silence you—what I've learned has really reinforced that my voice counts." Daphne Jennings also learned the value of a single voice. "I learned that I was important, and now I can speak out if I feel it's necessary."

Along with the persistence necessary to make change, women members found they needed focus. "You had to decide what it was you really wanted to do," said Mary Collins, "had to set some very specific goals, particularly as a cabinet minister." Otherwise public servants would keep you busy so your time would be dissipated, and you'd never really accomplish anything. If you don't focus on what you want done, said Lynn Stephens, "you're not going to be happy here. You have to be doing this job because you want to accomplish something."

But focus needs perspective. "Every person who sat around those tables for two, three, four years came to understand perspective," said Joan Sawicki. "Dan Miller and I may have disagreed on every single thing, but I understand his perspective better than I ever would have if I hadn't had that experience. Other people's perspectives are valid, and I now try to present issues in a way they will relate to."

"There are so many really genuine people on all sides of the fence," said Christy Clark. By the end of her career, her responses were "a lot less personal and a lot more about ideas. I've learned to separate the two." As Brenda Locke put it, "You learn to make your way around an issue—not in the negative sense. It's like a puzzle. You've got to try to put it together all the time."

That kind of thinking softens edges. "Things I thought were black and white became grey when I looked at things from all sides," said Lois Boone. "And, even if your policy is clear to you, it's hard to implement it clearly."

Gaining perspective enhanced Chong's sense of citizenship. "I learned about democracy. I know better what my rights are. I have a greater respect for politicians, a greater respect and admiration for our rights and constitution." Chong added that now she always sings the national anthem—well, maybe not every time, she allowed, but she pays attention. "I'm a better citizen, and I thank the people who elected me for that."

Margaret Mitchell, who had spent several years working abroad, "changed as a human being. I developed a much wider understanding, not only of Canada, but of the world." And Hedy Fry said, "I would not have known the plight of the indigenous people, in Canada and around the world. I would not have known what a remarkable group of young people we have nor met a huge number of women around the world who struggle every day for things we take for granted here as women." Women are still bought and sold in some places in the world. Children are working at the age of ten, married at the age of twelve. Now she has met them, not just read about them in a book. "I would not have met so many people who love this country and struggle every day to survive and maintain a sense of being Canadian. I found my Canadian roots from politics and learned really what it meant to be a Canadian."

However, the women also discovered how impatient the public could be. "We live in a disposable society," said Judi Tyabji Wilson, "and people are prepared to throw elected members away much too easily because they figure there's another one coming down the pike. It's like drive-through politics. People 'buy' a whole car-full of BC Liberals, and then get down the road and don't like them, so they chuck them out." People are too used to disposable or replaceable products, so they think that way about their government. "I had no idea how pervasive that thinking was."

Cathy McGregor became cynical about people's motivations and how they treated others. "It was very difficult to get used to being screamed at. I used to downplay it, but it was the most surprising thing how many people felt they had the right to decimate me as a person." On the other hand, she was "constantly amazed at what people do to help and support others. That's the other part of it—the humanity. The two ends of it. The organizations that work for peanuts to deliver services to important groups—seniors, kids, or women. The dedication those people put into their work, the hours they put into it. . . ."

A positive view of people in the community came as a gift to many of the women. Gretchen Mann Brewin observed, "Communities are great places, and the participants, the volunteers, are phenomenal." Wendy McMahon said, "There are a lot of great people out there, not just here in the riding but everywhere in the province. That's been a real plus." And Evelyn Gillespie remarked, "I know from some of the travelling committees that I've been on, there's a whole lot more in common around the province than not."

Margaret Mitchell "developed a much wider understanding, not only of Canada, but of the world." *Courtesy New Democratic Party.*

"The people, as a people, make mistakes," said Grace McCarthy, "but they can be trusted. I'm glad to have learned that collectively we're pretty smart—we the people."

In adapting to public life, women learned volumes about themselves. For one thing, they learned whether or not they were "political." Elizabeth Cull was. "Politics is my life whether I'm in it or not. Getting bitten by the political bug is like getting malaria: you're never cured— you're just in remission from time to time." Cull uses politics as the lens through which to view the world. "Political activity is one of the ways we make society work. It's the way to be involved, not just grumble around the coffee table and the water cooler." She sees the world in terms of power relationships: who's being served and who's not, who's marginalized and who's at the centre. "That's a whole world view. Others may look at it from an environmental or a First Nations point of view."

And Jan Pullinger knew she was a politician on her "watershed day" when the forest companies were organizing the grassroots to protest the Commission on Resources and Environment (CORE) process on Vancouver Island and bussed eighteen hundred loggers to the arena at Lake Cowichan. "The thing was stacked, and I was the target. I managed to turn that crowd, and that was the day I decided I would never be afraid on my feet again. Now I wouldn't be afraid to stand up in front of any crowd on any issue and do my bit."

Simma Holt was not political. She would loudly berate anyone who called her a politician. After one term, she asked herself, "Am I getting to like this job? Am I on a power trip or do I want to continue to serve?" Her conclusion: "I am a journalist. I will always be a journalist. I'm a reporter; I'm not even an author. My books are journalism." She has not regretted that she sat only one term.

All political women did things they had never expected they could. Besides learning to be humble about things she wished she'd done better but never managed, Anita Hagen became "a shrewder politician in terms of analyzing everything from motive to operational style." And Jackie Pement found she "learned to read people better, to understand different groupings of people that I had stereotyped in my own mind." Evelyn Gillespie offered an explanation. "When called to perform, you do what's necessary. And I haven't seen anybody in elected office who isn't capable of rising to that challenge."

Patty Sahota learned to be "a lot more careful," as did MacPhail, who said, "I had to learn that holding your tongue is often an effective vote. And pausing twenty-four hours on anything, as long as there would be no negative consequences to others, is always important."

Political experience cleared April Sanders's eyes. "I learned that I'm not the centre of the universe. It's a good lesson for people of my generation, the 'me society,' with the push for women to prove themselves—and basically kill themselves trying." She learned to see the big picture and recognized a lot of value for things she had been hostile to. She would never have considered being an at-home mother, for example, "and though I'm not now, I think that's a very hard job. In fact, it was too hard for me to even attempt." She has abandoned her "whole goal" of doing whatever guys have done—but better. No longer "particularly interested in having myself evaluated from an external mechanism that would pit me against some man and what he has done," she has developed better balance between her needs and the needs of those around her. "As a result, I'm quite a bit happier as an individual."

"You have big plans and visions, but the small things make the difference in the life of ordinary people," said Sindi Hawkins, who also related her lessons to family. "So don't take your private life for granted, your family and friendships." She made these comments even before she was diagnosed with leukemia and went through a long series of treatments, through which she was able to count on her family and friends.

In her five years in the legislature Carol Gran learned how important her family was. "I felt tremendous guilt when I realized how my husband had lived alone for five years," and her young teenaged kids probably needed her as much as when they were little. "Politics isn't my life. Here's my life, right here." It's "a wonderful thing," said Gran, that men are beginning to learn that about their jobs too.

Kwan, who had a baby in her second term, learned to really value her home, her family and even her dog. "When you are at the bottom, they are there to be supportive. A right decision or a wrong decision, they don't judge you. That is so valuable."

"Government is like family," said Priddy. "You have to make compromises, you have to put forward arguments, you have to be able to work with people and persuade them. In government as in family, the only power is in the collective." At the cabinet table, it was primarily a collective power—just because you were a minister, you didn't get to use all your power without agreement of the group. "That's an important lesson anywhere." And she learned strongly that governments are not all-powerful. "In some ways that's a very freeing notion, because it takes away some of the awe, if there's any left out there, for government."

GOOD SYSTEM,
COULD BE BETTER

"The party system works well," observed Sindi Hawkins. "We have used it for generations." She joined Pat Carney as an outspoken supporter of our democratic parliamentary system. "We have the most accessible political system in the world," said Carney. "Our biggest democratic asset and by far the most democratic freedom that Canadians enjoy is access to power. Anybody can run with minimum qualifications; they just need Canadian citizenship. You do not need a lot of money. Because of our federal laws, you can't buy a seat. In Vancouver Centre we could spend roughly a postage stamp per voter. So you have one of the cleanest systems, one of the most accessible systems in the world, and it's an honour to be elected." Lynn Stephens agreed, pointing out that in the USA "money needs would virtually eliminate people like me from even considering running for office," and preclude a good cross-section of the public as legislators.

Mary Collins has worked internationally since ending her political career. "We are so lucky in Canada," she said, "because basically, despite all its flaws and cracks, most decisions are made on the basis of what is perceived to be best for a broad spectrum of people, not just to serve a narrow interest. Most politicians are honest, and from what I'm seeing that is unusual in this world."

Rosemary Brown, who saw the system "in a whole different way" as a black woman, defended the system by saying politicians get bad reputations because "we're incompetent, for the most part," and every party makes bad decisions when they are government. Still, figuratively "throwing rocks at each other across the legislative floor is better than killing each other, which they do in other parts of the world, and what they used to do. Look at Israel, where they come to blows on the floor of the House. In Canada the issues that are being debated are very important for both sides of the House. Sometimes when feelings are running high, you don't stop to use the most correct grammar or the most polite way of expressing yourself. But you're not hitting each other; you're not hitting at each other. You're not pulling out your guns and shooting each other. I think it's one of the most civilized ways of dealing with very difficult issues anywhere in the world."

"Of course," she adds, "I was one of the worst offenders when I was there, so I'm probably rationalizing it. But I don't get upset about politicians screaming and yelling at each other, and I don't think the yelling is the basis of why people think politicians are terrible." Nobody would resist her daughter's marriage to a man because he had been called a scoundrel or a low-life. They resist someone who would take bribes—as would anyone. "But nobody remembers from one day to the other what one member called another across the floor unless it was funny." She cited the Newfoundland MP John Crosbie, who "used to say the most amazing things, but I don't know anybody who was ruined by anything he ever said. Our system is working. The people who don't stand up and shout sometimes don't feel passionately about anything."

I asked Brown if she subscribed to the axiom that power corrupts. "Very much so. It corrupts, but it doesn't have that wide corrupting influence it used to have or still has in some countries where democracy is not guarded as seriously as it is here. We have checks and balances. When a prime minister has to stand up and defend interfering with statutory boards [as former Prime Minister Jean Chrétien did in the Quebec sponsorship scandal], it makes a person think twice before getting into any kind of corrupting business. You don't have those checks and balances in some countries. So I don't think Canada will ever be as corrupt." And she concluded, "The system has a lot of flaws, but I don't know a better one."

Lynn Hunter also prefers our rough and ready assemblies to the political activities in some other countries. She remembered constituents visiting Parliament during a particularly raucous question period. The president of Mozambique was in the speaker's gallery that day, and one of her visitors said, "Well, I was just appalled," referring to what our Parliament would look like to a prestigious guest. Hunter said, "Their way of getting political attention is to nail women to trees and to cut their breasts off. That was during the RENAMO."[91] The visitor was astonished, and Hunter went on: "What we do in our Parliament isn't particularly nice, but it's far preferable to how some countries do it." Hunter believed we must get the public to realize that they're very well served by their representatives. She has travelled to a number of other countries to look at public institution building and concludes that "Canadians are very, very fortunate. We have all sorts of ways of expressing political dissent that are not available in other countries. We take our right to dissent for granted—and it shouldn't be. It's a really important freedom."

Joan Smallwood recalled having a conversation with Bob Skelly, former leader of her party, who said that "in other countries people are shot for what we do." "Like any democracy," Smallwood concluded, "we are on the cusp of the kind of discord we see in other countries. We think they aren't as sophisticated or civilized as we, but it hasn't a great deal to do with that. When you no longer can rely on your assembly, the power shifts back to the streets. And that's when you see violence." As a society we should understand that government collapse is a possibility. "I'd like people to understand more about how valuable democracy is and be more engaged to maintain it."

Despite these sincere votes of confidence for our system, many of the women suggested that our parliaments could use refurbishment. "It appalls me," Darlene Marzari said, "to see how our communities allow such corrupt, untransparent, idiotic systems to perpetuate themselves." The problems emerge "because you elect people to a position which you think has power to change things for the better and move your community into a better framework to make sure that your kids grow up healthy and don't get less than the best." Politicians can't produce, however, and for a really good reason: they operate inside a structure that isn't relevant to today's needs. But they are "unable under their party system to report out." They are forced into "this structure of bad guys, good guys—cutting the edge, dividing the middle, marginalizing the issues so that people will understand them in black and white." Without public consensus, the politicians are not capable of steering the ship, and they can't form consensus because the system fails to persuade people to discuss and to logically decide on the spending of taxpayers' dollars as long as they work within a hierarchy.

Sue Hammell also observed the difficulty of trying to work toward a consensus inside a pyramidal system. Before sitting on the backbench and later in cabinet, she came from the backrooms of her party where "you are constantly networking; you've got goals; you're making plans; you're moving groups of people toward a goal." But once her party was elected government, "caucus and cabinet immediately separated. The whole hierarchical nature of the place was not conducive to working together collectively. For backbenchers, it started on that very first day when all you guys were sworn in, and the rest of us were just flotsam and jetsam out in the audience. We actually thought we were effective, too, and so this whole hierarchy and the reward system and power at the top was very different than how we worked before." Still, she said, "caucus minus the cabinet worked very well together, and you could create that same world."

The cabinet system, in which only some members are given portfolios—which carry status, rewards and perks—leads to discussing problems and solutions issue by issue instead of on the broad canvas that party organizations provide when they are trying to make their overall policy hang together as a piece. Party policy discussions range broadly and involve anyone who holds a membership. But in government, as Joan Sawicki pointed out, too often decisions are compartmentalized, and nobody considers the whole structure. "In my mind things either fit into the puzzle or they don't. If they don't fit, they're not going to take you where you want to go. So you have to look at the whole puzzle. One of my most fundamental frustrations is that there's no place in the system to have a thoughtful consideration of where we're leading anybody, let alone where people are going to follow."

Public response to our system should also be more active in a democratic system. Women members see the signs and some of the causes. "I would like to see more respect for what people perceive government should be," said Katherine Whittred. "I am really concerned about the apathy of people" on a broad world canvas. On a holiday in England, fellow travellers told Whittred that in Britain hardly anybody votes. "The numbers were just appallingly low." How, Whittred wondered, could we change what we do so that members of the public feel they have a greater role? So they feel more in tune with their elected representatives? Many people say their elected representatives are not acceptable, and some think they run for election but just don't care. "I don't think that's true. Yet the public continues to feel alienated from their representatives.

We need initiatives to engage people. We have to address the issue of the public being disconnected from the people who represent them in government."

Public apathy worries Susan Brice too. "Our whole system is suffering from a huge lack of interest. People have written us off; they don't trust or accept politicians. Fewer people of quality are considering running. I see a whole segment of the population deciding not to get involved."

Sawicki outlined a trap politicians fall into that encourages public apathy. "One of the first lessons we learn is that we must give the media what they want if we are to get any coverage." Members also learn to give constituents what they want to hear so they feel represented. "We get into this trap in spite of ourselves. If there's a crisis we have to deliver an announcement to say we're going to fix it so that everybody can say, 'Okay, they're going to fix it, I can go back to my life.' We let the public and the media abdicate their part of the process. But the three groups are locked into this totally dysfunctional family, and we need to fix it. We're all saying our scripts, because they're the scripts we've been handed, and if you change the script, the other two don't recognize it. Yet all three know in their hearts it's impossible to deliver the quick fix, even when it's demanded. So why do we keep playing this silly game? It's dishonest."

The voters will not feel they are part of the process or help in making decisions, said Iona Campagnolo, until the media changes its approach. "The media want confrontation, which counteracts both the dialogue process and the philosophical leadership of the process, which is a rhythm. It's a creative process. It will never be complete; it will always be evolving. Creating something that is constantly evolving is really difficult because people want certainty. Well, they can't have it!"

Judi Tyabji Wilson would like people to be "better informed before they jump to conclusions. They say they don't trust the media, and then they run around quoting from it." And Brenda Locke said, "We have to create more opportunities for the public to learn about politics and take responsibility for it."

Apathy goes hand in hand with cynicism, or perhaps it is a stepping-stone to cynicism, a danger clearly seen—at the beginning of the twenty-first century—as entrenched. "Political cynicism is like a cancer on the body politic," Kim Campbell said when she was running for the Socred leadership in 1986. Eileen Dailly remarked that public cynicism could ruin our democracy. "I came away realizing how important the work is, and I never got cynical about it. I still take every opportunity to explain to people who are constantly criticizing politicians as all being corrupt that they came there to do something good. They're not corrupt." Nevertheless, Hunter pointed out, "If you say often enough, 'Politicians are all scumbags,' only scumbags will apply." The public, the politicians and the media need to see this consequence and rein in their cynicism.

Libby Davies wants democracy to spread. "The media deliberately turn people off; they don't want ordinary people to be engaged in politics. They're quite happy with the controls in the editorial rooms and some very large corporations of the Business Council on National Issues." Davies sees editorial staff as satisfied with corporate ownership and control, which excludes the viewpoints of many regular citizens. "It's up to us to

challenge that, and so Davies would change the political system by "democratizing the media so that people are actually getting real information and can begin to take a sense of ownership about what's going on and become engaged again." She is enthusiastic about the highly democratic spread of information on the internet.

Sawicki had an annual engagement to speak to journalism students at BCIT, so she regularly "worked through" issues about the media in BC. "I would like to see it more sincere, more substantial. The thirty-second news clip mentality is senseless and can't achieve anything. It's hypocritical and a discredit to just everybody." The basic synergy between the role of government as the only institution that can speak for the public and the media as the institution that carries public messages is thus distorted. "It's as fundamental as that." The public no longer accepts that government is the only institution that speaks for the people as a whole. "It's lumped with the corporations, the trade unions—we're all 'those assholes.' You somehow have to make the reconnection that government is us. And you have to make sure the public good is served." It's not easy. "In my worst moments, I just throw up my hands and say, 'This species deserves to be extinct. Maybe the next species will do a better job.'"

Judy Tyjabi Wilson encourages voters to be better informed.
Photo courtesy Judy Tyjabi Wilson.

WE'RE ALL IN THIS TOGETHER

If we want to save our parliamentary system from the cynicism and resistance of the public, we'll have to change it. Women politicians suggested a wealth of ways for us to practise politics better without losing the skeleton that has served us well.

Gretchen Mann Brewin was optimistic, looking to more consensual decision making which includes every responsible citizen. "There's a different breed of guy coming up through the system now, and more women are there to say, 'There's a better way to do this.' We're going to have to let go of some of the ways we thought were the only ways to run a parliamentary democracy. It's important that people continue to participate and others come into it."

"This life is very, very hard on families," said Wendy McMahon, so she would advocate moves that make politics more attractive to young parents. Young mothers, in particular, are scarce in the ranks. Said Joy Langan, "There's still that whole mentality of, 'How could you leave your children at home and become a parliamentarian?'" Sheila Orr would arrange for moms to have their babies with them. "In that way, maybe you'd get younger women. Even women whose children—and that's even tougher—are eight, nine and ten." Joy MacPhail, with first-hand experience, said, "I just wish there were some way that's easier to raise a family and be a politician. What we do now [three out of four weeks, no scheduled night sittings] isn't enough if you have children twelve or under." "Ban night sittings altogether," said Christy Clark, "and don't call caucus on weekends. We as a legislature need to think of family time as an important consideration."

And women of all ages, parties and locations want communities to lead policy decisions. Members would see that community-based decisions prevail before, during and after elections. Like the little girls with a soccer ball at a park (see page 182), they want to agree on the rules before they play, rather than just opposing the other player and adjusting the rules to increase the likelihood of scoring. Scoring should count only when the rules are reached by collaboration and everyone knows them.

Grace McCarthy observed, "I'd really like to see all people have more involvement, because the more people involved, the better the system, but I'm not so sure we're good at getting people involved. We're good in a crisis: if the train's coming we'll gather around to prevent people from being hurt. But just keeping the machinery going—I don't know any party that is good at that. We leave it to factions, and that's quite unhealthy because they get a voice they haven't earned, and it's also a narrow focus."

Iona Campagnolo has defined a dichotomy in government. "There are two basic processes we go through. Process number one is dialogue for everybody who's equal, so you come to a conclusion. Then you have to implement that. That's when the managers manage, when somebody is 'higher' than somebody else. We keep getting mixed up in these processes all the time, and the two are incompatible."

In our democracy each party goes through the dialogue process to define its policy. All party members are equally welcome to participate in the dialogue. Similarly, all voters have equal power to participate in the electoral dialogue which precedes the choice of a government. But when it comes to discussion in assemblies, a military-hierarchical system takes over, even though much of the discussion is still about policy setting.

Some women suggested jettisoning the party system, which they see as a basic source of conflict, without and within an assembly. "If we're going to change politics at all," said Bonnie McKinnon, "we're going to have to get away from the party system. We're going to have to allow an individual MLA to have some say for her community." Betty Hinton decried our chances for good government if fear of punishment through hierarchy motivates members to vote as they do on policy. A leader can alter every member's appointments. Sophia Leung described our system, in which power is centred in a very small number of people, as "not democracy but hypocrisy." But Sue Hammell thought we could fix the parliamentary system if we "curtail the power of the premier or prime minister and create a system where not all power resides in the centre."

The women proposed a range of measures to free members from the aggregation of power in the leader's office. Margaret Bridgman was committed to following party policy but rejected the power of the leader as opposed to that of her constituents. Members shouldn't have to vote by what the leader of the party says on issues that are not in party policy. "They should vote what a majority of their constituents want. Then when the government puts a bill in the House, it will know that it has to solicit support; it doesn't have it in the bag."

Libby Davies wants more openness and democracy within our political parties. She objects to having her views and her representation of her constituents lost within the party's parliamentary strategies. "I'm not a big fan of the whole party whip system. MPs could be more effective—individually or as people representing different regions or different issues and interests—if Parliament itself was much more democratic. And that's really not radical." Daphne Jennings would escape party bonds altogether "Nobody should have control of elected members except the people of this country." Jennings would "love to be an independent, because then you truly represent your constituents. And you can vote with any party."

Carol Gran would like ministers to wield "way more power in the cabinet, so that when a vote is taken, the premier might lose. All by itself that would make a huge difference. Cabinet ministers wouldn't be afraid anymore, and they wouldn't go to cabinet with a defeatist attitude. The concept of getting your colleagues to work with you would take on a whole new meaning." But Margaret Lord would democratize beyond the cabinet. "I felt that decisions were made elsewhere and brought to caucus," a feeling that Barb Copping echoed, saying she would "like to see elected people more in control of government than advisors." Copping referred to the numbers of unelected advisors who support the prime minister's and premier's offices. "I never had the feeling that the elected people were the main power, but I didn't think the advisors were the brains of the place." That they had paid their dues in most cases counted more than their expertise. Lord would establish a formal way for caucus members to get issues to cabinet—one that would be an assured conduit. What was needed was "open, meaningful caucus debate," Copping said. Then backbenchers wouldn't be "turning on the radio to hear what we did. We should at least have known we did it—and why—when we answered the phones in our offices."

Wanting to be completely independent of a party caucus, said Margaret Mitchell, is "not realistic. Your caucus gives you strength." Members fight out the issues inside caucus, with many differences of opinion. Such discussion is necessary if party principles are to be supported by members in public. "And we've got to be together on it." Still, Mitchell would support more opportunities for independent comments. "We had a nice system in my later years in Ottawa. When bills were being presented, we had a fifteen-minute period when we could stand up spontaneously and question the minister. Then we mailed out the Hansard record so people would know where we stood and could respond."

Val Meredith would take the issues right back to the voter. "The prime minister has sole control of appointments to all the important positions in our parliamentary system from federal court judges to senators to refugee appeal board members. That allows him to control his MPs. We have very little opposition in the senate. So we have to

Parliament itself could be more democratic, said Libby Davies, on a subject chewed over well by all women members: the function of parties in government. *Photo Anne Edwards.*

somehow convince the voters—whose numbers are diminishing—that it's important that they register their votes." Meredith would have an elected senate with equal representation for each province "so that there is regional representation." She also suggested freeing up members of Parliament to act more independently "and not be under the control and the domination of the prime minister," with free votes, more opportunity to introduce legislation and a different system for declaring confidence motions.

"If you could stop centralized decision making," Cathy McGregor said, you could "fundamentally shift the way government works. Because as much as you think you're working independently, if the premier's office thinks you're not doing it, you're not doing it. That's the way it was when I was in government, when you were in government, and obviously [responding to Gran's statement] when Carol Gran was in government." We shouldn't put all our eggs in the premier's basket. "It has to be more than what the premier wants, or else what are we in this for?" McGregor thought a woman premier would move that way.

Margaret Bridgman said, "In committees, some people couldn't put the political party in their back pocket and debate the issue and even play the devil's advocate. If a good point was made, I didn't give a damn if I was a Reformer or not, I would say it was a good point. I wrote a critique separate to my colleague on one of the studies—he was a man, by the way—because I said, 'I'm not going to damn this just for the sake of damning it.'" Opposing measures that are not exactly what the party demanded is "silly, absolutely silly."

Anita Hagen would change the committee system "in an ideal world," because parties in power have never been prepared "to yield one ounce of governing power to a collective of members." Hagen said, "It wouldn't be difficult to give a committee some issue where, by the very reason of their concern for the issue, members would get beyond conflict." When an issue challenges their community and the province, most elected people "have the potential to forget their partisanship."

"If you're going to change anything," said Rosemary Brown, "you have to change where the decisions are made," but she couldn't see it happening. "I don't see power going to committees in government because that would undermine the power of the minister. And if you undermine the minister, you undermine the power of the premier, who has to be able to exercise the right of veto." The conundrum—in which group decisions come up against the pyramid with its time constraints—has brought Carole James to prove Brown's point. While she fostered participation by her caucus after becoming leader of the official opposition, she maintained her veto. "Caucus members say they've never seen a leader who's taken more opportunity for discussion in caucus, and I think shared decision making is a strength. But having gone through the legislature now, I see the importance of the leader, who is ultimately responsible and accountable for decisions, being able to take that veto."

When governments strike a committee of Parliament or the legislature, members of all parties serve, but they are chosen to reflect the proportions in the assembly. As a result, Meredith reported, "our committee structure is controlled by a majority of government members, and thus the government controls the agenda, the way the agenda is handled, and the way the bills go through committee. They don't allow amendments, so there are few opportunities to change government legislation even if there are flaws in it." Meredith would remove such government control "so the committees can operate independently and actually challenge the government and challenge the prime minister through challenging his agenda, his legislation." Jackie Pement sees possibilities. "If we honestly used the tools that are there—the committee system to solve problems without partisanship—you wouldn't have to change the whole system. Maybe change the attitudes. A true committee system is more consensual."

McGregor would see more coalitions or cross-party initiatives coming up with solutions on issues of common concern if the committee system were not highly adversarial. Committees on which she served were "set up to come to certain conclusions and used to manipulate public opinion." She observed that in the United States, "daycare is a common issue to Republicans and Democrats, and they found a way to build a program that could meet everybody's expectations. It wasn't easy, but they did work together to reach an agreement. And it was largely amongst the women on both sides of the house that they came up with a strategy."

Mitchell saw no reason not to let the committees be "more balanced and less partisan—their reports still get processed through the party system when they get back in the House, so the checks and balances remain."

As well as more opportunity for all-party work, James wanted "more opportunity for the public to be involved in decisions. I see no reason why, if government is working on some kind of legislation, committees can't get more citizens involved." This might also encourage what James called "doing it for the right reasons" rather than "because it's going to get us elected." She saw a great reluctance to take things on politically unless you're "going to get an immediate bang for it, an immediate credit," but wanted to have the political system support forward-looking decisions. Shirley Bond also sought involvement in decision making beyond government precincts. "The system itself should reflect local decisions. It is most reasonable that the people closest to the problem make the decisions—while they are held accountable."

Campagnolo observed that people who hold public office often lament the constant conflict and say to her, "I can't stand the abuse any longer." In her view, "the only way to make it less abusive is to make it more inclusive." She used the example of the world economic and environmental summits beginning in the 1990s. Increasingly they have become targets for protests, and the police component has become greater and greater. "Don't use those great big walls to keep protestors out. Get great big circus tents to bring them in. These are people crying for inclusion. Some of them will be bad apples, yes, but a great number of them will be motivated very positively."

"I come from the community," said Jenny Kwan, "and I believe in the community development way of doing politics. Governments would have to be willing to relinquish control and trust in the people to make their own decisions. Every region is different. Let them make their own decisions within parameters, such as no clear-cutting. Whether it works or not, it's a partnership. If we can move politics into that realm, then there is some hope for real democracy—participation and legitimacy for youth and less partisanship."

Like Kwan a former municipal politician, Darlene Marzari pointed out that already "at civic and regional levels we've got flexible, workable city states. They need to be strengthened. We have a provincial-federal system which should be regulatory and legislative over "common good-issues such as public health." Provincial government would deal with issues like water and air quality control, for example, as well as dioxin release, agricultural land reserves and heritage, "those things in which the whole provincial population is involved." But critically, more and more effort would be put into empowering local government.

McGregor points out that we already have a good model for public participation. "I talk to people all the time about the CORE land use planning model that former Premier Mike Harcourt started. It brings multiple interests together, and people develop relationships and listen and talk—how extraordinary! The model is right there to use."

In another direction, Jan Pullinger recommends a different model for funding election campaigns. "If we're ever going to have anything approaching real democracy we'll have to limit election funds—take away any organizational donations to candidates, put a cap on donations. Ideally the elections should just be government-funded as they are in other countries, so you're running, not buying elections." Not going that way moves us further and further away from the democratic model "because the more we move to globalization, the more money interests are involved and the less democracy we have." Judi Tyabji Wilson would also

Jenny Kwan, centre, is just one former municipal politician who wants politics grounded more in communities. Another, Libby Davies, is on the left. *Courtesy Jenny Kwan's office.*

"level the playing field. I would like to be less dependent on money from outside sources. But there would have to be some publicly funded system to allow candidates to be on an even footing."

The media, because of its interdependence with politicians, drew critical attention. Changing it would constitute "a huge part" of what Davies wants. "The media plays such a critical role in turning people off." She would "reverse the alarmingly central control over media that's a huge factor in how we look at politics, how we receive information and what kind of perspectives there are."

Lynn Hunter said, "If the fourth estate would recognize that their responsibility extends to trying to convey some of the benefits of the system. . . ." She didn't complete her sentence, but she completed her thought by suggesting, "Maybe they should travel to Albania as I have and figure out that we've got it pretty good in Canada."

Decrease the isolation of capitals, Pat Carney advised, and originate some federal programs in BC. "Why can't federal committees use the provincial legislature when it's not sitting and vice versa, so that all members could experience the nation's many provincial cultures?" Davies also finds Ottawa remote in BC. "My biggest challenge is how to make Ottawa relevant so constituents feel as though it has something to do with their lives and they have a stake in what's going on. I would like to see the three levels of government operate much more interactively at the local level."

Even given all these changes, it still would not be easy—yet—for women to be elected. But increasing the number of women in assemblies is crucial. Said Brown, we need "a broader base of experience, a wider spectrum in the sense of diversity within Parliament. Every time you have a first ministers' meeting, you have all these men who look exactly alike. They dress exactly alike. You know they're thinking alike. Nothing's going to change as long as this is all we've got going for us."

Sheila Orr would like affirmative action to get more women into assemblies. "We could say, 'Okay, we're going to have five positions for women who don't have to be nominated.'" When federal Liberal leader Jean Chrétien appointed women candidates in the 1993 and 1997 federal elections, "that was a pretty bold move." The provincial NDP has developed an affirmative action plan to assure women take the nominations in seats vacated by incumbents for the 2009 election.

What can women do to bring their numbers up to half in Canadian assemblies? Can they do it while they are still trying to convince voters that they belong in public life? Politics will change, said McGregor, "when we have many more women knowing they have strength and capacity—in spades—recognizing that the skills they take to their day-to-day work are the very skills they need to be valued leaders in an organization." Then it will be easier to persuade voters to support women on the basis of having a different style, and given that voters scorn the system, to know that style would bring "substantive change to the political process." And Mitchell concluded, "There has to be real recognition in our own parties and in our governments that women have a contribution to make as members, not just as women."

Even with the understanding that consensual decision making takes huge amounts of organization and time, a commitment to inclusiveness would counter one of the surest enemies of democracy: cynicism.

As long as politicians flail at each other from either side of a no man's land, the media calculates political effectiveness as a warrior's strut and voters scorn their representatives—the ones they have chosen by their own systems—as greedy and conniving, no government will be able to constrain the huge power our societies have dispersed away from our assemblies.

Unless the public sees politicians as neighbours struggling with the issues of province and country, they will not see that government is the people. They will not fulfill the promise of those who fought for democracies so that the people have ultimate power through their government to choose which issues we will deal with and how we solve them.

In a world with all our technological tools and all our means to communicate quickly and broadly, we have to find new ways to give our representatives the power to make the people's decisions. Women politicians are not the only ones of their profession who see this, but most of the women who have served in assemblies are pointing the way beyond hierarchies to greater participation and consensus. As Val Meredith said, "It's important to recognize that we're all in this together, that there's a bigger picture. We're there to cross party lines—to accomplish something."

MY MOTHER'S DAUGHTER, MY SISTER'S SISTER

S hannon O'Neill is a practical person. Number one on her list of advice to new members was, "Be sure you have a warm suit to sit in the legislature. Otherwise you'll freeze." Number two was, "Get a convertible." She has a lively repertoire of stories about riding in parades in various open vehicles belonging to other people, sharing with other politicians or—preferably—not. But nobody can really tell a novice how being a member will affect her life. "It's a bit like parenthood. When you're pregnant, people try to tell you what it's going to be like, but they can't. You have to be a parent." But O'Neill would tell women newcomers "about the women's washroom that still has the urinals in it. You get the message: 'Don't get too comfortable, girls, you may not be here for long.'"

But women do intend to be around for a long time, and they do it with the help of other women. When Elizabeth Cull ran for election, for example, a local Victoria woman came out to work in the campaign and said, "Elizabeth, I'm going to be your personal services coordinator. I'll run your family life." Every Sunday morning she brought a week's worth of meals for the fridge and freezer and a menu list. She took clothes to the cleaner, shoes for repair and books back to the library. "For twenty-eight days she did everything a wife would have done, and after the campaign she gave me my bill for the groceries, the cleaning and so on."

Jan Pullinger enjoyed similar support. At a "rather uncomfortable election planning meeting," the committee asked what she needed, because they had never supported a woman before. Worried mostly about her son, she said, "I need a wife." The committee got the message. "They were fabulous. From the time I became candidate, somebody would turn up at my house and dinner would show up in the fridge." And they helped in other ways too. "They were just terrific."

"Get yourself a support network if you don't have one," Cull recommended to new members. "I would never have got through my political career without my incredibly supportive network of women, who seemed to know when to take me aside and say, 'By the way, we've arranged a babysitter for your son for the weekend. You and Terry are going away. We've booked you into . . .' I'm not joking. They just knew I might not have been sane. They knew when I needed a phone call. At difficult times they'd come into the legislature and sit in the gallery across from me. They were there when the budget was leaked [Cull was finance minister when the government released the budget before it was read in the legislature because it had been leaked, a rare move which launched a barrage of criticism]. They were the only ones in the gallery. Some took time off work."

"Ask for help," said Penny Priddy, who thought women did "least well" at that. "You need to have good people around you," said Libby Davies, "people that you can trust and who will give you honest advice and not just tell you what you want to hear." Within the system or in your personal life, Davies advised, women "have to work with other women, even across party lines. Because there are still a lot of biases and discrimination against women in politics and women generally—without that support it's overwhelming."

The good old boys' network (GOBN) or its female counterpart, the GOGN, can both work against you, Jackie Pement observed, so don't take them for granted. "The challenges haven't changed because of the women's movement. There are some opportunities for young women that were definitely not there for my mother, and probably not for me, but the main obstacles are still there." April Sanders said, "Beware of falling into stereotype, being pigeonholed. We love to pigeonhole our women in politics."

Many women cautioned against taking family for granted. "Give them priority," said Sheila Orr. "If there's a phone call, put their call first." Sanders was amazed at the number of divorces and separations "even in my five-year term." "You have to really make sure you protect your family," said Lois Boone. "We chose to get into politics, not they. We can stand up and defend ourselves." Christy Clark too said, "Families take such a beating in politics. And we're all going to be run out on a rail eventually. In British Columbia, this isn't a lifetime career." "Keep a long view," said Ida Chong. "At the end of the day, you will go back to being who you were, and you need your friends and family. I'm still my mother's daughter, my sister's sister, my niece's aunt, and my neighbour's neighbour."

As for their political style, Lynn Stephens advised women to "stand up and speak out" and men to "learn and listen." And Joan Sawicki said, "The advice I would give to men would be to do politics more like women." She didn't mean stepping back from the hard stuff. As Gillian Trumper put it, "If it gets too hot in the kitchen, then you shouldn't be there. When everyone's screaming at you over an issue that may not be too popular at the time, you've got to be able to put up with it, whether that's the right decision or not." If you can't, you've got to "get out of politics at any level." Hammell warned: "No whining, no complaining, no blaming. Just get the job done. My advice to women is, get off the issue of why you can't do things. Get on with figuring out how you can, because time spent figuring out why you can't is not productive. . . . Everybody is in the same boat, and those people who figure out how will be the ones who get ahead."

Sharon Hayes recommended choosing a single issue at a time. "Become the resource, and make your mark in that one issue. If you go in thinking you can do it all, you'll do nothing."

"Make sure that you're going in there to make change," Hedy Fry cautioned, "and that you're not just going to sit down and accept things as they are."

Try to learn the system so it gives you no surprises. "Understand the deficiencies of the system," said Darlene Marzari. "Understand exactly how powerless you can be inside a system that is in itself inadequate. If you want to be happy in the job, choose your issues, run for them, play the game. If you want to be thoughtful in the job, understand what you're up against, and do what you can do with the few collegial minds you may find." She recommended that as a member you should "let people know what you're trying to do and don't pretend you're going to be god saving. If you go in thinking you'll do a rational, logical approach to public policy making—you won't. That's not the way it works.

You have to balance. It's constant balancing, constant tension, constant conflict. It has to be." Marzari added, "If you have a single issue, you don't need to be in electoral politics. You can stay inside your advocacy group and push for your agenda."

A step back and a look forward was Sawicki's advice. "Spend time learning how decisions get made and power gets exercised." You don't have to adopt those ways, but if you don't know them, you'll spend a lot of time standing on your soap box, hoping to convince everybody to agree, when what you are saying is "not even relevant to the decision makers."

As for getting into the political trade, the women recommend that rookies know their community by getting involved as volunteers or serving on boards or councils to establish the reputation needed to gain voter support. Anita Hagen said, "Get yourself really rooted in your community in an ethical way—not in an opportunistic way—a way where you find some work to do that is generally related to your passion, to what you feel strongly about, and put a lot of energy into that, to learn and to challenge yourself, and to become known as somebody a community can respect and count on." Kim Campbell called it getting "a positive identity that precedes your entry into provincial or federal politics." She added, "It's not always easy to establish that you have an identity."

Darlene Marzari advises rookie politicians to "let people know what you're trying to do and don't pretend you're going to be god-saving. Learn to play hockey." *Courtesy New Democratic Party.*

Said Karen Sanford, "For a budding politician the important thing is to get out to meet people, to know them and what their problems are, and to be available. You've got to be willing to work. People who let their names stand for nomination must realize that they have to work to get the nomination—and if they get the nomination, that the work has just begun."

Don't rush it. "Take your time and get your feet wet in municipal politics," said Orr. "I wasn't going to do that. I thought I could win a provincial seat, and I ran and lost—the best thing that happened to me. There's so much to learn." One of those things to learn—and never forget, said Erda Walsh—is "who your boss is." It's not yourself, it's not your friends, it's not the government. "It's the people who put you there."

Mary Collins would warn women to "know that you're sometimes going to be trivialized, . . . observed in a way that men aren't, whether it includes your dress or your voice, how you behave yourself or your relationships. So you'd better not do anything you'd be embarrassed about seeing on the front page of the newspaper. Women are judged much more harshly than men in that respect. So if they look dowdy or if they're perceived to be having an affair, the judgment is more critical."

Sue Hammell, who leads election workshops for women candidates in Third World countries, says, "No whining, no complaining, no blaming. Just get the job done. Use your time to figure out how it can be done. " *Photo courtesy Patrick Tam/ FlungingPictures.com*

"Don't lose your temper publicly ever," said Betty Hinton, "and never cry. If a man loses his temper, that's okay; if you lose your temper, you go back to that label again—bitch." Women might get away with crying now in some cases, "if it's out of sympathy for someone. But if you're crying out of frustration they never let you forget it. Personally I wouldn't trust anybody who couldn't cry, but you don't cry in public." You will be judged as too emotional, someone who can't control herself.

Hammell called women's lack of self-confidence "their greatest barrier in politics," and would counsel women not to "take stuff personally. Learn to separate your person from the issue. For young men, it's part of their culture. They do that more easily." Rosemary Brown gave the same advice. "The criticism is directed not at you, but at the political party to which you belong, the constituency, the riding. Anybody else in your place at this time is going to get the same kind of stuff, so why would you take it personally?" Jenny Kwan counselled understanding where criticism comes from so you don't lose your sense of self. "Don't let people undermine you, even though they will try very hard to do so at every turn."

Women have reason to feel confident. "You bring skills that your male colleagues don't bring," said Priddy. "Not better, but different. In all of our communities, our kids will be worse off if those skills don't get to the table. You're doing this for me and you're doing it for my grandchild. You have every right to be there." Recognizing that "women have more self-doubt about their ability," Joyce Murray advised, "Go out there with a yes-I-can attitude and draw the people that will support that attitude; then jump off at the deep end and trust that they can swim." Barbara Wallace quoted Tommy Douglas, a long-time provincial and federal politician who was known for his wit. "Tommy Douglas had two pieces of advice. The second was, whenever you get the chance, go to the bathroom because you never know when you'll get another chance. But the first was, never think you're less competent than anybody else."

Not all the advice was precautionary; initiates should know that there are rewards. "I think elected office empowers women," commented Pement. And Joy MacPhail advised that elected members "are well-paid, well-recognized and honoured in the community." This respect exists, paradoxically, right along with the suspicions that attach to politicians.

Linda Reid said warmly, "It'll be the most incredible intellectual journey you'll ever be on, in terms of assimilating, analyzing, hearing a lot of viewpoints you didn't originally think you wanted to hear." Members give that information back, and "that's what makes the democratic process survive. With all the nuances out there about what an indelicate system we have—I'm always open to hear of a better one."

The rewards of being a member do not always extend to the monetary field, said Joy Langan. "You're not going to get rich being a politician. Whether you get your pension or not, it's a very expensive lifestyle, even if you're frugal." Therefore, she said, "Make sure you've got something to fall back on after politics because otherwise you end up grabbing for the brass ring and hanging on for dear life, compromising your principles to stay there. I saw politicians whose personae became that they were MPs because they really hadn't established any other niche before they were elected. Do some other things first."

Kim Campbell, like Langan, was back in the world looking to her future after a single term in Parliament. "Think about financial security," she warned. "I left without a pension. Another thing about being a woman: you don't have all the old boys running around looking after you." Her experience and reputation in the US brought her better rewards than her political career in Canada. "I don't sit on any Canadian corporate boards, although I sit on American corporate boards."

Make sure to enjoy your time in office, said Priddy. "Nine and a half years [her time as an MLA] is way too long a time to spend if you can't have a good time more times than you can't." Eileen Dailly got similar advice early in her career. "On my first day at the legislature, W. A. C. Bennett met me in the corridor going into the house. He put his arm around my shoulder and said, 'Now, Mrs. Dailly, I'll tell you how to laugh in this place.' He was no taller than I was, you know. He had interesting eyes that pierced right through you, and he said, 'First of all, you must maintain a sense of humour.' I never forgot that. There are too many people—and I saw it in our own members—who don't last, who don't want to run again, or it's taking a terrible toll—the ones who can't roll with it. One member came out of the house every day with a headache. Old Bennett was right. Take it seriously—there's nothing more serious than that place—but learn to roll with it."

A good sense of humour will help you "maintain good physical health," as Hunter advises, "just because of the energy demands." So will having a plan. Margaret Mitchell reported that "in the last two years I got smart and scheduled my down time. There were times when I had to . . . refresh and take care of my body." Dawn Black advised, "Be good to yourself. Take time . . . off out of the province where you're away from the phones, away from your constituents."

It's temporary work—or at best, continues term by term. "I look at elected service as a relay race," said Kwan. "You pass the baton, and maybe one of your dreams is one of their dreams. Reaching that star comes closer and closer as time evolves. When you get up one day and you feel tired, and you don't want to do the work that you have set out for the day, or if that dream is no longer a reality for you—it's time to step aside. Not because you are bad but because you are tired, and it's time for someone else to carry the baton for the next race. Otherwise, the goal will never be reached."

Glossary

ADM: assistant deputy minister

BPW: Business and Professional Women, an international organization

CA: constituency assistant

CCF: Co-operative Commonwealth Federation

CORE: Commission on Resources and Environment

DM: deputy minister

GOBN: good old boys' network

Grits: historical name for Liberals, still used informally

GST: General Services Tax, generally called by the public Goods and Services Tax

IWY: International Women's Year

LCW: Local Council of Women

MLA: member of the legislative assembly

MP: member of Parliament

NAFTA: North American Free Trade Agreement

NCW: National Council of Women

NDP: New Democratic Party

P&P: planning and priorities (committee), often existing within cabinets

PEL: Political Equality League

Plain brown envelope: A package of official information sent anonymously—usually by a civil servant—to a politician, reporter or other person.

Qs & As: questions and answers, often prepared to go with members' speeches

QP: question period

ROC: rest of Canada

SFU: Simon Fraser University, Burnaby

Socred: BC Social Credit Party member

SWC: Status of Women Canada is a federal government organization that was set up to promote the full participation of women in the economic, social and democratic life of Canada. Some referred to it as **SOW:** for Status of Women

Tories: historical name for Conservatives, still used informally

UBC: University of British Columbia, Vancouver

UNBC: University of Northern British Columbia, Prince George

VL: Voters' League

WI: Women's Institute

Woodward's Squat: In 2004 homeless people set up tents and shelters near the former Woodward's Department Store building while the provincial government and the city of Vancouver decided on a development plan for the building, including how much of it to dedicate to affordable housing. The gathering was called the Woodward's Squat.

WRC: Women's Rights Committee

YWCA: Young Women's Christian Association

FURTHER READING

Arscott, Jane, and Linda Trimble. *In the Presence of Women: Representation in Canadian Governments.* Toronto: Harcourt Brace and Company, 1997.

Bennett, Judith Antonik, and Frederike Verspoor. *British Columbia Executive Council Appointments: 1871–1986.* Victoria: British Columbia Legislative Library, 1989.

Brodie, Janine, and Jane Jenson. *Crisis, Challenge and Change: Party and Class in Canada Revisited.* Carleton Library Series 148. Ottawa: Carleton University Press, 1988.

Brodsky, Gwen, and Shelagh Day. *Canadian Charter Equality Rights for Women: One Step Forward or Two Steps Back?* Ottawa: Canadian Advisory Council on the Status of Women, 1989.

Brown, Rosemary. *Being Brown: a Very Public Life.* Toronto: Random House of Canada, 1989.

Campbell, Kim. *Time and Chance: the Political Memoirs of Canada's First Woman Prime Minister.* Toronto: Seal Books, 1997.

Carney, Pat. *Trade Secrets: A Memoir.* Toronto: Key Porter Books, 2000.

Converse, Cathy. *Mainstays: Women Who Shaped BC.* Victoria: Horsdal & Schubart, 1998.

Creese, Gillian, and Veronica Strong-Boag, eds. *British Columbia Reconsidered: Essays on Women.* Vancouver: Press Gang Publishers, 1992.

Electoral History of British Columbia 1871-1986. Victoria: Government of British Columbia, Elections BC and the Legislative Library, 1988.

Farrell, Ann. *Grace MacInnis: a Story of Love and Integrity.* Markham: Fitzhenry & Whiteside, 1994.

Gough, Lyn. *As Wise as Serpents: Five Women & an Organization that Changed British Columbia.* Victoria: Swan Lake Publishing, 1988.

Jamieson, Laura E. *Women Dry Those Tears.* Vancouver: CCF Women's Council of British Columbia, 1940.

Kome, Penney. *The Taking of Twenty-eight: Women Challenge the Constitution.* Toronto: Women's Press, 1983.

Kome, Penney. *Women of Influence: Canadian Women and Politics.* Toronto: Doubleday Canada Limited, 1985.

Latham, Barbara, and Cathy Kess, eds. *In Her Own Right: Selected Essays on Women's History in BC.* Victoria: Camosun College, 1980.

Latham, Barbara K. and Roberta Pazdro, eds. *Not Just Pin Money: Selected Essays on the History of Women's Work in British Columbia.* Victoria: Camosun College, 1984.

Lewis, S.P. *Grace: The Life of Grace MacInnis.* Madeira Park, BC: Harbour Publishing, 1993.

MacEwan, Grant. *Mighty Women: Stories of Western Canadian Pioneers.* Vancouver: Greystone Press, Douglas & McIntyre, 1995.

MacInnis, Grace. *J. S. Woodsworth: A Man to Remember.* Toronto: Mac-Millan Company of Canada, 1953.

Masuch, Cristi Leanne. "Man-Haters, Militants and Aggressive Women: Young Women, Media Representations and Feminist Identity." Master's thesis, Queen's University, 2004.

McKenzie, Judith. *Pauline Jewett: a Passion for Canada.* Montreal and Kingston: McGill-Queen's University Press, 1999.

McLaughlin, Audrey, with Rick Archbold. *A Woman's Place: My Life and Politics.* Toronto: MacFarlane Walter & Ross, 1992.

Mitchell, Margaret. *No Laughing Matter: Adventure, Activism & Politics.* Vancouver: Granville Island Publishing, 2008.

Norcross, E. Blanche. "Queen of the Hustings: British Columbia's Fighting First Lady of the Legislature." Unpublished manuscript. Nanaimo, BC: Nanaimo Historical Society, 1986.

Sharpe, Sydney. *The Gilded Ghetto: Women and Political Power in Canada.* Toronto: Harper Collins, 1994.

Tyabji, Judi. *Political Affairs.* Victoria: Horsdal & Schubart, 1994.

Walsh, Susan. "Equality, Emancipation and a More Just World: Leading Women in the British Columbia Co-operative Commonwealth Federation." Master's thesis, Simon Fraser University, 1983.

Webster, Daisy. *Growth of the NDP in BC: 1900-1970, 81 Political Biographies.* Vancouver: New Democratic Party, 1970.

Endnotes

1. "With Its Face to the West," *The Face of Canada,* 1959. Quoted in *BC Bookworld,* Spring 1997, 27.

2. Stephen Hume, "Cold Reality Pushes Liberals off Their High Horses," *Vancouver Sun*, November 8, 2001.

3. Martin Robin, ed. *Canadian Provincial Politics: The Party Systems of the Ten Provinces. 2nd ed.* (Scarborough, ON: Prentice-Hall of Canada, 1978), 40.

4. Bob Groeneveld, editor of The *Langley Advance,* in an email response to the author, October 7, 2004.

5. The Victoria *Daily Colonist,* June 19, 1884.

6. The Victoria *Daily Colonist*, June 18, 1908.

7. *WCTU Year Book*, 1910, 62.

8. The *Champion*, March, 1914.

9. The *Champion*, February, 1914.

10. "Whose Husbands Are to Get All the Portfolios?" The Vancouver *Province,* March 16, 1916.

11. The Victoria *Daily Times,* April 6, 1917.

12. The Victoria *Daily Times,* April 14, 1917.

13. Grant MacEwan, *Mighty Women*, 33–37. Quoted from House of Commons debates, June 5, 1895.

14. Lyn Gough, *As Wise as Serpents: Five women and an Organization That Changed British Columbia.* (Victoria: Swan Lake Publishing, 1988), 3.

15. Gloria Whelan, "Maria Grant, 1854-1937: The Life and Times of an Early Twentieth Century Christian," in Barbara Latham & Cathy Kess, [eds.], *In Her Own Right* (Victoria: Camosun College, 1980), 127.

16. *WCTU Yearbook,* 1886.

17. *Daily Colonist,* March 24, 1907.

18. Jane Arscott and Linda Trimble, *In the Presence of Women: Representation in Canadian Governments. (*Toronto: Harcourt Brace, Canada, 1997), 110.

19. Stephanie L. Montgomery, "Women and the Reform Party." Master's thesis, University of Western Ontario, 1997.

20. Sydney Sharpe, *The Gilded Ghetto: Women and Political Power in Canada*

(Toronto: Harper Perennial, a Phyllis Bruce Book, 1995), 141.

21. John Keen to John Oliver, July 23, 1920, Oliver Papers, PABC. Cited in Margaret Ormsby, *British Columbia: a History* (Toronto: The MacMillans in Canada, 1958), 413.

22. Helen Doherty, Secretary, "Report: First Assembly of the National Federation of Liberal Women of Canada" (Ottawa, April 17–18), 1928, 5.

23. "Why Were Women in the Gunsights?" "Killer's Letter Blames Feminists" [page heading], The *Globe and Mail,* December 6, 1997.

24. Thomas E. Patterson, *Out of Order* (New York: Alfred A. Knopf, 1993), 205.

25. Helen Doherty, Secretary, "Report: First Assembly of the National Federation of the Liberal Women of Canada" (Ottawa, April 17–18, 1928), 13.

26. Gordon Hamilton, "A Work in Progress," The *Vancouver Sun,* November 24, 2004.

27. The *Toronto Star,* September 22, 2006.

28. The *Vancouver Sun,* September 24, 1977.

29. Don Collins, superscript "Acclaimed on All Sides at End of 5-day Filibuster," The *Daily Colonist,* September 24, 1977.

30. Michael Smyth, "Just an Innocent Prank in the House?" and "Toying with Our Time and Money," The Vancouver *Province,* July 11, 1997.

31. Don Hauka, "Apology Good Enough for Me, Says Victim of Sex-Toy 'joke,'" The Vancouver *Province,* July 13, 1997.

32. Michael Smyth, "Party Prank Riles Readers," The Vancouver *Province,* July 13, 1997.

33. Michael Smyth, "'I Am So Saddened,'" The Vancouver *Province,* July 14, 1997.

34. Susan Martinuk, "Double Standard of Legislative 'Sisterhood,'" The Vancouver *Province,* July 14, 1997.

35. Michael Smyth, "Clark Plays Safe by Axing Bill 44," The Vancouver *Province,* July 17, 1997.

36. William Parsons, "A Little Disciplinary Action for 'Penis Platoon,'" The *Province,* July 16, 1997.

37. Vaughn Palmer, "Gordon Campbell Seems to Be the One Who Just Doesn't Get It," The *Vancouver Sun,* July 12, 1997.

38. Jim Beatty, "Speaker Plans No Discipline for Female MLAs Over Prank," The *Vancouver Sun,* July 12, 1997.

39. This is based on the report—also in this piece—that the women apologized

and Nebbeling accepted their apology. Jim Beatty, "Penis Joke Women Right to Say Sorry, Prof Says," The *Vancouver Sun*, July 15, 1997.

40. Susan Chung, "Victorians tell MLAs to Grow Up," The Victoria *Times Colonist*, July 12, 1997.

41. "Oh, Oh: Some Members Not So Honorable," The Victoria *Times Colonist*, July 12, 1997.

42. Les Leyne, "'Enemies of B.C.' Lurking in Clark's Own Party," Ibid.

43. Jim Gibson, "Winding Down from Late-Night MLAs' Windup," The Victoria *Times Colonist*, July 17, 1997.

44. Jody Paterson, "Part-time Decency in Leaders Simply Isn't Good Enough," The Victoria *Times Colonist*, July 18, 1997.

45. Quoted by Vaughn Palmer, "Gordon Campbell Seems to Be the One Who Just Doesn't Get It," The *Vancouver Sun*, July 12, 1997.

46. Eleanor Maccoby and Carol Jacklin, The Psychology of Sex Differences (Stanford, CA: Stanford University Press, 1974), 368.

47. David M. Buss, *Evolutionary Psychology: The New Science of the Mind* (Toronto: Allyn and Bacon, 1999), 368.

48. Truism voiced by Clint Eastwood's character in *Million Dollar Baby*, DVD, directed by Clint Eastwood (2004; Burbank, CA; Warner Home Video, 2005). The movie is about a woman boxing star.

49. Sydney Sharpe, *The Gilded Ghetto: Women and Political Power in Canada* (Toronto: Harper Perennial, a Phyllis Bruce Book, 1995), 16.

50. Vaughn Palmer, "Tales on the Campaign Trail—and Not in Lloydminster, Either," The *Vancouver Sun*, May 6, 2005.

51. "Councillor Cries Over Defence Plans," The *Vancouver Sun*, April 21, 1959.

52. Paddy Sherman, "Sneers, Tears Lower House," The Vancouver *Province*, March 16, 1962.

53. Peter Bruton, "'Politics' Charge Draws Tears Sets Off Battle," The Victoria *Daily Colonist*, March 15, 1962.

54. Ibid.

55. Ed Cosgrove, "Her Tears Pack a Punch," The Victoria *Daily Colonist*, March 17, 1962.

56. Herb Capozzi, MLA 1966–72, in a letter to the editor, "Warning: This Letter is Not Appropriate for Readers under 19," *Orders of the Day*, Vol. 12, No. 5, June 2006, 14.

57. Interview with Sydney Sharpe, quoted in *The Gilded Ghetto*, 18.

58. Jeff Lee, "Leaving the Political Life Behind," The *Vancouver Sun,* November 13, 2004.

59. Tyabji Wilson was the youngest person ever elected to the BC legislature.

60. Judi Tyabji, *Political Affairs.* (Victoria: Horsdal and Schubart, 1994), 114.

61. Carolee Chute, "You Made Your Bed, Judi, . . ." The *Vancouver Sun*, February 18, 1993.

62. Lori Culbert, "Child of Politics Awaits her Firstborn," The *Vancouver Sun,* June 10, 2001.

63. Anna Elphinstone, letter to the editor, The *Vancouver Sun,* August 18, 2001.

64. Jim Beatty, "Deputy Premier Quits to Raise Son," The *Vancouver Sun,* September 17, 2004.

65. "Changing the Gender Agenda of Politics," *Canadian Parliamentary Review,* Summer 1994.

66. "If Women Vote for a Woman—But Will They?" The Vancouver *Province*, January 22, 1918.

67. Joe Paraskevas, "Tory MPs Show Support for Nina Grewal," The *Vancouver Sun,* June 9, 2005.

68. Penney Kome, *Women of Influence: Canadian Women and Politics.* (Toronto: Doubleday Canada Limited, 1985), 17.

69. Ibid., 7.

70. *Being Brown: A Very Public Life* (Toronto: Random House, 1989), 231.

71. Sydney Sharpe, *The Gilded Ghetto: Women and Political Power in Canada* (Toronto: Harper Perennial, a Phyllis Bruce Book, 1995), 9.

72. Ibid.

73. "House Shamed by MPs," May 14, 1982, A 15.

74. Rosemary Speirs, Chair Equal Voice, news release, June 29, 2004.

75. Rosemary Brown, *Being Brown: A Very Public Life* (Toronto: Ballantine Books, 1990), 149.

76. Sylvia Bashevkin, *Women and Politics in English Canada.* (Toronto: University of Toronto Press, 1985). Quoted in Audrey McLaughlin, *A Woman's Place: My Life and Politics.* (Toronto: Macfarlane Walter and Ross, 1992), 63.

77. CBC, December 17, 2003.

78. Bill Curry, CanWest News Service, "Liberal 'Pit Bull' Forecasts Minority," The *Vancouver Sun,* April 1, 2004. Kinsella is identified as the author of *Kicking Ass in Canadian Politics.*

79. Adam Radwanski, "Jack Layton Is Good for Canadian Democracy," *Ottawa Citizen,* The *Vancouver Sun,* January 5, 2004.

80. "Quotes," The Vancouver *Province*, September 27, 2006.

81. *Being Brown: A Very Public Life (*Toronto: Random House, 1989), 152.

82. Ibid., 178.

83. The CCF-NDP has consistently been a third party in the Canadian House of Commons.

84. Janine Brodie, "Restructuring and the Politics of Marginalization," pp. 20–37 in *Women and Political Representation in Canada,* Manon Tremblay and Caroline Andrew, eds. (Ottawa: University of Ottawa Press, 1998), 21.

85. The *Globe and Mail,* June 5, 1993.

86. Sir John A. Macdonald was elected in Victoria riding from 1878 to 1882 after he had lost his Kingston seat and the Victoria member resigned to create a by-election. He was Prime Minister, but no one claimed he was a British Columbian.

87. Gordon Hamilton, "The lonely job of reviving a party: She has spent a lot of time touring the province, pushing her message of moderation. For voters, she is slowly coming into focus, but is she too nice?" The *Vancouver Sun,* April 16, 2005.

88. Vaughn Palmer, "Suddenly, Belatedly, the Liberals Discover NDP's Carole James," The *Vancouver Sun,* April 1, 2004.

89. Quoted in Savage, Candace, *Our Nell: A Scrapbook Biography of Nellie McClung* (Saskatoon: Western Producer Books, 1979), 53.

90. Quoted by Joy MacPhail, *Hansard* (April 28, 2003), p. 6252.

91. RENAMO was a terrorist organization in Mozambique. It operated for a long time outside of the government system, but was finally recognized as an official political party.

Appendix A

Order (2006)
BC's 96 Women MLAs and MPs in Alphabetical Listing

Surname	Given	Position	Years	Constituency	Party	Terms	Deceased
Arsens	Lydia	MLA	1953–56	Victoria City	SC	1	y
Bell	Catherine	MP	2006–	Vancouver Island North	NDP	1	
Black	Dawn	MP	1988–93, '06–	NW–Coquitlam–Bby	NDP	2	
Bond	Shirley	MLA	2001–	Pr. George–Mt. Robson	LIB	2	
Boone	Lois	MLA	1986–2001	Pr. Geo.–N/PG–Mt. Rob.	NDP	3	
Brenzinger	Elayne	MLA	2001–5	Surrey–Whalley	LIB	1	
Brewin	Gretchen	MLA	1991–2001	Victoria–Beacon Hill	NDP	2	
Brice	Susan	MLA	2001–5	Saanich South	LIB	1	
Bridgman	Margaret	MP	1993–97	Surrey North	REF	1	
Brown	Buda	MLA	1956–63	Vancouver–Pt. Grey	SC	2	y
Brown	Rosemary	MLA	1972–86	Van–Burr/B'by–Edmonds	NDP	4	y
Campagnolo	Iona	MP	1974–79	Skeena	LIB	1	
Campbell	Kim	MLA	1986–88	Vancouver–Pt. Grey	SC	1	
Campbell	Kim	MP	1988–93	Vancouver Centre	PC	1	
Carney	Pat	MP	1980–88	Vancouver Centre	PC	2	
Chong	Ida	MLA	1996–	Oak Bay–Gordon Head	LIB	3	
Clark	Christy	MLA	1996–2005	Port Moody–B'by Mtn.	LIB	2	
Collins	Mary	MP	1984–93	Capil/Cap–Howe Snd	PC	2	
Conroy	Katrine	MLA	2005–	W Kootenay–Boundary	NDP	1	
Copping	Barbara .	MLA	1991–96	Port Moody–B'by Mtn.	NDP	1	
Crowder	Jean	MP	2004–	Nanaimo–Cowichan	NDP	2	
Cull	Elizabeth	MLA	1989–96	Oak Bay–Gordon Head	NDP	2	
Dailly	Eileen	MLA	1966–86	Burnaby North	NDP	6	
Davies	Libby	MP	1997–	Vancouver East	NDP	4	
Dawson	Isabel	MLA	1966–72	Mackenzie	SC	2	y
Edwards	Anne	MLA	1986–96	Kootenay	NDP	2	
Fry	Hedy	MP	1993–	Vancouver Centre	LIB	5	
Gillespie	Evelyn	MLA	1996–2001	Comox Valley	NDP	1	

Surname	Given	Position	Years	Constituency	Party	Terms	Deceased
Gran	Carol	MLA	1986–91	Langley	SC	1	
Grewal	Nina	MP	2004–	Fleetwood–Port Kells	CONS	2	
Hagen	Anita	MLA	1986–96	New Westminster	NDP	2	
Haggen	Lois	MLA	1956–66	Gr. Forks–Grnwood	CCF–NDP	3	y
Hammell	Sue	MLA	1991–2001, 2005–	Surrey–Green Timbers	NDP	3	
Hawkins	Sindi	MLA	1996–	OK West/Kel–Mission	LIB	3	
Hayes	Sharon	MP	1993–2000	Port Moody–Coquitlam	REF	2	
Hinton	Betty	MP	2000–	Klps–Thom–H'land Vall	ALL/CONS	3	
Hobbs	Margaret	MLA	1962–63	Revelstoke	NDP	1	y
Hodges	Nancy	MLA	1941–53	Victoria/Victoria City	LIB	4	y
Holt	Simma	MP	1974–79	Vancouver–Kingsway	LIB	1	
Hunter	Lynn	MP	1988–93	Saanich–Gulf Islands	NDP	1	
Ilich	Olga	MLA	2005–	Richmond Centre	LIB	1	
James	Carole	MLA	2005–	Victoria–Beacon Hill	NDP	1	
Jamieson	Laura	MLA	1939–45,'52–'53	Vancouver Centre	CCF	3	y
Jennings	Daphne	MP	1993–97	Mission–Coquitlam	REF	1	
Jewett	Pauline	MP	1979–88	NW–Coquitlam	NDP	3	y
Johnston	Rita M.	MLA	1983–91	Surrey/Surrey–Newton	SC	2	
Jordan	Patricia	MLA	1966–83	North Okanagan	SC	5	y
Karagianis	Maurine	MLA	2005–	Esquimalt–Metchosin	NDP	1	
Kripps	Agnes	MLA	1969–72	Vancouver South	SC	1	
Kwan	Jenny	MLA	1996–	Vancouver–Mt. Pleasant	NDP	3	
Langan	Joy	MP	1988–93	Mission–Coquitlam	NDP	1	
Leung	Sophia	MP	1997–2004	Vancouver–Kingsway	LIB	2	
Locke	Brenda	MLA	2001–5	Surrey–Green Timbers	LIB	1	
Lord	Margaret	MLA	1991–96	Comox Valley	NDP	1	
MacInnis	Grace	MP	1965–74	Vancouver–Kingsway	NDP	3	y
MacInnis	Grace	MLA	1941–45	Vancouver–Burrard	CCF	1	y
MacPhail	Joy K	MLA	1991–05	Vancouver–Hastings	NDP	3	
Marzari	Darlene	MLA	1986–96	Vancouver–Pt. Grey	NDP	2	
Mather	Camille	MLA	1960–63	Delta	CCF–NDP	1	
McCarthy	Grace	MLA	1966–72,'75–'91	Vancouver–Little Mount.	SC	6	
McGregor	Cathy	MLA	1996–2001	Kamloops	NDP	1	
McIntyre	Joan	MLA	2005–	West Van–Garibaldi	LIB	1	
McKinnon	Bonnie	MLA	1996–2001	Surrey–Cloverdale	LIB/IND	1	

Surname	Given	Position	Years	Constituency	Party	Terms	Deceased
McMahon	Wendy	MLA	2001–05	Columbia River–Revel.	LIB	1	
Meredith	Val	MP	1993–2004	S Surr–W Rock–Langley	REF/ALL/ CONS	3	
Mitchell	Margaret	MP	1979–93	Vancouver East	NDP	4	
Murray	Joyce	MLA	2001–05	New Westminster	LIB	1	
Murray	Joyce	MP	2008–	Vancouver Quadra	LIB	1	
O'Neill	Shannon	MLA	1991–96	Shuswap	NDP	1	
Orr	Sheila	MLA	2001–05	Victoria–Hillside	LIB	1	
Pement	Jackie	MLA	1991–96	Bulkley Valley–Stikine	NDP	1	
Polak	Mary	MLA	2005–	Langley	LIB	1	
Priddy	Penny	MLA	1991–2001	Surrey–Newton	NDP	2	
Priddy	Penny	MP	2006–	Surrey North	NDP	1	
Pullinger	Jan	MLA	1989–01	Nanaimo/Cow'n–L'smith	NDP	3	
Reid	Judith	MLA	1998–05	P'ville–Qual/Nan.–P'ville	LIB	2	
Reid	Linda	MLA	1991–	Richmond East	LIB	4	
Roddick	Val	MLA	1999–	Delta South	LIB	3	
Rolston	Tilly Jean	MLA	1941–53	Vancouver–Pt. Grey	CONS	4	y
Sahota	Patty	MLA	2001–05	Burnaby Edmonds	LIB	1	
Sanders	April	MLA	1996–2001	Okanagan–Vernon	LIB	1	
Sanford	Karen	MLA	1972–86	Comox	NDP	4	
Savoie	Denise	MP	2006–	Victoria	NDP	1	
Sawicki	Joan	MLA	1991–2001	Burnaby–Willingdon	NDP	2	
Smallwood	Joan	MLA	1986–2001	Surr–Guildford–Whalley	NDP	3	
Smith	Helen	MLA	1933–41	Vancouver–Burrard	LIB	2	y
Smith	Mary Ellen	MLA	1918–28	Vancouver City	IND/LIB	3	y
Steeves	Dorothy	MLA	1934–45	Vancouver Centre	CCF	3	y
Stephens	Lynn	MLA	1991–2005	Langley	LIB	3	
Taylor	Carole	MLA	2005–	Vancouver–Langara	LIB	1	
Terrana	Anna	MP	1993–97	Vancouver East	LIB	1	
Thorne	Diane	MLA	2005–	Coquitlam–Maillardville	NDP	1	
Trevena	Claire	MLA	2005–	North Island	NDP	1	
Trumper	Gillian	MLA	2001–05	Alberni–Qualicum	LIB	1	
Tyabji	Judy K.	MLA	1991–96	Okanagan East	LIB/PDA	1	
Wallace	Barbara	MLA	1975–86	Cowichan–Malahat	NDP	3	
Walsh	Erda	MLA	1996–2001	Kootenay	NDP	1	
Webster	Daisy	MLA	1972–75	Vancouver South	NDP	1	y
Whittred	Katherine	MLA	1996–	N Vancouver–Lonsdale	LIB	3	
Young	Phyllis	MLA	1972–75	Van–Little Mountain	NDP	1	y

APPENDIX B

Questions for interview with Anne Edwards on BC women in federal and provincial politics.

1. What got you into politics? Was there some particular person who encouraged you? Was there an issue? Did you initiate the process or were you inducted?

2. Did you ever think you would like to be leader of the party?

3. What was your greatest success as a politician?

4. What did your family think of your choice to go into politics? What did they think of you as a politician?

5. Was gender an issue when you got into politics? Later? Did the party help you? Did other women help?

6. Are/were you a feminist?

7. Describe the difference between men and women as politicians.

8. How did you work as a politician? Were you like other women in politics or more like the men? Margaret Thatcher has said: "If you want something said, ask a man to say it. If you want something done, ask a woman to do it." Is there any truth to her observation?

9. Would politics be different if there were more women elected? If there were more women than men?

10. Do you encourage other women to stand for election? Would you want your daughter to stand for election? Your son?

11. How do you see British Columbia as a spawning stream for politicians? What makes BC different politically than the rest of Canada?

12. Would you do politics in Ontario, if you moved there? Alberta? Etc.

13. What were your greatest barriers?

14. Is it true that for politicians, timing is everything?

15. How would you like to see the political system changed?

16. What did you learn from your political career? How did it fit with the rest of your life?

17. Are you glad you did it? Could you have achieved what you did in some other way?

18. When St. Peter asks what was your occupation, what will you say?

19. What advice would you give rookie politicians? Would it be different for men and women?

INDEX